Daily Intentions

by
Ann Blakely Rice

Robert D. Reed Publishers • Bandon, OR

Robert D. Reed Publishers
P.O. Box 1992
Bandon, OR 97411
Phone: 541-347-9882 • Fax: -9883
E-mail: 4bobreed@msn.com
web site: www.rdrpublishers.com

Typesetter: **Barbara Kruger**
Cover Designer: **Cleone Lyvonne**

ISBN 1-931741-20-4

Library of Congress Control Number 2002102463

Manufactured, typeset and printed in the United States of America

In loving memory of my parents,
Browne Botts Rice, Jr., and
Ann Townes Rice

Acknowledgments

How does one thank the universe for placing so many people in my life who have helped this book to materialize?

On an autumn night in Houston, I was talking with some good friends about spirituality and how many of the day-by-day books had helped me so much. One friend suggested that I write my own. Her name is Virginia Magliolo and I will be forever grateful to her for planting this "book-seed" in my mind, heart and soul.

I sincerely want to thank God, the program of Alcoholics Anonymous and the courageous people therein, who, like this book, take life one day at a time.

I thank all of my loyal friends and my immediate and extended family who continued to support me on this journey of writing Daily Intentions. (Hey! John, Browne, Katie, Tina! The Blakelys and the Townes family.)

Special thanks to Nancy Farr, who helped in proofreading this book in its adolescence. She remains one of my dearest friends and confidantes.

Thank you, Mindy, and the Author's Assistant, who also believes in this book.

To all those who I would read a daily entry to in person or over the phone to see where I was and to get their feedback. I respect their opinions and support, including Loretta and my sister Katie.

I thank Nonie for her support and for being silently relieved that this was not another poetry book!

I thank Mary Norris for her Energy Body Clinic and for introducing me to the concept of God as actually being our Universal Parents. She has inspired me with her humor and brilliant insights and gifts.

I thank all the owners of the dining rooms and cafes all over the world that allowed me to write and edit, taking up tables at their establishments.

To all those at the Warwick for helping make my life so much easier.

Special thanks to Kevin for his patience, friendship and support.

To the Kanaly Group for their trusted support.

Thank you ever so much to my Oncologist, Rebecca, whose humor and expert care helped so much in overcoming cancer.

I thank Dane Petersen and Bob Reed for the hard work and attention to details to this book, and Bob for his marketing skills, of which I have none whatsoever. I thank Bob again for his time and our pleasant conversations over the years.

I have to thank Jane and Penny for first typing this book from my somewhat unreadable original longhand writing.

So many, many others to thank. If I forgot to name you, I am sorry and must blame it on my momentary middleaged memory loss. Yet, I want to mention Shakti, Caroline, and Lisa for their wisdom. Many thanks to Eric for his interest in this project.

Last, but not least, from my heart and soul, I thank one of my most beloved teachers, Janellen, whose support and inspiratiion made this book a reality. Wherever you are, Janellen, please know that I love you.

Prologue

Daily Intentions was written in 1995-1996. I decided to write it one day at a time, writing one daily entry per day. It was done this way because I thought that each day was unique in its own way and that how I felt each day would most likely cover most of the emotions human beings had felt in their lives at one time, as well. Whether at home or travelling, I would write in the morning, asking for Divine Guidance and Inspiration. I would then light a white candle and begin setting my pen to paper. Naturally, the book was completed in 365 days. Because of the contents of each entry, I think this book would read more easily with the reader reading only one or two daily entries a day. This book does not read or work like a continuous novel. The individual entries were written for the reader to reflect upon or contemplate each specific day. Of course, there is no one way to read *any* book,. yet I just thought I would make the above suggestion.

While meditating one evening while working on the book, I received a message from my Spirit Guide that this book would be published in time, and that I would be able to recognize that particular time.

With that message in mind, I did not hurry to find a publisher, yet after being edited and proofread several times, I did send it to a few publishing houses. Some were interested in the book, yet nothing solid came of the submissions. During the next years, after its completion, I seemed to find in my life every single challenge that was possible to a human being and everything that was brought up in the book to overcome. While *Daily Intentions* was written solely for the purpose of helping others, I found the entries a refuge in my own storms!

I want to mention here that simply because I have written a spiritual book does not make me a saint nor free from afflictions or daily problems. I, indeed, like to have fun in life. (You should see me in Las Vegas!) I think that is what is on the other side of suffering—more serenity, more joy, more fun and lightness of spirit.

With all of the unavoidable interruptions involved with just now having completed the book for print, I hope it uplifts those who would want to read it. This book is my way of giving back to people all of the help they have given me over the years.

May God bless you.

Ann Blakely Rice

P.S. My references to an all-loving Supreme Power are used merely to simplify, rather than to claim as the only names for one's Higher Power. The reader is openly invited to insert any reference term(s) that they call their own Highest Source of Goodness.

If we can find something positive in obstacles,
we can create a festivity.

FESTIVITIES

January 1

May we make every day a festive one with our Creator in our hearts.

Holidays can be joyous and festive, providing that we are in the spirit of gratitude and rejoicing in the meaning of the particular day. Let us remember that we can make every day a holiday by understanding that we do, indeed, create our own realities for each day, beginning with our attitudes.

Let us make today a festive one, celebrating the miracle that we are alive, coupled with the potential for the vast amount of Love that the Creator has given each of us in our hearts. We can always ask our Guardian Angels for the creative imagination to make every day a special one.

May we have a real holiday today, one accompanied by a positive and God-given creative attitude, celebrating the endless magic that surrounds us, if we but attune to it.

We found something to celebrate this day. It is easy with Angelic inspiration.

We are all perfect children in our individuation, only comparison makes us think otherwise.

PERFECTION IS INDEED ACHIEVABLE

January 2

May we realize that perfection is achievable on Earth by humans, and that we are created Divine in nature.

Our old conditioning states that no one is perfect. The Angels tell us this is a gross misunderstanding. Our Creator resides in each of us. Acknowledgment of this Divinity within can gradually bring about perfection in our lives, providing that our hearts are thoroughly sincere and humble.

With our growing curiosity for more awareness and consciousness, we naturally become more like the Creator. Therefore, it follows that outdated habits, unloving thoughts, old beliefs, hate, bitterness, and the like will slowly or abruptly fall away. This is a promise to all, if we sincerely seek out Divine Will and invite the sunlight of the Spirit into our souls.

May we know that we are perfect as we seek the ways of the Creator.

Love God and all beings, and know that perfection is attainable inside and out. With humility and Grace, perfection is ours.

*Sometimes we have to think fast. This does not mean
we must create havoc.*

HURRY

January 3

May we take time for the Creator and listen to what the
Angels have to say.

We have twenty-four hours a day to take care of ourselves, to
accomplish what is in front of us and to find the joy in living and
in giving. Let us always remember to take time for our Creator in
prayer and meditation. We all have Guardian Angels.

Let us learn to ask them for help when needed. If we find
ourselves in too much of a hurry to find the joy in life, perhaps
our Angels can assist us in these situations. In just a few minutes
of contemplative thought, surrounding ourselves in Divine
Spiritual Light frees us from aversion and fear, enveloping us in
a loving Peace, shedding intuitive light onto any obstacles
presented to us throughout the day.

May we always take time for spiritual matters first, and then
witness the peaceful flow of our busy day.

*Work a little, eat a little, and rest a little. Pray and meditate,
and find the joy in life according to the Creator's interwoven
plan.*

*Heaven on Earth is practicing spiritual laws in all
we do, think, say, and feel.*

SPIRITUAL HUNGER

January 4

May we hunger and thirst for spiritual concerns—the
Unconditional Love and Light of the Highest Source.

Universally, there is a gross spiritual deficit. Deficit means a
scarcity in amount and usually applies to income. Yet, if we apply
this term to spiritual matters, we can see the need for all beings
to be aware of a totally loving and forgiving Creator. The Creator
can provide each of us with Abundance, Joy, and Peace in
accordance to the degree of our needs on our souls' journeys. To
lift the deficit, let us begin with each individual's personal
relationship with the Creator.

There exists a telepathic wave of energy transmitted to others
from one in a spiritual healing process. If we have made a
connection to the Creator, then it is our responsibility to share our
Light with all others. We do not have to be a fanatic about
spreading good news. We can teach by mere example, a smile, or
a kind gesture to all humankind and creatures. Some people are
gifted teachers. We can learn great insights from them about
spiritual matters, while we spread the found Love and Light.
However, the Creator is the greatest and wisest teacher.
Ultimately, the Creator has supplied us with all the answers we
need to live healthy, happy, prosperous lives.

May we become enthusiastic about connecting or
reconnecting with the inspiration of the Universal Love and Light
of the All Intelligent Creator.

*We are well aware of the national debt, hunger, and global
disharmony. Yet, we can fill our spiritual cup with thoughts of the
Divine and affect the world tremendously.*

*Sometimes we can have more success if we surrender what
exists and begin again—fresh with renewed understanding
and creative intuition.*

SURRENDER

January 5

May we learn how to surrender our self-will and all of our
cares to our Creator, creating room inside ourselves for peace of
mind and service to others.

According to the dictionary, to surrender means to yield to a
power of another and to give up completely. In a spiritual sense,
this does not connote weakness, but strength in giving our cares,
burdens, and ego-directed willfulness into the hands of a loving
Creator. There exists a paradox here, some may say. Yet, to
depend upon a Creator actually gives a person more independence, as she or he becomes free of guilt, fear, worry, and all
obstacles to serenity.

When we practice giving these fears to an omnipotent Power,
an all-intelligent Creator who possesses all knowledge to handle
all problems concerning *all* people, places, and situations, we
naturally have more peace of mind. We begin to cultivate the
deep meaning of Faith. We find that by surrendering our bodies,
minds, and spirits to God, we discover a newfound freedom in the
guidance of Divine Will.

May we find daily victory in relinquishing all of ourselves—
body, mind, and spirit—to a caring Creator.

*In offering ourselves totally to the Divine, the Will of the
Creator becomes ours, and the peaceful flow of our lives begins.*

Some people must think that dwelling on trivial matters
is why the telephone was created.

PETTINESS

January 6

May we learn to rise above the world's trivialities and learn to distinguish between pettiness and what is truly meaningful. We rest in the calm reassurance that the Creator is in control of all situations.

There are those times when we can become so bogged down with the actions, words, and gestures of other people, that we let unpleasant situations rule our lives. When we find ourselves entangled in the world's trivialities, let us remember our True selves, found in prayer, a smile, or in deep meditation. Our True selves are love, beauty, and wisdom—exactly the way we were created.

The Creator is found in all people and in all situations in greater or lesser degrees. When we keep our Creator as the main focus, the larger picture is more visible, and the worrisome pettiness of the day vanishes. Contact with the Creator keeps us intuitively aware of the Truth. By living in the creative solutions of the Truth, we disregard unnecessary details of situations and know that all is well in the Universe without our having to control every little thing therein.

May we try to see the spiritual significance in each and every person, place, or situation.

God is within all beings and all things. When we tune into God, we see that we are all little godlings. We thirst for Love, and we long for the Divine Light. The journey of each of us is spiritual and meaningful to the Creator.

If you truly want to know something,
always go to the Highest Source.

KNOWING

January 7

May we possess a deep knowing that we are beautiful in the sight of our Creator and our Angels, and that they will always take excellent care of us.

We all have our days or moments when self-condemnation creeps into our thoughts. This could be referred to as low self-esteem, psychologically speaking. All of us could really use some comforting thoughts about ourselves. Let us comfort ourselves in the knowing that our Creator loves and accepts us unconditionally, and that Our Angels also see us as beautiful, spiritual beings, who have souls that long to be nearer to the sunlight of God. Let our knowing be that of joy, that we are loved exactly the way we were created, no matter how we may feel at any particular time.

Knowing is more than believing. It is our insight from lessons well learned, as well as our hard-earned truths. When we can look at ourselves in the mirror, squarely in the eyes, and know that we are human reflections of the Creator's Unconditional Love and Divine Light, we, too, can begin to love ourselves unconditionally. We can begin to feel safe in the Universe, knowing that our path is Divinely Guided.

May we carry the deep insights and the *knowings* found on our journey into the light of peace and safety that shines continuously within the window of our sacred homes.

"Arise! And walk in the sunlight!" said our Angel. "For you have a glorious story to tell!"

The moment we know we have choices is the moment
we begin to mature.

CHOICE

January 8

May we choose to grow toward the light daily, making wise choices with the assistance of the Divine.

By virtue of the fact that we all have free will, we encounter in our lives the right to choose. All choices are God-given, and they are tools for our learning. As we grow in our *life education* and find what *works* for us, and what does not, let us be comforted in the knowing that we are always growing and evolving toward the Light. Each day, our souls move further along the path toward *Home*, where we are One with our Creator. Each soul has its own journey to walk back into the loving arms of the Divine, or whatever Source it considers to be the Highest and Best Power in the Universe.

Let us not judge our choices as *good* or *bad*. Yet, let us possess the profound knowledge that we are always learning to choose the path toward the Light, our Greater good, and the good of the whole.

May we fine-tune our path back to our Source—that Source is Infinite Love.

Love is ours forever. May we walk in the Light. Our journeys are underway, and our hearts have taken flight into the skies of freedom.

*The soul is fed by the living waters from the river
of a positive mind.*

FEEDING THE SOUL

January 9

May we feel and nurture our souls with good thoughts of Love, Light, and True Wisdom.

There are those elements in the world that, once accepted by our bodies, minds, and spirits, can prove more destructive to our souls than constructive. Although we can have realistic opinions about the world and the people in it, we do not have to accept any negativity into our lives or our belief systems. We possess the Power, through our Creator, to change our thoughts, what we put into our bodies, and even our self-seeking prayers.

Let us send our prayers to become more like our Creator up to Heaven, like incense. Let us feed our souls with pure and gentle thoughts. Let us nurture our bodies with physical exercise and healthy food, and most importantly, let us feed our souls with the Spirit of the Highest Good for all concerned.

May we choose to feed our minds, bodies, and souls with healthy spiritual food.

Let all of humanity do what it will. It cannot jolt the calmness of our souls, which are quiet and still. Let us seek the Divine in our own way and leave all unnecessary negativity behind.

Ultimately, it is up to the individual to follow
his or her own Truth.

INDIVIDUAL RELIGION

January 10

May we decide, by Providence and personal truth, to create our own religion.

Providence is Divine guidance. Let us be open-minded enough to think for ourselves and learn to become our own *gurus*, while still learning from others, taking what fits for us, discarding the hype, the fanaticism, and somebody *else's* truth, which may not fit with our experience. Always ask yourself, "What is *my* Truth, and what are the spiritual principles that *I* live by?" As long as your principles are in the spirit of the Highest Good for all concerned, there is no harm in living by your *own truth*. The difference between religion and spirituality is this: Religion was and is created by mankind, for mankind, with a dogma or an agenda attached, whereas spirituality is accepted as a free gift and blessing from the Creator to follow a Spiritual path guided by the spirit of Higher Will. Of course, we each have an individual relationship with God, as we understand the Divine.

Let us study many different religions and philosophies to become knowledgeable enough to choose our own way to have a personal relationship with our Creator in our lives. We expound upon the gift and Grace, which our Creator has benevolently bestowed upon us.

May we increase our knowledge toward having an individual religion, according to our life experiences, values, morals, beliefs, and spiritual truths, as to what part the Creator plays in our own life.

We opened our hearts and saw Love standing there. We opened our minds to allow our Creator to prepare the way of Peace, Light, and Truth. At last, we saw our confusion, guilt, and worry take flight.

Let our Angels get the tasks done. We'll get out of the way.

COMPLETING TASKS

January 11

May we begin and complete our necessary tasks today with the help of our Angels.

At times, we may become overwhelmed by all the tasks we need to complete in one day. We might want to begin by making a priority list and eliminating those items that are not as urgent. If nothing can be eliminated, let us ask our Angels or the Divine for assistance in our performance that day. Usually, we feel a sense of satisfaction by finishing what we begin. Let us prepare by pausing, taking in a few deep breaths, and getting mentally organized by the Divine intervention of our Angels. Angels are incredible motivators. All we need to do is call on them. With assistance, we can work more joyfully, peacefully, and unfettered with any given task. No job is too big for our Angels, who always work for our Highest and Best.

Let us always remember, after our work is done, to give thanks to the Divine and breathe deeply once again, this time with a sense of accomplishment.

May we thank our Angels for their Divine guidance in assisting our greatest and smallest tasks throughout any given day or night.

We felt overwhelmed by the work at hand, yet it became much easier with the help of the Divine.

For those who truly love God, finding the good comes naturally.

FINDING THE GOOD

January 12

May we find the good in ourselves and all others and expound upon it.

We all have goodness within us. Even when, at times, we cannot see the good in ourselves or others, the light or spark of the Divine is there. The Creator placed this Godspark within each of us. Let it be our choice to humbly see the good within ourselves, for when we find it in our own being we can more easily and readily see it in others. Let us not fall prey to gossip or criticism; yet instead, spread positive thoughts about others. When we place our thoughts with the Creator, we can see how this generates more loving thoughts toward all in our hearts and minds.

Let us be the bearers of good cheer, as what we give away will naturally come back to us. Let us *fan* the Divine spark in our hearts to create a Loving Fire within our souls. Let us expand this Fire to include *all* others, void of our judgments. In this way, we create a more harmonious state for ourselves and world around us, as we vibrate in that loving space of Peace, Power, Wisdom, and Eternal Light. We can then offer this Light to others and perhaps help them upon their spiritual journey as well.

May we look upon ourselves and others with a new pair of eyes—the eyes of the Divine.

Now we see each other as our brothers and our sisters. With God in our hearts, we find that loving one soul expands into loving many more, as each soul is filled and enlightened. This healing is passed on and on, from one soul to the other, to the next, and so on. Let us seek to uplift each other.

A starving man would not turn down food
offered to him with love.

ACCEPTING GOD'S LOVE

January 13

May we accept the Unconditional Love of the Creator.

Our finite minds cannot fathom the type of Unconditional Love and Acceptance that the Creator has for each of us, yet we can learn to accept this incredible Love more and more each day. The practice of meditation, when we *lose* ourselves in God, lets us know and feel the immensity of that special Love. At times, we may feel unworthy of receiving such intense Love and brilliant Light.

Yet the truth is that the Creator can help us to allow our minds, bodies, and souls to accept these free gifts. When we accept the Highest Good, we are saying "Yes" to life, as we grow in the mirroring of our Creator's Love. When we receive Love, we are more equipped to share this Divine Light with all whom we come into contact with each day. When we open our hearts and minds to the Creative Divine, we are allowing Infinite Possibilities of God's Love, Intuition, and Peace to naturally flow into us, becoming a part of us—thus, being filled, we naturally give this Love to others.

May we wholeheartedly trust that our Creator loves us, forgives our shortcomings, and totally accepts us exactly at this phase of our development and evolution.

We may not be all that we could be. Still, we know that our Creator cares about us. For how else could we be allowed to mature, except for God's impeccable, loving nature?

*It is primarily the ego's fear that prohibits us
from asking for help.*

JUST ASK

January 14

May we remember to ask for guidance and inspiration from
our Angels and the Divine.

We all have those moments when we do not feel inspired, are
not motivated, and are filled with apathy. Let us remember that
there are unseen (or perhaps you are one who has had the
privilege to see) Angels: the messengers of the Divine, who are
omnipresent. Angels love to inspire and uplift; all we have to do
is ask for inspiration, motivation, and the energy to perform any
task. Does it seem too simple? Just try it! We can also ask the
Divine to help us learn how to pray and to place the necessary
knowledge and people in our lives as vehicles toward a more
spiritual life.

Sometimes, it is the ego's fear tactic that prohibits us from
asking precisely the questions for which we need solutions. Our
intuition gives us the best opportunity to understand the
particulars about our lives and how to best handle certain
situations. When we feel ready, let us try a few moments of
meditation. Go within; ask for guidance; listen and receive. The
answers have always been within us, yet perhaps we were not
ready to be quiet, still, and enveloped in the presence of God long
enough for the messages to come through. Truth is always
available to us. We only need ask to hear it. Then, let us wait for
the answer patiently and quietly.

May we trust the intangible, and know deep within that we
are not alone, and that we can ask for uplifting guidance at any
time.

*At last! An inspired thought comes to us from above. In
gratitude, we offer a pink rose in pure and simple Love.*

Be careful whom you judge as ignorant, for they may
possess the wisdom of a sage.

WISDOM AND IGNORANCE

January 15

May we gently shake off guilt and the concepts of *good* and *evil*, for, in reality, there exists only wisdom and ignorance.

We all know the dogmatic Western concept of the battle between *good* and *evil*. In a sense, there are positive and negative forces at work in the universe. However, these could also be called the shadow and the light, whereby both are necessary to create a balance. Let us slowly begin to change our guilt-ridden judgment of "we are good," "we are evil," and think about another concept: wisdom and ignorance. Spiritually speaking, we could say that wisdom is about the acknowledgment of a Primal Energy Force, God, or Creative Universal Intelligence coupled with the awareness of the soul's learned lessons. Ignorance, on the other hand, could be referred to as something that is hidden from the Light, or lessons not yet learned. This is not a derogatory statement; it is simply a fact about one's state of mind.

Let us pray that the veils of ignorance be removed from our awareness and be replaced by the wisdom of the heart, mind, and soul. With this kind of reasoning, there is less judgment and guilt of *pleasing* or *displeasing* God. Only the bright Light of the Spirit remains.

May we pray that the dense layers of ignorance around ourselves be gently removed. May we be open to the Divine Brilliance of Wisdom.

Love is wisdom; fear is ignorance. We trust in the Power of the Creator to deliver us from fear, or, better termed, the veils of hidden Truth.

One who lives in fear, knows no Love. One who lives
in Love, knows no fear.

EMBRACING OUR FEARS

January 16

May we learn to embrace our fears, integrating them into the entire pattern of who we are.

All human beings have fears. It is what we *do* with the fear that makes or breaks us. When we feel fearful or anxious, let us take a moment to go within and ask for the honest, root cause of our fear. Usually we will find that some portion of the *ego* is threatened or that we have given too much power away to a person or a situation. Even if our fears overwhelm us at times, we can pray and remind ourselves that, spiritually; all is well in the Universe. Fear unattended to can be fatal. An open heart and mind is the solution. Remember to surrender the fear to the Creator, offering it up as incense to be transformed into a more loving, constructive learning tool. If we can acknowledge the fear, embrace it as part of who we are, and utilize it as a learning system, we are already in the solution.

Let us not deny the fear or the shadow. Let us stand tall in the Divine Light and work with it until it is rewoven back into the beautiful essence of who we truly are, which is Love, Wisdom, and Innocence. We also need to remember that we are not wholly the fear itself; this temporal sense of insecurity does not identify our whole personhood.

May we rest assured that the Creator has the solution to all of our founded and unfounded fears.

Relax and bathe in the sunlight of a loving Creator. Let us drink in the strength of our Divine Ones who watch over us.

May we never lose our childlike imagination.

PLAY

January 17

May we not take our little trials and ourselves too seriously. Instead, may we learn the art of play.

Can you remember when you were a child, and how you played, pretended, and were engrossed in your own God-given imagination? Children are very close to the Spirit world. Let us have a more childlike, play-like spirit today. We still have access to that incredible imagination now, even if we think that we have left that world behind.

When we find ourselves uptight or stressed, let us find the part of ourselves that is loving, playful, creative, and humorous. We are not on Earth to lose our sense of humor, yet instead, to find the humor in even the gravest of circumstances. Let us be creative today and work on finding the humor in something, where, normally we would be *serious adults*. Perhaps we can practice this day to retrieve our childlike creativity, which may be filled with profound insights into ordinary, everyday problems. Today, let us touch the hearts of our imaginary inner children.

May we remember to play, laugh, and sing a little tune in the midst of our work.

We whistled a tune in the heat and havoc of our day. Our Angel laughed aloud and said, "Now this is not that tragic!!"

*We each have a purpose on this Earth. Let us accept it
with dignity and joy.*

WE ARE NEEDED

January 18

May we have a deep understanding that we are needed in this
world.

Whatever our occupations, our roles, our duties, or
responsibilities in life are, let us remember that we are needed for
that purpose at the time. If your talent lies with being a parent, an
artist, a secretary, a doctor, or simply living your life seeking
truth, you are needed where you are right at that given moment.
This is not to say, however, that your career identifies you totally,
rather, you respect yourself where you are now in your life's
journey.

Let us rest in the comfort of the Creator's Divine Plan for us
all, which is that everything and everyone is interwoven into the
Universal Tapestry, working together for balance and harmony.
In meditation, we can ask our Higher Selves for the revelation of
our Divine Purposes. We are living our Divine Purposes if we
love what we do and do what we love, according to our Highest
Potentialized Selves in the Highest Good for all concerned.

May we realize our Divine purpose, and know that we are
working to integrate this aspect into the Highest Good for
ourselves and all others.

*Be the best you can be at each moment. Create love within
and be confident and serene.*

If one believes and intuitively "knows," one is never alone.

ANGEL'S COMFORT

January 19

May we be comforted in the belief and the inner knowledge of our Angels.

Do you believe in Angels? Sometimes they also are referred to as our guides. Even though most of us cannot see them, we can still maintain the *knowing* of their presence, perhaps in the witnessing of miracles, which can be one way of confirming their existence. The next time we feel sad or are in need of comfort, we can ask our Angels for nurturing support. They are in the business of helping us to adjust our lives back onto the path to the Divine.

Nothing is too overwhelming for the Angels, as they possess the Infinite Intelligence and Grace, being held closely in the arms of the Creator. Let us intently listen to these Messengers, for their voices whisper the secrets of the Universe.

May we learn more about Angels—our Guides—and call upon them in times of need, while remembering to thank them for their support and healing.

A teardrop fell from our disheartened eyes, and we called upon our Angel for nurturing and wisdom. The tears soon dried, as new inspiration filled our heart and mind, and we found creative solutions to our problems.

Even if we cannot trust totally in people, we can still
trust in the law of the Universe.

TRUST

January 20

May we remember that, according to the Creator's Divine Plan, we are exactly where we are supposed to be in our healing process. We trust this process and know that the Universe is safe and well.

We are all constantly in a healing process—whether it is conscious or unconscious—and have been since the moment we were incarnated on Earth. The Earth is also in a healing process. Let us have faith in our Creator that the Earth and *all* beings are part of a Divine Plan, and that it is unfolding perfectly, even though we may not be able to trust this in totality. Trust means a firm reliance or a confident belief or faith. With this definition in mind, even though we may not be where we would like to be in our healing processes, let us have the trust that we are changing and evolving with the rhythm of the Universe.

Let us carry this faith and not allow expectations, which could possibly undermine the natural healing processes with guilt, fear, and shame, thus causing more mistrust and deeper disappointment. Let us, then, be grateful for who and what we are, which can spiritually be defined as Love, Beauty, and Wisdom; all steadfast in the ever-changing winds of time.

May we learn to trust the Perfect Intelligence of our Creator, and know that we are essentially Truth itself in the eyes of the God within us.

When we align ourselves with Higher Will, we know the
process of life is simply food for our spirit.

One does not need eyesight to follow the vision of the heart.

FOLLOWING THE HEART

January 21

May we always follow our heart, for therein lies the Intelligence of the Universe and the Unconditional Love of the Creator.

Following the heart is being true to ourselves, as we pursue our Divine Quest with confidence, love, and assurance. We all have interests in our lives—those subjects that speak to us not only through the mind, but through the heart as well. You may ask yourself the question of why you are drawn to certain subjects and certain people. In each instance, the answer most likely lies deep within the heart, where intuition speaks invariably louder than intellect. There are people in our lives with whom we may feel a strong connection, those who uplift or inspire us, and those to whom we are quickly drawn. Although the attraction may be founded in past-life experiences with that person, we are still using the eyes of the heart to see them.

Let us, then, place more trust in our God-given intuition, which is inside the heart and soul of every creature in this Universe. When we choose to live more intuitively and spontaneously, we find the reassurance of joy in places where we may have never before conceived them to exist.

May we learn to live more intuitively and know that we are drawn to certain beliefs, people, and situations through the language of the heart.

When we see another through the eyes of the heart, there is a connection between our souls that nothing can destroy.

Forgiveness is not denial. It is being responsible.

WORKING ON FORGIVENESS

January 22

May we continue to forgive ourselves and any other being that we feel has the potential to rob us of our peace of mind.

There comes a time in a person's life when she or he can no longer afford to hold onto resentments of any kind. For those on a spiritual path, we will find that harboring any *ill feeling* toward ourselves or another is simply a deterrent to peace of mind. One of the most effective ways to rid ourselves of resentment and forgive others is to practice Metta meditation. Metta is one of the Buddhists' ways of enlightenment or self-actualization, meaning, freedom from all suffering.

When we practice Metta for ourselves and all others, we are, in Western terminology, praying for the health, happiness, and prosperity, which we wish for ourselves, to be also shed as a Light upon those we resent, for those we love, and for the whole planet. After sincerely practicing Metta for a short while, we will find that the bitterness harbored toward another will naturally turn into understanding and compassion and, eventually, Love. Peace of mind and serenity are ours once again. You may create your own words of goodwill for yourself and others. Forgiveness is essential for peace of mind, and it may take a lifetime of effort to achieve.

Here is an example of Metta Meditation:

May I be at peace.
May I be free from suffering.
May my heart be open.
May I awaken to the Light of my True nature.
May I be healed.
May I be a source of healing for all other beings.

First, we pray for ourselves to be balanced, in order that we may better pray for others. We then pray the Metta for our loved ones and friends, followed by prayers for any and all those whom we may resent. Finally we pray the Metta for *all* beings.

May we remember to practice Metta daily and celebrate the freedom that comes with true forgiveness.

Learn to love yourself, even in the throes of anger.

ANGER

January 23

May we learn to handle our anger appropriately and be as compassionate as possible with ourselves should it pour out in ways that may not be as graceful as we may want them to be.

All beings experience anger. It is merely a human emotion. When we feel threatened, or our sacred space and boundaries are violated, or if we have been abused in some way, we feel anger. Yet, underneath the anger lies deep hurt and/or fear for our primary survival. When we want to show our incisors, let us take a step back, and take our anger to another level of expression. Let us take a look within, and nurture our hurts or fears.

When we take a deep breath and pause, we then have more of a choice as to how we act in the situation. We need either time to walk away or to give as appropriate responses as we can. We may have to be firm, yet we do not have to reside on the same heated level as our offender. We do not blame or avoid, only take responsibility for what may be our part. We can learn much about how to react when angry by studying the spiritual Masters, some who use humor to transform it into something joyful, yet effective. We then pray for our offenders so as to not hold onto resentment, apologize if we were inappropriate, and eventually let it go. We need to wonder if we will even *remember* the situation in three weeks. Know that all is well.

May we deal with our anger the best way we know how, as we acknowledge that it is there, and may we learn different methods of letting it go after it has been expressed.

When we raised our voice, we heard our Angel say: "Next time, sing it out, and see that there is no reason for anger."

*If we are truly honest, we can see our weak points. If we are
truly humble, we can see our strengths.*

TAKING INVENTORY

January 24

May we always remember to sweep our own porch first.

Every good business takes an inventory. An inventory is a
survey of goods or stock. How many times do we take another
person's inventory without taking ours first? Usually, all the
things we like or dislike in another are mirrored in what we like
and dislike about ourselves. Most of us, in the midst of the angst
and hurry of this world, are quick to judge another without
looking honestly at what our own inventory looks like.

Let us take a good survey of our own personalities, before we
come to conclusions about another. Let us remember that all
people are struggling in their own way toward the Light and Love
of our Creator.

May we disengage from our false pride and remember that
the Creator is in control of our thoughts, words, and deeds.

*When we look out the window and see sheer beauty, we are
seeing the reflection of all the joy within us.*

When we consciously choose Love, we will know less fear.

CHOOSING LOVE

January 25

May we choose Love over fear and integrate that Love into all aspects of our being.

Did you know that we can choose how to think and feel? Emotions begin with thought. We can consciously change our thoughts and not be enslaved by them or our emotions even when we *feel* overwhelmed. The choice to Love is the greatest work we shall ever do in life. We all feel fear at times, yet we can overcome it with our choice to be free of it.

We do this by identifying the fear first, then thanking the fear for protecting us. We then embrace the fear and integrate it, with Love, into our whole being. With the guidance of our Creator and the Love of our Angels, we will find that there is nothing to fear that Love cannot make right again.

May we choose to be master of our thoughts today, and to remember that the art of loving is our natural state.

Our nature is Light, Love, and Spirit. We are not slaves to fear, for our Creator does not let us out of Divine Sight.

Love confined limits goodwill.

LOVE ALL

January 26

May we learn to love all beings and creatures with equanimity.

Do you place limits or conditions on your love? Do you feel love for only a chosen few? If so, let us learn to expand this love to all persons and creatures. We are all an integral part of the Creator and the Universe. We are interconnected with a common Source. This source is Love. May we observe the teaching of the Great Masters and try to act accordingly. We may not agree with the actions of all people, yet let us remember that they, too, have the capacity to love and to be loved.

Let us not consolidate our love for only those to whom we feel close to, yet, through prayer and meditation, learn to love, if only in thought, all beings and creatures in this Universe. We will see that, in return, the Universal Love comes back to us.

May we use the power of our thoughts to send love and goodwill to all humanity—to all who dwell upon this Earth, excluding no one.

There extends a beacon of white light from our heart to all on Earth through which we send unconditional Love, Goodwill, and Mirth.

Filling the intellect with too much knowledge leaves
little room for intuition.

INSPIRATIONAL READING

January 27

May we read the words of the masters to be inspired to lead a more God-centered life.

The human mind is like a computer: garbage in—garbage out. The opposite of course is true as well—Divine messages in—Divine messages out. Let us be more selective in our reading and be inspired to think and act with wisdom and illumination.

The words of the Bible, the Koran, the Bhagavad-Gita, and other teachings can bring insight into ourselves and others, as well as help us to walk the same path as the Masters. We are all Masters of our Spiritual journeys, being intuitively guided by the Unconditional Love and Light of the Creator.

May we be inspired to read and learn to the very best of our ability and to find the hidden secrets of the mystics to comprehend the true meaning of life.

We surround ourselves with Divine teachings, and we lose interest in material frivolities and unnecessary worldly things.

The slightest shift in attitude can bring the most profound happiness.

ACCEPTING OTHERS

January 28

May we accept others as they are, relinquishing our need to control them.

Do we appoint ourselves "Directors-In-Chief of the Universe?" If only people thought, said, and did what we wanted, everything would be rosy, right? If so, let us let go of this unrealistic responsibility. What a burden to carry! Instead, let us take delight in the fact that we are all individuals. We each have different personalities and are unique to the extent of our past experiences and our spiritual evolution.

When we can appreciate the differences in others, we can more readily see the similarities. By the same token, we can discipline our children without infringing upon their individual character. We can bring assurance and love to them by being uplifting and inspiring. We can accept people without necessarily approving of their behavior at times. Total acceptance means being less critical of another's character, as we lovingly let go of all judgments. When we learn to accept ourselves more, we naturally will accept others, flaws and all.

May we learn to accept others as they are, not for who we would like them to be.

We know our Highest potential. Let us enjoy each other now on this lifetime journey.

We all deserve gifts that delight the heart.

GIVE YOURSELF A GIFT

January 29

May we release ourselves from all guilt and give ourselves a meaningful gift.

Let us pause for a moment and ask ourselves if we have given ourselves a gift package lately. If not, then let us ask our Creator for the creative inspiration to do just that—and not feel guilty about it. Gift packages come in all shapes and sizes, yet there is always something inside the box that brings a smile. We do not feel guilty about giving someone else a gift, therefore, let us give ourselves a gift, too, that we truly deserve and would cherish.

We do indeed deserve a gift today. Remember that the Angels' Love makes us happy, and, if we search our hearts, we find that happiness is our birthright and natural state, and it is only society's conditioning and our attitudes that make that loving state otherwise.

May we honor ourselves with a gift today.

We are here on Earth to enjoy being alive and well. Breathe in the gift of living, and feel your heartsong.

Be creative! Go into nonsense gear and laugh!

FRIVOLITY

January 30

May we indulge ourselves in a little healthy frivolity each day to relieve the monotony of tedious work.

If our minds need a little break from the work and arduous tasks we do daily, then let us indulge in the playfulness of healthy frivolity for a time. Our Creator loves us and knows our need for a *mind-break*. The inspiration of the Angels is about Divine balance. Sometimes we need the nonsensical to keep our minds more sound. When was the last time we had a good belly laugh? As long as we are not harming ourselves or others, any type of "goofing off" can be beneficial. We were not created to be working machines with no humor in our lives. We can wear our *own* selves out by being overly serious and/or too intense! This is the time to call a fun friend or to watch some comedy.

Let us do and think of something a little more uplifting and natural to keep our mind-body mechanism in good working order. Over time, we can learn to live harmoniously in giving the necessary nurturance to our bodies, our minds, and our spirits. It is all within the Divine Balance.

May we enjoy ourselves for a time today without being detrimental to our overall well-being.

We hummed a song of happiness and whistled a tune, as Angels caressed us.

*Caution: Sensationalism may be hazardous
to your spiritual health!*

SAFETY

January 31

May we exercise caution as we travel about in this world and utilize the power of prayer in all situations.

We live in a world of exaggerated fear most of the time. If we listen to radio or watch TV news, we hear the most sensational reports of crime, weather, and anything else that would induce our fears and prevent us from even leaving the house! This is media manipulation. There are also wonderful events that happen daily throughout the world.

Let us realize that, indeed, we need to have caution, yet we need to be able to move around in our lives with the confidence that our Creator surrounds us with protective white light and will take care of us. If we share the interest in the common good of humankind, then we have no fear—we will be comforted by our prayers to have caution, but overall, confidence, poise, and self-assurance from our loving Creator and the power that this Highest Angel places in our hearts. Try taking a long break from watching or even listening to the news. We may find that we remember that we live in a beautiful world, as well. Nature is never too far away.

May we use caution in our daily affairs, yet know, ultimately; that we will be all right no matter what the circumstances. Nothing can separate us from the Love of God.

Whistle in the dark if you must, but know that you are in the Light. Trust in your Creator.

There is nothing sadder than the drought of the spirit within.

QUENCHING THIRST

February 1

May we quench our thirst with the life-giving waters of our Creator.

How simple is the concept of the body's natural way of quenching thirst—we drink water or liquids to satisfy this biological need. The soul also thirsts, as well, for the Love of the Divine. What benefits us if we are overflowing with physical strength and material goods, yet are dehydrated spiritually? Without fulfilling ourselves with the Water of Life, which continuously flows freely from the Undying Source, our bodies soon wither and our possessions prove meaningless. There are many different ways of filling the spiritual cup. It is up to each of us as to how to do so constructively.

Let us drink in the water of the Highest Good to become more of who we truly and naturally are—we are children of the Eternal Creator, and we shall be forever satisfied by the drink of Love and Light from the Eternal Spirit within.

May we drink in and absorb all of our Creator's Love.

Thirst is always quenched. In drawing from our Creator's well, we are awakened and purified.

Those of a generous nature touch people's lives
without even knowing it.

GENEROSITY

February 2

May we be generous in kindness of character, always remembering that we do, indeed, always have something to give others.

Generosity means to be giving. We do not have to be philanthropists or *big spenders* to be called generous. We can act with kindness for everyone we meet today. Even if we encounter adverse types of people, we can still have compassion for them.

Being rich in character means to be humble, as well as knowing how to love others, respect others, and to feel the real joy of living and giving. We may never know when another appreciates our smile.

May we be generous and have the willingness to give.

The Angels gave us a prayer to offer "May you be at peace and share goodwill, and know that, no matter what, you are loved."

Keeping warm is much more than mere survival.
It is a way of life.

KEEPING WARM

February 3

May we be kept warm by the understanding that the Grace of our Creator forever surrounds us.

If we live in a part of the world that has harsh winters, then we know the importance of taking care of ourselves by keeping warm. Keeping warm makes us feel cozy, as well as protects us from the elements. In another sense, we can protect ourselves from harm and the world's harshness by visualizing the warm, White Light of the Creator surrounding us at all times. Not only does this Grace surround us, it is held within us at all times. This Grace is merely a thought away.

Let us keep warmth in our hearts by thinking warm and loving thoughts. We find that as we invite these heartwarming thoughts into ourselves, we are also feeling those same thoughts for others.

May we utilize the Creator's warmth in all aspects of our life today.

We built a fire and found warmth in our home. We also found warmth in our heart, given to us by our Creator, to give to someone else.

One begins to mature when the point is reached in life to ask,
"What really matters?"

WHAT MATTERS

February 4

May we learn to separate what matters in our life and what
does not actually have great effect in the long run.

What really matters in life? Is it a monetary possession, or
what the Jones' are doing? Or is it keeping physically, mentally,
or spiritually fit? We can see how trivial we can be at times. What
really matters is a balance in leading a fulfilling life, with
acknowledgment of our soul's journey leading back to our
Creator. What matters are the lessons that we learn each day from
our experiences on this life-path. What matters is our unique
connection with the Divine, celebrating the joy therein. What
matters is those we love, including how we grow to love
ourselves in humility.

Let us learn to differentiate what really matters in life and act
accordingly. Simple beatitudes can have profound meaning. Let
us look for ways of joy, not ways of harm. Let us learn to see
where we can be of service to others. May our song be, "How can
I help?"

May we learn to live more mindfully each moment.

What did we learn today? We needed what our Angels had to
say. What did our Angels tell us? Find joy and faith and live
spontaneously.

We truly begin to see when we see with the eyes of the Creator.

WE ARE SPIRIT

February 5

May we have the realization that we are Spirit—One with our Creator—and that no harm shall come to us.

Can we even imagine what this world would be like if each individual were to have the self-realization that the self is actually Spirit—one of Pure Love and Pure Light? Can we imagine perfect harmony and peace in the world? If we cannot, try to imagine this: it is indeed possible!

Let us begin to heal the world by meditating on our Creator's immeasurable Love for us and all creations. Let us pray for self-realization, and for the realization of each individual—truly wanting for them what we want for ourselves. Let us pray to be free of judgments, critical thoughts, and anything negative that keeps us bound to the ego. While the ego is necessary for our survival, we are not the Ego. We are Pure and Spiritual beings on our journey to Peace and Harmony with God.

May we pray and meditate not only for our own souls, but also for freedom of spirit for each individual.

We are Light vibrations of Power and Love. Let that power be Peace and hold the thought that "so below is as above."

The past can be a nightmare, or it can be an adventure story filled with valuable lessons.

FREEING OURSELVES FROM THE PAST

February 6

May we find healthy, alternative ways to free ourselves from our past.

For some, childhood and adolescence may have been trying times. We may have regrets from our earlier years, or we may have wished people, places, or situations to have been different. As we watch our minds, let us be aware of how much time we spend living in the past. We know well, that we cannot change what has already happened. We also know that we can learn certain techniques to gently bring our minds back to the present. Praying for right attitude is one technique. This can call for forgiveness for ourselves and others. Another technique is meditating. This changes our focus from the past or future to the immediate present, as we commune with the Divine or simply watch the breath for a period of time.

There is little peace of mind in living in the past, yet there is peace in prayer and meditation if we make the concentrated effort. Living in the past is a signal to us that we are refusing to live in the present. Let us separate what was then and what is now. We can ask ourselves quietly, "What in ourselves are we afraid to see?" We may be pleasantly surprised to see our basic goodness.

May we always keep in mind that we have the choice and power, instilled in us by our Creator, to focus on the present.

We learn from the past. We do not let it intimidate or frustrate us. We simply contemplate the Peace of the Divine and let it go.

What on the surface may look still and silent, may be
working diligently within.

DORMANCY

February 7

May we understand that our personal cycles are like that of
the seasons.

At times, we may feel as if we are not traveling on a spiritual
path, or we may feel like we are not accomplishing as much as
we would like on our souls' journeys. Let us understand that
these are cycles or phases in our life rhythms, and that we may be
germinating under the soil, like a planted seed, hoping for new
sprouts to show their faces in the next cycle. Dormancy is
necessary for activity. Even when we are resting, we are doing
something: taking care of ourselves or nurturing the planted seed.

Let us understand that all of our cycles are extremely
necessary in order to move on to the next phase. Humans are not
too unlike the four seasons of the year—we also have times when
we pull back, perhaps to observe, and then move forward with
more natural reassurance. Contrasting this waiting period, as in
our winter season, we may soon burst forth with newfound
energy once again, followed by another season of deep rest,
allowing our productive actions to *mature*—as in Autumn, the
season of maturity.

May we be as gentle with ourselves during dormancy as we
would be to a sleeping child. All is a process to be trusted, a
rhythm to be celebrated, and a cycle to be completed—only to
begin again, refreshed with newfound energy.

Our Creator designed the seasons for a purpose. When we
tune in to our own rhythms, we find the Divine cycles within us.

There is a spiritual teaching in the angry words of a lover,
as well as in the profound wisdom of a sage.

SPIRITUAL TEACHING

February 8

May we acquaint ourselves with the Highest Spiritual teachings of the mystics, saints, and all those who follow the path toward the Creator.

There are thousands of pages written about the different paths to the One—the Divine Source. May we keep our minds open to the many philosophies of different religions and cultures to get a well-rounded idea of spiritual aspirations.

Let us be Universalists, who explore and study all spiritual paths, which ultimately lead to the same God. Closing our hearts and minds to other paths can lead to self-righteousness and stubbornness, which ultimately defeat the Higher Good for which the path was originally embarked upon.

May we appreciate all paths to God and learn even more about them, knowing that Our Creator will gently urge us to grow—whether we follow one particular path or accept all paths as Divine Teachings.

Whatever your path, keep the Creator as your single focus.

To look fearlessly within is absolute honesty.

LOOKING WITHIN

February 9

May we have no fear to look deeply within ourselves for the insight needed to be aware of our full potential.

Does looking incisively inward with clear perception frighten you? You can be assured that deep within the heart and soul lies a beautiful paradise. It is true that at times in our lives we need to sort out the shadows and *boogiemen*, yet it is not to say that we should fear these dragons. To look fearlessly within, means to love ourselves in our totality and to incorporate all aspects of ourselves into a healing whole.

Our Creator will only reveal to us that which we are entirely ready to see at a particular phase in our lives. This is a progressive, growing process, and if persistence is applied, looking within means discovering who we naturally are: loving children of the Creator.

May we be willing to look within our whole self, and feel the blessing of the Divine.

We are created in Love, and to love this Divine realization of who we are. All fears are merely traps to hold us from seeing the Light and acknowledging the One Loving Source of Creation.

Silence can be an entire filibuster.

SPEAKING YOUR MIND

February 10

May we learn to speak our mind quietly and clearly.

Are there any people in your life to whom you would like to "speak your mind"? If so, search your heart for the true intent and motive, and then courageously confront that person should the opportunity arise. There are many ways to get the point across without harming the basic character of any other.

Sometimes, we must speak diplomatically in order to meet our own needs, yet without bluntly offending the other person. Speaking harshly could only exacerbate the problem. An affirmation such as, "my thoughts and speech are perfectly controlled by God for good communication with others" may be helpful to repeat silently to oneself before speaking one's mind.

May we choose our words carefully when speaking directly to such a person who may have harmed us or threatened our serenity in some way. May we pray to make our point very clear, yet say it with the intention of the Highest Good for all concerned to create a "win-win" situation.

When we speak emotionally, sometimes the floodgates open. When we are clear-headed, we know our Angel is choosing the most effective words.

To understand life's cycles, watch thunderstorms pass.

THE ASCENT TO JOY

February 11

May we gently awaken to our joy ascending upward from the depths of our pain.

Nothing in life is permanent except the unconditional Love and Light of a Forgiving Creator. Should we find ourselves in the dark caverns of our emotional pain, let us know, beyond a shadow of a doubt, that there is also joy that brilliantly awaits us. We change during each and every breath and cannot expect a *mood* or *feeling* to last forever.

Therein lies the hope of new beginnings, which are always present for each and every one of us. Like the Phoenix rising from her ashes, let us be reborn again into life's joy. Even if we deny our pain and even our joy, let us encourage our soul to know that all is changeable on the emotional plane, and that should we choose, the Higher Self can guide us to balance and harmony in Divine Totality.

May we enjoy our ascent into a newfound joy and realize that it is the depth of our pain that has given us the eyes to see the Light again.

The Phoenix builds her own funeral pyre and then arises triumphantly from the ashes, purified, refreshed, and new.

Loving ourselves is knowing when to nurture ourselves.

GENTLENESS

February 12

May we be gentle with ourselves today, taking special care of our physical, emotional and spiritual needs.

It is true that humans can be overly critical and harshly judgmental of themselves. Let us give ourselves a gentle break from this habitual way of treating ourselves. We deserve to have good thoughts about ourselves, and for surviving the "slings and arrows" of our lives thus far.

Let us be more loving and nurturing to every aspect of ourselves today, and bask in the sunlight of our own Divine essence. As we take care of our needs, we are more available to help and serve others.

May we nurture ourselves with loving and confident thoughts about ourselves today.

As the Divine Mother takes care of her children tenderly, let us model ourselves after this loving kindness for ourselves and all of humanity.

One who carries himself in Peace, resonates louder
than any gunshot.

THE POWER OF PEACE

February 13

May we feel at Peace with ourselves, our world, and all beings, acknowledging the immense Power therein.

One of the most powerful forces in the Universe is Total Peace. This means to act calmly, and confidently, in even the most extreme circumstance. The calm comes from the inherent knowing that the Creator is always within us. The confidence comes by also acknowledging that the Divine guides us in all that we do, say, think, and feel.

When we merge with the Divine in meditation, we keep the Power that is bestowed in us through that very Source. The source is Love. This Love and Light constitutes what we call True Power. Our quiet times can reconnect us with this Loving Source and all that we know to be universally true.

May we know the true source of Pure Peace and Power. That which empowers us is the ever-flowing river of Divine Love found accessible within us at all times.

Physical strength has little to do with True Power. The Divine is the Loving Force that empowers us in our weakest hour.

Every day, find one person with whom you can identify.

ONE CULTURE

February 14

May we stand united within ourselves, knowing that every single soul in this world can be united as well.

When listening to others from different cultures or studying about them, let us see our *unified* souls rather than the differences. Let us attempt to see the similarities in all humans instead of our judgmental likes and dislikes. In the knowing that a Creator gave birth to all, with a soul that longs to love and be loved, we can more easily see our similarities. Prejudice is not within our true selves, it is the result of conditioning, experience, and false programming. There is a solid freedom in not allowing society to dictate how we should think or feel.

Let us respect ourselves in our lives' journeys, and respect others in their journeys as well. Let us look into the eyes of others and see through into the windows to their souls.

May we look for ways to connect with all others, understanding that what we may not like in them is a perfect mirror to what we dislike in ourselves.

We see you as our sister and our brother. We are all connected by the heartstrings of the Divine Mother.

A soft heart may break. Yet, there remains the abundance
to soothe it again.

SOFTENING

February 15

May we accept the Unconditional Love of the Creator into our heart and feel our entire essence begin to soften.

How difficult most of our lessons have been! How hard we have been on ourselves! Does not a soft touch for the body, mind, and soul sound precious? We can do this in a creative meditation, whereby we visualize the soft white glow and illumination of Our Creator surrounding us and enfolding us.

We then take this glow and gently place it around our hearts. We feel our hearts open and soften with the Healing Power of the Divine energy. We let in this tender light. We begin to feel safe and loved. We then extend this Healing Light to others who may be suffering. We feel connected to the Creator through the umbilical cord of Divine Unity. We are gradually awakened. We extend this beautiful cord of Love to all others. We are healing ourselves and the entire planet, one by one, with Universal, Unconditional Love and Healing Light.

May we soften enough to see, hear, feel, taste, and touch the Divine Light within our soul and realize that all souls also are in need of this same Healing Energy.

Soft, Divine Light is all around us. Soft, Divine Light is within us. Together we heal the tumultuous waters at last, and merge into the bliss of a calming sea.

Align your will to the Highest Star, that is,
believe in your Spiritual self.

SELF-HEALING

February 16

May we remain openhearted and open-minded to all forms of self-healing, maintaining the aspiration that we *can* totally heal.

Today, there are many types of self-healing techniques available to us. Let us explore the ones that are the most well-rounded and beneficial for the body-mind-spirit. Yoga, for example, is a wonderful way to unite *all* three aspects of the self, using the breath, postures, and meditation for a healthy body, mind, and spirit.

Let us find our own methods of healing that speak clearly to us and our specific needs. Various holistic and integrative medicine procedures can also prove useful. Attending lectures, 12-step programs, workshops, and reading books on the subject of emotional, spiritual, and physical healing can also be advantageous to us. Most important is the Divine Discipline that we need to take action to heal ourselves in times of need.

May we continue to explore all areas of health and healing to enrich our life and, in turn, help others to lead more fulfilled and quality lives.

Our Angels whispered words of wisdom. The message that came from the Creator is clear, "Have faith and fun in life. Look within for Me, your most plentiful resource, and know Peace."

It is only when we honor our own boundaries, that we can honor the boundaries of others.

UNDERSTANDING BOUNDARIES

February 17

May we respect our boundaries, as we respect others' sacred spaces, and keep Peace in the Divine center.

We all have invisible sacred spaces that surround us at all times, and are to be respected and honored as, indeed, sacred. How do you feel when someone, even a loved one, invades your boundaries? Suppose you want to hug someone. Usually, this is a beautiful, unspoken gesture of the heart and is equally understood and reciprocated. Yet there are times when we need to say, "I could use a hug," or "May I hug you?" This is respecting both people's boundaries appropriately.

Let us not be overly pushy, nor deny ourselves when we wish to become closer to someone else. Let us keep our own boundaries clear with others, while honoring their boundaries as well. We each have a right to sacred spaces.

May we reserve our space of honor for our Creator, as well as use discernment of who may enter there.

There is a time to unite and a time to maintain honor. Ask the Creator for wisdom and perception, whether or not you are seeking space or union.

If we can create karma, we can also uncreate it.

KARMA

February 18

May we create good thoughts, words, and deeds and realize that each has a profound impact in the Universe.

We have all heard the expression, "What goes around, comes around." These words are very true. Another word to define our actions and their impact is karma. While deeds are obvious gestures, let us also fine-tune our thoughts and words, realizing that they, too, have immense effect on the course of right action. This is difficult to achieve. Yet, when we realize the importance and the profundity of thoughts themselves, we will know that we can control our own thoughts, choose our own words, and act in accordance with the harmonious flow. Know that the karma that we incur will travel back to our thoughts, words, and deeds.

Let us create good karma and watch our own minds, speech, and behavior. If we buck the system, it inevitably creates disharmony in our lives, which also keeps manifesting chaos in the world like a boomerang affect. Let us learn to be gentle and kind to ourselves and others, wishing only Healing and Goodwill to all.

May we satiate our mind with Unconditional Love and Forgiveness, ever filling our thoughts with goodness and beauty.

Love given from the heart creates more of the same. Adversity in thought and deed have never created a "win-win" situation.

*To appreciate the celestial, we must also appreciate
the mundane.*

ONE FOOT IN FRONT OF THE OTHER

February 19

May we trust our Creator inherently and know that some
days are simply a matter of putting one foot in front of the other,
with our Angels guiding us.

Some days are filled with mundane tasks, which we may or
may not like. With a prayer for guidance and a cheerful attitude,
we can perform these tasks, however great or small. We can be
grateful for responsibilities and challenges in our lives, rather
than complain that we would prefer being somewhere else
or have the attitude of "We *have* to do this, ugh!" It is truly
amazing how our entire attitudes can change with simple prayer.
Maybe simply being grateful that we possess a healthy mind and
body to even *do* these tasks can be enough to get us through an
uneventful day.

Let us take time to ask for guidance from our Angels or the
Creator and place one foot in front of the other and then, walk
assuredly.

May we understand that we are guided by our Creator in all
ways, however great or small.

*As we go through the day, we concentrate on one task at a
time. Placing full concentration on each task brings gratitude our
way.*

When we let go of our victim role in life, we let go of our anger.

LETTING GO OF ANGER

February 20

May we recognize when we are angry, and without antagonizing ourselves or anyone else further, may we find the strength and understanding to let it go.

By definition, anger is a strong emotion of displeasure, excited by a sense of injury. Do we want to hold on to displeasure in our lives? When we understand that anger usually masks a deep hurt or a fear, it will be easier to let it go. We can let it go by using our breath. By deep breathing into the physical body, where the anger has manifested, and surrounding that place with love and compassion, we can then breathe it out. Strong emotions, if not acknowledged, will take their place in our physical body and lead to serious illness if not addressed.

There is a science behind breathing in the Life Energy into our bodies, minds, and spirits. Once we feel more at ease and learn how to forgive ourselves and others, we can then find more pleasure in our lives. Our pain subsides. We are on the road to recovery.

May we use the breath to let go of anger and finally breathe in the spirit of forgiveness.

We pray that our Creator helps us find the understanding deeply embedded underneath our anger. When we feel more of a sense of unity with humanity, we find that we are released from any negative emotion.

To be mature does not mean to lose one's sense of humor.

MATURATION

February 21

May we embrace the process of emotional, physical, and spiritual maturation.

To mature means to be brought by natural process to completeness of growth and development. Our entire lives are a maturation process. Let us absorb how much we have already matured up to this day and continue to nurture our bodies, minds, and spirits for even more fine-tuning and development. If we are more mature in some areas than others, we can see this by practicing self-awareness exercises.

Reading up on the areas where we may be somewhat weaker, practicing new ways to mature, and incorporating these new ways into our behavior and lifestyle are how we can more fully grow. Being inspired by masters and experts in the field can also help us to come full circle. Let us also be gentle on ourselves if we have not matured as much as we would like, and love ourselves in the process as much as possible. We are not perfect in all areas. Perfection is not the goal, nor is being overly serious. Progress is where we *all* shine.

May we ask our Creator for guidance to become more mature in some area every day.

We are growing and ripening every single day in our awareness of our soul's journey to wholeness and peace.

One does not need to know how to cook to follow this recipe!

RECIPE FOR FULFILLMENT

February 22

May we utilize the ingredients for a rich, full life to make a nutritious meal, healthy for each day.

Just as we use different ingredients in cooking, let us use these ingredients, in any order, for a healthy fulfilling life:

1 cup—Healing Light
1 cup—Grace from the Divine
1 cup—Unconditional Love
1 cup—Total Loving Acceptance of Ourselves and Others
1 cup—Discernment
1 cup—Humor
1 cup—Prayer and Meditation
1 cup—Positive Attitude
1 cup—Physical Exercise
1 cup—Discipline

Mix all ingredients thoroughly and apply every day for a wholesome life of richness, fun, and adventure.

God is always a breath away from the innocence of every heart.

SEEKING GOD

February 23

May we seek God with all of our compassionate heart, our questing mind, and our longing soul.

To seek God alone with all that we and our inner resources possess is to know that we are children of Divine Grace. The Creator brings up different images for different people, yet the goal is all the same: to realize that our lives are never-ending, even though we all must shed the body at some point. Our spirits, however, belong to the Creator. When we know, with our deepest knowledge, that God is within us, we truly know that we are the immortal children in Grace of the Divine Light. Seeking God does not mean that we have to become "nuns and monks." It simply means living in gratitude while we are doing what we were meant to do on this Earth.

Let us seek our Creator with all the zealous energy and passion within us, asking that the Divine reveal itself in our every thought, word, and deed.

May we become willing to seek the essence of our Creator within ourselves and within all things.

Seek God with all your heart and soul and walk within the Divine Light.

We are all chosen by God to sojourn on our Spiritual Path.

WE ARE BLESSED

February 24

May we understand that the Creator has blessed us and all others with the same Love.

Each and every creature alike on Earth breathes in the same air and life force that sustains us. Our Creator has blessed us all with lives to live. The only differences in people's lives are how they choose to live within a 24-hour period. As God's children, we are not judged and differentiated. However, the law of karma is a Universal Law, and we do indeed reap what we sow. Yet there is a spark of the Divine in every single living and multiplying cell in the pulse of eternity.

Let it be a comfort to us to feel blessed by the Living Spirit and look with our eyes and see this same living Spirit of the Divine in all others.

May God bless all in the Divine Harmony of an everlasting Peace within the Healing Light.

When we know we are blessed, we more readily see Divine Light in everything and everyone.

Your inner self is the wisest teacher.

BE YOUR OWN GURU

February 25

May we be guided by the Divine Love within our own soul.

Throughout our lives, we may have many good spiritual teachers, and we can learn much from each. In actuality, we can learn much from anyone with whom we come into contact or read about. Each soul has its own story to tell. However, if we draw deeply from the wells of our own spirits, we can take what we have learned from all, assimilate it, and use it to become our own "gurus." Our main focus is on the Creator or whatever name we choose to give to Spirit.

Let us let the impersonal Divine manifest into our personal guru by the art of meditation and by living a healthy life, well balanced in body, mind, and soul. We become sure-footed and honest, living by our Higher Standards, which is the Divine working through us.

May we learn from all, maintaining autonomy and individualism, following our own Divine spiritual path.

If all paths lead to God, who is to say any individual path is not worthy to tread?

The Mother is both underfoot and overhead.

GROUNDED

February 26

May we always be sure-footed and grounded onto Mother Earth, for this is where our strength lies.

When those days arise when we feel less than balanced, or are consumed by fear or some other threatening emotion, let us take a moment to remember this: our feet are said to be sacred if firmly planted on Mother Earth. We can soon feel reconnected and calmed. We can close our eyes, breathe deeply, and visualize that we are like a tree, with roots extending downward, deep into Mother Earth. With a firm foundation, we are free to grow, branch out, and eventually bloom.

The Mother is where we take in our sustenance, trust, and courage and where we find the most support. May we find our little patch of nature, our favorite garden, or our sacred ground today to feel sound and strong.

May we remember to become grounded this day, open to more meaningful and fulfilled life experiences.

Let our heads rest in the clouds, while our moccasins remain firmly planted on the Earth. We draw our strength from the Earth, giver and sustainer of life, the Mother who gave us birth.

There is an Angel inside of you. Take her by the hand and
hug her with your heart.

ANGELS EVERYWHERE

February 27

May we remember to ask our Angels for assistance in all undertakings.

While writing this book, one daily entry per day, I always asked my Inspirational Angel to guide me in writing these daily thoughts. She never disappointed me. We all can attest to the fact that the well of inspiration never runs dry, thanks to our Angels.

Let us, in whatever we do, think, or feel, remember to ask our Angels for guidance. We have many Angels—for Creativity, Protection, Humor, Love, Sleep, Healing, Work, *ad infinitum*. It is simply a matter of *asking* our Angels to help us in different ways. We are wanted, needed, and deeply Loved by the Angels. When we know this in our heart of hearts, we can begin to heal, help others, and walk more confidently, knowing that we are walking in the spirit of the Divine Goodness.

May we hold our heads up and acknowledge our Angels in gratitude.

If we feel overwhelmed at times, we can ask our Angel to calm us. Breathing in inspiration from above, we can make each undertaking an act of Love.

Now you see yourself. Now you don't.
Now, look again with new eyes.

THE PHOENIX

February 28

May we rise from the ashes of our past, renewed and refreshed, like the Phoenix.

The Phoenix is an ancient, mythical, Egyptian bird that was the embodiment of the Sun God. It was said to have lived 500 years, then consumed itself in the fire of its own making. The miraculous bird was to rise again from the ashes, rejuvenated and youthful. The Phoenix is one of the emblems of immortality.

Let us consider our past, whether it be an unhappy childhood or perhaps remorse over mistakes made, as the ashes from which we are reborn and rejuvenated. In a sense, we have built our own funeral pyre. Let us deal with our past issues and then continue on in the Light of the path that our Creator intended us to walk— one that is more happy, joyous, and free.

May we choose not to dwell in the consuming fire built by our own actions in the past, yet find the strength to regain momentum in the present, rebuilt and blessed with new energy.

If we learn from our past, the pain will not repeat itself. The past is a lesson, not something in which to continuously delve. Prayer for freedom and wisdom is a worthy aspiration.

Concentrate until you become One with what you are doing.

CONCENTRATION

February 29

May we learn to concentrate and focus, to the best of our ability and see projects all the way through.

On those days where we may feel somewhat scattered and "out there," let us use the art of prayer and meditation to come back down to Earth and to focus more intently on that which is in front of us to do. We can ask the Angel of Concentration to help us come back to center.

In our minds, we can visualize a white beam of Light from the Creator going directly into our *third eye*—the point between the eyebrows. This Light is Love. This *Love Light* helps us to put love into doing the next right move, or to simply be still and take in a few deep breaths to regroup. With that practice of creative visualization, we can love what we do and do what we love.

May we concentrate on loving our projects and, coupled with perseverance, see this Divine project to the end.

Because we all possess the spark of the Divine, all that we do is either Divine or led by the light of that spark. The spark never totally goes out by itself, yet it can transform into a flame of passion that directs our lives toward harmony.

To silence the mind is Peace from the Creator.

SILENCE

March 1

May we find Divine solace in the quiet depths of our mind.

Are you comfortable with complete silence? If not, ask yourself "what is the origin of the fear?" There is such a quality known as *comfortable* silence. When we are comfortable enough inside the body/mind/soul, we can acknowledge the spirit within. Do you have persons in your life with whom you find no words need be spoken to give and receive the loving energy that is being silently exuded? Then you know what comfortable silence is.

Another way to find comfortable silence is in the practice of meditation. In a walking meditation outdoors, we only hear the beautiful sounds of nature. Meditating indoors, there need be no other sound than the sound of one's own heartbeat. With these natural rhythms we can hear the Love of the Creator. With understanding, we find that we are not alone at all in silence and that we can embrace the entire world with our hearts.

May we come to feel comfortable with the natural rhythm of silence.

We listened to our inner knowing and found the ever-flowing Grace of the Divine Spirit.

Lessons never cease in the human world
or in the spiritual world.

GETTING *THERE*

March 2

May we realize that there will always be another *there* awaiting us.

Are you always striving to *get there*, be it in a physical, psychological, or spiritual sense? Granted, it is admirable to achieve the strength to perhaps overcome an outdated habit or lifestyle that no longer serves us and is not healthy for us. There can be the achievement of a particular state of mind, a state of financial security, or many other desirable aspirations.

Let us remember that there will always be other areas in our lives that we may wish to improve upon. *There* is a lesson—a human lesson for our spiritual growth. When we learn that lesson, there will be another lesson to learn. Lessons never stop—this is what makes life an adventure. If we desire to learn a lesson for good, then the Creator will set up a series of obstacles for us to consider. Let this not discourage us in our spiritual or emotional growth, nor in physical terms, as well. We may be trying to create a certain outward image or appearance. *There* is like an unspoken rule for being human: when we think we are *there* or have arrived at a particular goal, there will always be another *there*. Getting *there* is like a stepping stone to help us keep moving ahead in life. It may help to remember that the true goal is individual peace of mind, and Peace with our relationship with Spirit. Lessons can also be learned through joy and positive situations. Let us be humble and good students; there is always a time to be the teacher.

May we know that we are guided by the Divine Spirit in all things, and that all lessons are necessary for the Divine Plan.

When we learn a lesson, let us say thank you to the Divine.
We can dwell in our newfound freedom knowing there will always
be more to discover.

Want to buy the Highest Potentialized Mind? Call the Creator.
Meditative installment plan offered.

CHANGING OUR MIND

March 3

May we realize that we always have a choice in changing our mind.

It is true that we always can, indeed, change our mind in any event, and that we have total permission and a right by the Divine Power within us to do so. Yet there is another meaning to the literal phrase, *changing our mind!* By prayer and communion with the Divine, we can surrender all thoughts—both high and low—to the Creator and find a change in our perception as to how we view life. If we have been negative and pessimistic, we can be more positive and optimistic through the desire to live a more joy-filled life. Whichever way we choose to meditate is up to us, as the various ways to do so are so vast. Five minutes a day may be all we need.

Let us remember that we can, by persistent desire and with the practice of meditation, change our attitudes, views, and our entire mind for the better.

May we work toward changing our perception of ourselves, the world, and spiritual views for the Highest Good available by surrendering ourselves to an omnipotent Creator.

When others see a change in us, it is usually first noted in the eyes. It is when we are filled with new life and joy that the old perceptions of darkness leave us.

An entire day can be colored by a single thought.

STARTING THE DAY

March 4

May we always begin our day with a reconnection to our Creator.

Usually the day will go a little more smoothly if we start it off with a remembrance of the Divine. Perhaps we could read an inspirational passage from a spiritual book or a quote from a spiritual master. We can also meditate for a little while on the spiritual message or calm our busy minds while meditating in any fashion to which we may be accustomed. Prayer is a beautiful way to start off the day, as well as to set the stage for a more God-centered assurance with which to walk, talk, and take action. Prayer and/or meditation may be for us or not. Perhaps a simple thought of a spiritual word or phrase will suffice.

Let us breathe deeply and focus for a moment on the gift of life and its meaning. This can place us in a state of gratitude, which humbles us and helps us to open our hearts.

May we choose a meaningful way to begin each day for a Higher cause.

When we align ourselves with the Spirit of the Creator, that moment is carried on throughout our day with grace.

Never compromise your Truth.

COMPROMISE

March 5

May we learn the art of give and take.

All people and situations cannot always meet all our needs all the time. There is definitely an art to compromising. First, we may want to place our own special needs in the hands of the Creator and trust that all of these needs will be met. When dealing with others, we must be as giving as possible, without totally negating or denying our needs at the same time. The Creator is the Master problem-solver and will, if we put out trust in Divine hands, help both parties to adjust accordingly.

Let us also remember that we are—for the most part—doing the very best we can do at the time.

May we trust that, with the involvement of others of different points of view, our Creator will look after all the specific needs and will act as mediator concerning the Highest Good for all.

Give a little, take a little. Love all and know that the Creator is with you.

If you don't like the old tape, see how you can make it sound on CD.

TAPES

March 6

May we begin recording our own tape—a new tape of positive messages that have been recorded over the old, possibly negative, responses of society, institutions, family members, or any other unhealthy messages we have received in the past, which do not work for us in the present.

The next time we feel guilty or have unrealistic expectations of ourselves, or when the old "committee" meets in our heads, let us ask ourselves whose tape is actually playing in our minds. Is it our mother's voice or our father's? Could it be the tape of a teacher, unkind peers, or a boss? Whoever's voice it is, let us now record our own voice, giving ourselves kind and compassionate messages to enhance our emotional balance. We are each unique and special in the eyes of God, whose tape is loving, when truly heard with the heart.

Let us listen to our hearts' messages, which contain the spark of the Divine.

When we awaken to the Light of who we are and how God sees us, we shall be listening to the tapes of our own heartbeats.

May we record over the harmful words that used to guide our actions, and produce our own messages, with whisperings of the Creator's compassionate words to move forward on our journeys in life.

We are grateful for the words from our Creator's voice, wherein Love resides, giving us direction and freedom to choose supporting and uplifting messages to give ourselves.

*One of the most difficult undertakings a human being has
is to perceive themselves objectively.*

STEP BACK AND WATCH

March 7

May we extricate ourselves from our subjective ego-self and practice watching ourselves as an objective outsider.

There are times when we become far too subjective about ourselves, too involved with the ego, and overly consumed with *self.* With the practice of meditation and mindfulness, we can begin to separate the True Self, the God Self, from the ego-self and take a more objective view of our lives and how we live them. By stepping back and watching, we can usually see the two selves sometimes in a struggle. The more we meditate on the God Self or Higher Self, the more we can make peace upon the *battlefield* between heart and mind. We can do this by identifying more with the loving heart and less with the fearful mind. The art of meditation helps us to tame the mind and runaway thoughts that do not always serve our best interest. Try dropping your mind down into your heart when you meditate, for the true intelligence is in the heart center.

May we learn to take a more objective view of our *self,* aligning our self-will with Higher Will.

Our lives are like an endless movie, with all of the scenes unedited, until we reach a point where we may want to begin fine-tuning and editing some of our scenes.

*If you have a yard, plant a tree. If you have no yard,
plant a seed.*

BACK TO BASICS

March 8

May we return to our roots, look at the shadows under the trees, and feel the warmth in a patch of sunlight.

We live in a harried, almost frantic world these days. Do not despair if you have a somewhat difficult time keeping abreast of all the details of change and progress. Spiritual progress is the only progress that the Creator sees. Try not to become attached to outcomes, possessions, money, and superficial sensationalism of the media. Some humans try to run the world on fear.

Let us try to be guided more by infinite Divine Love rather than limited, erroneous human fear. When we grow spiritually, our sense of values change. We begin to see the Truth and gently release all else. When we are moved more by looking into the eyes of a beautiful and precious animal, by a campfire on a cold night, or the warmth of natural sunlight on our skin instead of by stressful work in an artificially lighted office for capital gain, then we will indeed have more of a sense of our special place and purpose in the Universe.

May we relish in the Light of God's natural wonders— simple, breathtaking, and meaningful.

When we stopped being a slave to money and fear, we found Spiritual Freedom within the Divine Light of our own Soul.

Gain as much insight from and into others and take it within.

ALL ANSWERS ARE WITHIN

March 9

May we go within and find all the answers to our questions about ourselves

When we are feeling introspective, contemplative, or the least bit uneasy regarding any aspect of ourselves, this is the time to embrace our fears and go within. To go within means to quiet the body and mind in order to find the infinite supply of peace that is available to us. Meditation is the most effective way to achieve this state of inner knowing. While quiet and still, we can ask the Creator, directly, to reveal the true nature of our unfolding soul, to know the answers which lie inside of us and have been there for eons. Our souls reveal the hidden answers, unavailable to us when the body, mind, and spirit are in a constant state of disruption.

Let us ask the Higher Self or the God Self for answers, which will be revealed to us slowly or quickly, depending on the sincerity of earnest search.

May we be gladdened by the revelations that the Divine awakens in us.

When we take time to observe the Self, we know the pertinent questions to ask; then we wait patiently for the answers we already know.

You don't have to "get good" enough for God; just "get good"
enough to live comfortably in your own skin.

KNOW THAT YOU ARE LOVED

March 10

May we integrate the truth that God loves all of who we are.

Do you ever think that you have to be "good enough" for God to love you? Do you still entertain the idea that you have to perform good deeds to win God's love? This is missing God's true message, for we are loved at all times for exactly who we are on our life's journey. This does not give us permission to hurt others or ourselves. Yet, on a deeper level, it is the clear recognition that the Divine loves us, whether we are acting lovingly toward ourselves or not.

No matter how we *feel* about ourselves or about the Creator, the Divine Love is like the North Star—ever constant. This image is analogous to our being able to see the star better when no clouds obscure it from our view. Yet, even with heavy cloud cover, the star is still shining. It is only from *our* perspective that we cannot see it, yet when the clouds move away, we can see the star more clearly. Like God's Love, it is always there; it is only the clouds of our minds that make our mistrust.

May we remove the layers of the cloud cover that conceals the Divine spark within others and ourselves.

Ever constant is God's Love for each person. It is merely a
passing cloud that diminishes our Vision.

Be a pioneer in the new millennium.

AGE OF AQUARIUS

March 11

May we change and evolve with the times.

We are moving out of the Age of Pisces, which has ruled the Earth since the birth of the Christ. We are moving into the Age of Aquarius, where the Christ consciousness is becoming more generally ingrained in us. Now, we are learning healing and wholeness of body/mind/soul. We are becoming more aware of the Earth, ecologically and environmentally. We are evolving into mind-body medicine, where holistic approaches to physical healing involve the healing of body, mind, and spirit. We cannot avoid this change nor our conscious progress of more awareness inside ourselves and in the outside world.

Let us try to "go with the flow," and evolve into this new consciousness at our own paces. The change is taking place rapidly. Therefore, we may feel disrupted, confused, and turned upside down at times. We are like new pups that eventually grow into their skin, where the Creator has allowed the perfect amount of room for us to grow into conscious beings of the Divine Light.

May we enjoy the changes that are taking place in us and in our brothers and sisters.

At last, the sun shines upon us. The world is unfolding at a tremendous rate. Let us reach for a sunbeam and hold on for the ride, knowing that the Creator has entered each and every heart for the betterment of humanity and our environment.

Angels only charge their clients with an asking.

ANGEL THERAPY

March 12

May we live under the counsel of our special Angels.

The Angels are excellent therapists. Their counsel is simple, wise, and profound.

Let us tune into our special guardian Angels and listen to what they may have to tell us. We can take any problem to a celestial level. When we quiet our bodies and our minds, the spirits of the Angels are but a whisper away. Whether we believe in Angels or not, the Creator itself may have an important message to send to us.

Angel therapy can entail humor and joy. After our sessions with the Angels, we will find that we feel better and can take ourselves more lightly just as the Angels take themselves lightly.

May we begin to ask our Angels for answers and find that we already have the inner resources available to us. The Angels simply help us to access this wise reservoir for our betterment and the betterment of the world.

We go to the Angels for peace of mind, humor, and wisdom. We acknowledge the voice of the Universal Spirit with gratitude.

One need not bathe in Holy Waters to be totally cleansed.

CLEAN SPIRIT

March 13

May we be totally washed and cleansed by Spirit.

We may think that because we bathe, wash our hair, faces, and hands that we are totally, squeaky clean from head to toe. We also may feel that because we do not drink alcohol, coffee, smoke cigarettes, eat fat, sugar, and salt, that we are totally inwardly clean. Although these cleansing qualities are admirable and virtuous, we still may feel that we are not immaculate, healed and thoroughly washed inside and out. To be clean in Spirit means to sweep the cobwebs out of our minds, hearts, and souls.

Let us accomplish this thorough cleansing by prayer and meditation, which opens our hearts, minds, and spirits in order to let in the Light of Spirit. Getting quiet and still, visualizing each and every cell washed and rejuvenated by Unconditional Love and Healing Light, and finally, breathing in the Divine Light into our focused minds, new cells, and hearts, we create new auras of Love and Light. It is then that we find ourselves more cleansed inside and out.

May we let the Light of Spirit cleanse our mind/body/soul.

We use the power of the breath to become focused—it brings in the Living Light that resurrects us from spiritual darkness.

*One needs to weed out the garden so as to not
choke out the healthy plants.*

SPRING CLEANING

March 14

May we simplify our life.

Simple means to be free from complexity. Although we may have complex personalities, we may still accomplish the art of living simple and natural lives. Let us free ourselves of the bondage of excess. In America, we may have become accustomed to living the old adage that "more is better"—more money, more food, more things, more, more, more. While it is all right to have these material things, let us comprehend the motto over the arch at the oracle of Delphi in Greece, where it states "nothing in excess" and "know thyself." It takes a lifetime to understand the true meaning of these words. We can reduce the excess in our physical environments and also in our minds and spirits. To acquire success is to learn to live moderately and resourcefully in all three—body/mind/soul.

Let us not mistake this for a limited mind, as the mind and creativity are limitless when guided by the intuitive Power of the Divine.

May we weed out all the unnecessary aspects of our life.

When we examine ourselves and our lifestyles to get rid of excess, we remain simple, truthful, and natural. These are qualities the Creator appreciates.

If you don't know how to call the shots,
send for an Angelic referee.

BEING FAIR

March 15

May we be fair in dealing with others, while not sacrificing our own sense of values.

Fair means equal treatment for all concerned, or to be *Just.* Our Creator is fair and sees us all, each and every individual, in a beautiful, Spiritual Light. The Ultimate Spirit does not favor anyone in particular over another. The Divine knows no prejudice. Can we, as opinionated and judgmental humans, imagine a world where we do not favor any one or any group over the other, treating each individual fairly? World peace begins with our own healing and our own sense of fairness to all.

Let us, in a family microcosm, begin this work, realizing that, as we are fair with ourselves, calmly keeping our spiritual values intact, we can more easily be fair with all family members. Families then learn to treat others fairly, and will then grow in serene equanimity within themselves and onto others outside the family as well.

May we always keep our Spiritual values close at hand, in order to treat ourselves and others in accordance with the Highest Good for all concerned.

A rock, a tree, a horse, a brother, a sister and all nations are our loved ones. Deep within the imagination is found the desire to treat all creation as brothers, sisters, sons, and daughters in the Spirit of Love.

Warning: Taking any toxic emotion to bed at night can be hazardous to your health.

FREE YOURSELF FROM TOXIC EMOTIONS

March 16

May we know that our emotions do not have to control us and that we have a choice to overpower, with the Creator's help, any non-beneficial feelings.

When we feel that we are in the throes of some uncomfortable emotions, let us realize that the feeling is neither right nor wrong, but is a reflection of our past experiences and a current perception of our lives. We do not have to struggle with an emotion like jealousy, for example, for as soon as we feel it, we can bring in other circumstances and emotions to replace it— in other words, it will pass.

Let us pray to our Creator and the Angels for a new, more positive and wholesome perspective of the situation when we feel an unsettling emotion. Also, negative emotions are not who we truly are. We are particles of Love and Light—spiritual beings who experience all human emotions, thoughts, and sensations. We are on a journey of *humanness* to understand better the refuge and solace that can come from trusting the Unconditional Love of God, or if you prefer, the Universal Spirit.

May we not be caught in a struggle over human emotions. Rather, may we free ourselves from the uncomfortable feeling by acknowledging it and preferring to move beyond it and on to the Light of Life.

The Creator knows who we truly are. The answers can be found in asking our Angels, who are never far from us.

Let an Angel do the Driving.

ATTITUDE ADJUSTMENT

March 17

May we ask our Angels for an attitude adjustment whenever necessary.

There are those times when something or someone may upset us. Rather than judging or blaming another person or a situation, try asking your own special Angel for a quick fix. Perhaps an attitude adjustment is needed. Knowing that we cannot change other people or a past situation, let us look more to changing ourselves. Our Angels are always on duty. Angels never sleep on the job, so they are close by to help in any given situation. When confronted with a problem, take a moment out for some deep, slow breaths, then ask your Angels to help you identify what you can do to change your thoughts. More uplifting feelings will follow most assuredly.

Let us allow our Angels to help with remedies directly from the Divine Source. Changing our attitudes is our spiritual responsibility. Let us accept it with honor and Grace.

May we look to see our part in any adverse situation and, with the Angels' help, adjust our attitude accordingly.

The more positive we become, the closer we are to winning most any battle.

A healthy escape airs the soul.

TAKE A DAY FOR YOURSELF

March 18

May we remember to take a day off for ourselves and our healing.

Sometimes, in times of illness or stress, the Angels just want us to take a day off from our busy schedules and rest. We are doing something when we rest; we are healing. Maybe we want to listen to beautiful music or watch an inspiring movie. Whatever way we find to take a day off, let us remember to do this upon occasion. After our rest time, we can then resume our responsibilities with more energy and enthusiasm.

Let us, when we hear our bodies or our minds calling for rest, take action. The paradoxical *action* is to rest or, simply, *just be.* While simply and silently sitting, meditating, or just staring into space, daydreaming, we may be helping ourselves more than the busy mind would allow us to realize. Sound sleep is also extremely rejuvenating, giving our minds and bodies time to heal.

May we rejoice in our rest-time, realizing that we are, in actuality, helping our mind, body, and spirit to regroup, readjust, and rejuvenate.

We heal when we rest deeply in the comfort of the enfolding wings of our Protective Angels. In a busy world, let us take the time to gather our energy.

Do not always rely totally on doctors. Begin healing yourself.

THE HEALING ARTS

March 19

May we actively get involved in the healing arts.

The healing arts are extremely popular today. They are found in massage, acupuncture, yoga, the martial arts, Tai Chi, Reflexology, Reiki, Rolfing, Aromatherapy, and countless other forms of holistic healing. Any of the Healing Arts can be a spiritual experience, if we perceive them that way. They were founded in ancient times and have come into a renaissance today.

Let us take advantage of some of these techniques to improve the mind/body/spirit, in an all-encompassing wholeness for well-being. Remember, when one person heals, the rest of the world is that much healthier. The healing arts can work in conjunction with the medical field. Sometimes they are referred to as *alternative* or integrative medicine and promote prayer and also meditation as healthy breakthroughs. I like to use the term *complementary medicine* that the British use, because it can work in conjunction with conventional medicine.

May we find one or more of the healing arts that speaks to us and incorporate it into our life for better health.

The spirit of healing comes from within. When one person is totally healed, world healing can begin.

*Listen intently to the sounds of nature, and know
the genesis of music.*

FIRST DAY OF SPRING

March 20

May we enjoy this first day of spring, a sign of growth and renewal.

In the northwestern hemisphere, most calendars claim this day as the first day of spring. This is the season for the sprouting of new growth, which was dormant in the winter. Another introspective winter has passed for humans and nature, and now we can replace the unexpressed, darker gestation period with regenerated, fertile expression, full of color and creativity. This is the day of perfect balance—the amount of daylight is exactly equal to the amount of darkness in this vernal equinox. Whether one finds themselves with snow still on the ground or lives in a warmer climate, the signs of springtime are most likely there. We are shedding more light on ourselves. Most trees, plants, and flowers are beginning to show signs of new growth, small or large. We are not unlike Nature's seasons. The days are getting longer. More sunlight is now available to all who live on or in this Earth. Ice is beginning to melt or will soon again, just like the year before. More water is available. It is a comfort to know that in our busy, ever-changing world, Nature and the seasons are constant. All things change in time like the seasons, year after year. The sun will rise and set, day after day. Still, no two seasons are exactly alike each year and no two sunrises are the same each day. The paradox is that no matter what we do, Nature *will* happen according to Natural Laws.

Let us enjoy our season's new awakening and splendor with enthusiasm and appreciation, for this particular day, as do all days, holds gifts from the Divine Cycle.

May we breathe the breath of new beginnings.

We can celebrate spring and the new warmth with glad tidings and gratitude.

*If you cannot consciously change your thoughts, ask the
Creator to change them for you.*

CHANGING OUR HURTFUL THOUGHTS

March 21

May we understand that we can change any negative thought
into a positive one.

Most people truly underestimate the power of their thoughts.
If only we could understand the incredible effect our thoughts
have in relationship to others and ourselves. Negative thoughts
can undermine a body's entire immune system. Yes, this is true.
We can make ourselves ill. The solution is to realize that we have
the power to change toxic thoughts by accepting the Creator
within.

Let us control a runaway mind by using the art of concentration. Here is a simple exercise to increase concentration.
Darken the room and light one candle in a draft-free area. Stare
at the flame for five to ten minutes. Notice all the qualities of the
flame, the colors, and the glow around the cone-shaped center.
Then close the eyes and see the image of the flame between the
eyebrows. Try to hold the image still in the mind's eye for as long
as possible, without struggling. Practice this often and know
that the flame is your Creator shining within. Try being more
observant of your thoughts, and concentrate more on the positive
rather than the negative.

May we learn to change thoughts that hurt others and
ourselves and replace them with positive, uplifting, and joyful
thoughts.

*By concentrating, we can learn to tame the wild frontier of
our mind. We can uplift ourselves and others, instead of being
unkind and hurtful.*

*Graceful and delicate, birds teach us that life does
not have to be a struggle.*

BIRDS

March 22

May we take the time to watch the birds and incorporate their lightness into our souls.

In the spring, we see more birds in our yards as the weather warms a little more. What a beautiful sight: birds in all of their numerous and diverse species. Perhaps you want to feed and water the birds that delight your home. Some of them have traveled a long, long way to come to you. The freedom represented by birds is so appealing to humans that we even have tried to imitate their wings in the air, like the Wright brothers. Birds bless us with their songs, colors, and their simple habits.

Let us learn from these simple and free habits. Let us take ourselves a little lighter today. Let us hum or sing a little tune, while we go about our daily tasks. Let us eat moderately and feel the lightness of our bodies; let us think soaring thoughts and lighten our minds, let us feel the spontaneity of this season in joy and peace; let us begin spending a little more time outdoors, feeling the sun's warmth and breathing in fresh air.

May we learn to lighten our souls and become more like the delicate, beautiful souls of our feathered friends.

Like the birds, we too can be light, and experience life's uplifting qualities.

Learn as much as you can from those you meet, and fine-tune it within your own inner wisdom.

BEING WISE

March 23

May we be wise in earthly and spiritual matters.

To be wise means to be discreet, using good judgment, and to be guided by wisdom. It can also mean Divination or magic. We all have this internal *Divine magic*. Let us open ourselves to the wisdom of the Universe and act and think along these ideal lines. To be wise does not mean to be boring or *better than*. Rather, it means to have wit, humor, and awareness to perceive a situation in a discerning way. Wisdom is a *knowing*; it is applying our knowledge in all our affairs. It is fun to be wise. The Angels are extremely wise.

Let us ask the Angels to guide us in our thinking and in our every action. Each individual has their own internal wisdom, guided by their own wise Angels. We can better tap into these wise teachings by becoming quiet and still, opening our hearts to the Divine Wisdom within ourselves. It is true that other people can teach or guide us, yet deep inside ourselves is the Wisdom of the Universe.

May we tune into our wise self, our Higher self, and know of that Spirit within.

We all possess the wisdom of eons past, present, and future. It is the still voice within that we nurture and listen to in our quiet times.

Think of love as a gentle spirit that cradles your heart
in its hands.

IN LOVE

March 24

May we fall in Love with life, the Universe, and Spirit.

We have all experienced the feeling of romantically falling in love with another person. Maybe it was a childhood "crush" on someone, or perhaps a future spouse, or a teacher, or a movie star, or a person who represented spiritual ideals. We can have this same feeling of falling in *love* with the Divine or simply with this incredible Universe as it manifests itself in our daily lives. If we already have a spouse or "significant other," we can all consider falling *back* in love with them, creating the same feelings we had for them in the beginning of the relationship. Perhaps we can bring a spiritual touch into a renewal of vows. While many people also live alone in this day and age, it does not mean they cannot be in the *spirit of love*, touching many people's lives daily. Being in love can mean many different things to many different people.

There are two basic forces at work in the Universe today— Love and fear. When we are in the spirit of Love, fear cannot exist. In contrast, when we are in the grips of fear-based consciousness, Love cannot exist. Which will be your choice?

May we always consciously choose Love as our Higher Power.

When lost in fear, we thank God it is only temporary. Perfect Love does, indeed, rule this Universe.

One may help another and have no idea of it.

SERVING OTHERS

March 25

May we serve others with joy, compassion, and gentleness, knowing that Divine Will guides us.

There are many ways to serve the Creator and humanity: perhaps volunteering for a worthy organization, getting involved with the healing arts, or helping a friend in need. If we have careers of being of service to others, we can consider ourselves blessed. There are always ways that we can be helpful and give of our time for a Greater Concern. Supporting a needy child is another way to serve.

Let us know that our efforts are worthy and very much needed. When we help another, we naturally feel good about ourselves, so we are actually helping two people—ourselves and another. Let us be a candle, one that lights many other candles in this world. Let us maintain a sense of well-being by being of service to others, knowing that all work is for the Love of the Universe.

May we find deep joy in being helpful in ways that benefit Spirit and all others with whom we come in contact.

Teach only Love, Peace, and Healing.

Reason by means of your heart.   •

REASON

March 26

May we keep our power to reason intact, with the aid of the Creator.

Reason means confirming a belief or a cause that, in reality, makes any fact intelligible. It also means motive and right thinking. The intellect has its place in humans. The power to reason is what separates humans from all other creatures. Yet let us not place ourselves upon pedestals, as human judgment is not always sane and sound, making for much of the chaos in the world today. There are two types of ways to reason, according to great mathematicians: inductive and deductive. Inductive reasoning stems from the specific or individual to the general or universal. Deductive reasoning is the opposite, where we take the general idea and go to the specific.

Let us not get too tied up with details and try to have a more broad, universal approach to life by inductive reasoning. Although minute details are important at times, let us always try to see the larger picture and spiritual concept of given situations. Let us always remember that intelligence has its base in the heart.

May we know that our intellect can serve us in choices that we make each day for right living.

God's breath is behind our heart and mind, and we reason with ease. Let all of our motives be pure, good, and kind.

After looking into the eyes of another person or creature,
one can feel the heart connection.

HUMANENESS

March 27

May we be humane in thought, word, and deed to all of God's creations.

To be humane is to be kind. Let us be grateful to all of the Divine Creations and treat all with a consciousness of benevolence. Everything in the Universe works together for a Higher Purpose and is interwoven into the Divine Tapestry. Every thread of this tapestry has its place to make the entirety a beautiful work of art. We all have a right to be here on Earth, and if one Creature is mistreated, it creates a loose thread in the whole tapestry, causing an imbalance therein.

Let us work together to maintain the intricate Tapestry in beauty, function, and good condition, weaving only strong threads of Love, Beauty, and Wisdom—what we are truly designed to do. I am reminded of Plato's old adage to be kind—for we are all fighting a hard battle.

May we be a helpful thread in God's Humane Tapestry.

God's Tapestry is strong, yet each thread is sensitive. Let us treat each part humanely, seeing how we can benevolently give to all.

A silent commitment to oneself is the highest form of honoring oneself and one's contract with Spirit.

HONOR YOUR CONTRACT

March 28

May we honor the contract that we made with the Divine before we were born.

We all made contracts with the Creator before we were born to come back to Earth and fulfill our Divine purpose. Our Divine purpose may or may not be revealed to us early in life, yet our persistence in seeking it is part of our spiritual journey and is also a part of the contract. Let us continue to search our hearts and souls for the best ways to honor the Divine Contracts. Once our Purpose is revealed, let us align our total energies with that of the Will of Heaven. One part of the contract is to overcome obstacles and to learn the necessary lessons for spiritual growth.

Let us remember that we have free will and may or may not choose to learn the lessons given to us. There is no judgment or blame, for our souls know their true Divinity and will follow their courses according to Divine Will.

May we find our Life Purpose and work on that in joy, while we are being true to ourselves and following the will of the Creator deep within our hearts.

Let us be humble on our Spiritual journey, for we made the Spiritual contract eons ago to do our best in this particular lifetime. When we pray for the revelation of our Life Purpose, we remember the words of our Angel and receive acknowledgment.

*There is a reason why every being is on this Earth
at this exact time.*

DIVINE PURPOSE

March 29

May we discover our Divine Purpose on Earth and work diligently and joyfully in fulfilling it.

We each have a Divine Purpose in life. Some would say it is a *calling* to a specific type of work. Remember that we work for the Highest Universal Good or Spirit. There are many ways to discover your Divine Purpose. It could be found during meditation, when we ask for it to be revealed by the Creator or the Angels. It could be found during a creative endeavor, through the arts, through brainstorming with colleagues, through a spiritual teacher, through our children, or through unexpected situations—many ways are available. We simply need the Divine Awareness of our innermost souls and the remembrance from where they came—our Divine birthright.

When we do find our Highest Purpose, let us rejoice and know, without a shadow of a doubt, that we are led by the Will of Heaven.

May we know our Divine Purpose. When it comes, the work shall be easy, joyous, and of Higher Will. We will know how to overcome any obstacle in our way, by simply remembering what our soul came here to do.

We will know our Divine Purpose by its Loving Nature, and we will align all of our energies with our Higher Will in fulfilling it .

A garden of flowers and the kind gesture of a mother
are synonymous.

GARDENS

March 30

May we cherish the memory of a garden that we have seen to remind us of our natural state of total innocence.

Have you ever been in a garden that evoked certain memories by colors, aromas, or a feeling of peacefulness? If you have had a wonderful feeling in someone's garden or in your own garden, your soul memory is probably that of perfect innocence, when harmony and peace reigned. This is the soul's natural state, and is a remembrance of the spiritual realm from which we evolved.

Let us take time to visit a garden and absorb all the qualities that delight our physical senses, as well as our soul's yearning to return to that Divine State of Purity. The pleasurable and peaceful feelings can also remind us of nurturing compassion—be it from a maternal source of being carried inside the harmony of the womb, or simply a remembrance of a time filled with magic, delight, and intense joy.

May we find refuge in a garden and rest our soul within its gates.

The innocence of a beautiful garden invites the soul to rest and remember the spiritual realm. Take in the fragrance of a flower, and lay your back against an old tree. Breathe in the freshness that surrounds your entire being, and remember that it is a glimpse of the Creator.

*Try to take delight in all situations, realizing that
all is part of a* Cosmic Dance.

MAKE IT FUN

March 31

May we take ourselves more lightly and try to make life more
fun with the help of the Angels.

There are always many ways to look at any given situation.
During those times when we become too negative, let us
remember that we have more options in which we can view this
same situation. Making life fun does not mean that we rest on our
spiritual laurels and let ourselves go into a destructive mode.
Rather, it means to take a grave situation and try to think about it
in a more positive tone. I have had the good fortune of having a
true "Auntie Mame," who was an extremely compassionate and
lighthearted individual who made an art of turning grave
situations into humorous, lighter stories. She was truly a teacher
for me, especially in this specific area. Making life fun is using
our creative minds. This is our birthright and a free gift from the
Creator.

We *all* have the ability to think creatively, if we learn *how* to
use the mind given to us by the Creator and always remember
that we are on Earth for a short span. Let us make it as enjoyable
as possible.

May we learn to have a light heart and make life creative
and fun.

*We took the worst situation of our life and laughed. We were
able to do this because the Angels helped us lighten and brighten
any heavy burden we have had to bear.*

*We worry so about outcomes, but the Creator already
has it figured out.*

OUTCOMES

April 1

May we not be as attached to the outcomes of deeds well
done.

I learned a little secret a long time ago when I heard a man
lecture on the quality of life. He said to try to do something good
for someone else as often as possible, and never tell anyone about
it. I like to pass this on when and wherever I can because of its
simple profundity. God sees our hearts and our intentions as well
as our motives.

Let us not let pride, either false or true, be our ally. Instead,
let us go about our daily work, helping as many people as
possible, without an anticipation of reward, monetary or
otherwise. Furthermore, let us not be too attached to the outcome
of any given plan or situation. If it is meant to be, it will turn out
according to the will of Heaven. Let us search our souls for the
lessons in each thought, word, and deed that we have.

May we be in the flow of the will of Heaven and seek no
earthly rewards for helping others. We will naturally feel good
about our assistance to others. Let that be enough.

*Let us remember that in the afterworld, it is the silent deed of
charity that is important. No one else has to know.*

Take a "Thinking Detour."

REDIRECT

April 2

May we learn to redirect our negative thoughts and feelings toward the positive aspects of the Highest Source.

In the world today, there are times when we are bombarded with negativity. Negativity can be the result of many things. It can come from exposure to free radicals, from being unmotivated, from not taking care of the body/mind/soul, or from emotional telepathy—picking up the negative thoughts and fears of other people. Instead of suppressing negative thoughts and feelings, let us learn to redirect and channel them into the Highest Best for all concerned. This is a matter of perception. We *can* change thoughts and feelings. Thoughts are as powerful as feelings. The Rosicrucians teach ways to control and expand the mind through esoteric philosophy. It is a school of thought that may be worthy of looking into for new, fresh ideas about our thinking.

Let us be open to the wisdom of the Great Mystics in order to have more control over ourselves in thought and action, and to live more fulfilled lives.

May we use the power of prayer and meditation to overcome any obstacles in our life.

We used our mind, and our body and emotions obeyed. The Higher Thought was the result of how we redirected lower vibrations into an enlightened pathway of thinking.

*If we all lived by our highest ideals, there would be
total Peace in the world.*

LIVING OUR IDEALS

April 3

May we have High Ideals and strive to reach them, weaving them into every waking hour of our lives.

High Ideals or aspirations can be inspirational to us, providing they are in direct harmony with the Highest Source. This does not mean that we are unrealistic and overly idealistic, living in a fantasy world. It means to always persevere, to try to be of better character, and to live by Spiritual and Natural laws. The Divine is the greatest inspiration to achieve our goals and to have eternal peace of mind. Let us always have our ideals in balance with Spirit and try to live in accordance with the Will of the Heavens. It is when we are able to make applicable all of our Highest thoughts and incorporate them into everyday life and our interactions with others that we, indeed, are living our Highest Truth. This is so much easier said than done. Yet our Creator sees our spiritual progress at all times. Mistakes are always going to be made, yet we pick ourselves up and keep going.

Let us allow ourselves to be the best we can be at all times, while acknowledging our shortcomings.

May our every thought, word, and deed be a positive statement to our Creator and all of humanity.

We rose up from worldly desires to Divine Principles. Now we understand the lessons taught by our greatest obstacles in life.

*Many new awakenings have been experienced through a
detoxification process.*

DETOXIFICATION

April 4

May we be willing to cleanse our mind, body, and spirit from
any poisons.

We usually think of poison as venom from a snake, old
tainted food, or a substance like arsenic. However, we could also
view poison as food with chemicals added, or as addictive drugs
and alcohol, or as something or someone who destroys moral
character. In order to have good health of body, mind, and soul,
we need to detoxify from anything or anyone who prohibits us
from having a total sense of well-being. Let us be discreet in
choosing healthy foods for our body, healthy thoughts for our
mind, and healthy spirituality for our soul.

Let us refrain from being corrupted by excess worldly
pleasures and from damaging, negatively oriented people. This
detoxification process may be painful and difficult, and could be
termed as a *healing crisis*. Like the darkness before the dawn, we
may have to do some soul-searching deep down to see how other
people may truly be affecting our well-being, or how a particular
state of mind may undermine our entire immune system.

May we learn how and when to detoxify ourselves from
hazardous situations, people, foods, drugs, and thoughts.

*All things work together and with a balance of
body/mind/spirit. We learn to discreetly listen to each, to cleanse,
and to have no fear as we progress in life's journey.*

To truly know others, one must first know oneself.

INSIGHT

April 5

May we have keen insight into ourselves and others in order to understand, to console, and to love.

Insight is having an unshakable knowing and understanding by the power of innate instinct. To be insightful is to be intuitive. This inner knowing helps us to understand ourselves better and to have more insight into others. Insight helps us navigate a little more easily through our days. Some call it a "gut reaction" to specific people or situations. Others may call it the still, small voice inside. To look deeper into life—to look beyond what appears on the outside of people, places, and circumstances is an innate gift of all beings. To cultivate more of it, we can close our eyes during our quiet times, when we need answers, or just to get a sense of ourselves and/or others. Usually, we gain more insight into life the more we experience life and interact with others.

Let us be wise and intuitive at all times and pray to learn from our experiences, whether pleasurable or painful. With insight, we can more fully understand ourselves, how we relate to others, and how our Creator manifests the Divine in us.

May we have the insight to use impeccable discernment in life—today and always.

If we intuit that the Creator will always take care of us, there is no room for fear—only greater insight.

If you want to truly see yourself, close your eyes.

THIRD EYE

April 6

May we use our second sight and our third eye to bask in the Purest Light.

In meditation, usually (yet not always) performed with the eyes closed, we learn to use second sight. If we candle-gaze for five minutes, then close our eyes, we see the imprint of the glowing flame in the mind's eye. This is the place between the eyebrows where mental images occur when the eyes are closed. After the image of the flame disappears, we have illuminated the second sight, where we may see pictures, religious symbols, or have particular visions and insights.

As we focus the mind inward on the Creator, we can know our inner self as it relates to the Divine. When the inner mind and the total self are filled with the True Light of the Divine, we and the Creator are One in Spirit. This peaceful and meaningful time in meditation spills over to every aspect of our lives. We are totally and completely in the mystical trinity of mind/body/soul.

May we be illuminated by the inner light of the Divine.

We have second sight and our mind is free. We are One with the Creator and nothing can make us incomplete or distraught.

Self cannot get one out of self.

THINKING OF OTHERS

April 7

May we think of how we can help others, especially when we feel somewhat low in spirit.

There are those times when we may have low energy and may have *the blues*. Those are the times when we can ask the Angels to comfort us with our troubled mind. Instead of recycling negative thoughts, let us also ask our Angels how we could help someone else who has trouble in their spirit. When we are able to help someone else, we get out of ourselves, forget our own worries, and live the life of service, even if it is done by only listening to another who may be in conflict.

Let us also remember to have a sense of humor, which is a real gift from the Creator, and shed joy in the depths of sorrow. This does not mean to minimize the problem at all. It means getting a new perspective on any situation.

May we be unselfish and think of how someone else may feel, and act accordingly.

In universal life, the paradox still stands. To find self-love, reach out to another.

God is the source of all prosperity. Give credit where it is due.

GOD PROVIDES

April 8

May we know deep within that God provides for our every need.

In our finite minds, we cannot always know what God intends for us. However, we trust that *all* of our needs are provided for. In prayer, we do not ask for specific things to be miraculously given to us, rather we affirm that God knows our needs and they are already in the process of materializing. In meditation, we can program the mind with positive affirmations that settles into our subconscious mind. This way, the conscious mind acts as if our needs are already being supplied. We then assume a posture that is affirmative, positive, and God-centered.

Let us remember that our benevolent Creator will bestow upon us that which we need, and not necessarily what we may desire.

May we program the mind affirmatively, knowing that in our God-mind, all things are in the process of materializing for our Highest Good and the Good of all concerned.

We are open to new ideas that enhance our spirituality. We are in positive motion and attuned to our intuitive sensitivity.

One can practice mysticism in a clothing store, at work, or
alone in the woods. It has no limitation of setting
or circumstance.

PRACTICAL MYSTICISM

April 9

May we incorporate the wisdom of the Mystic Masters into
our everyday lives.

We have reached a point in the course of the Universe where
those who are loyal to their spiritual paths are seeking more
practical approaches to incorporating their wisdom and truth into
every aspect of life to bring love, peace, harmony, fulfillment,
and prosperity to themselves and others. Now, we are in a time of
walking a mystical path with practical feet firmly planted on
Mother Earth. We know and trust that the Creator guides us in all
thought, word, and deed for the betterment of our own lives and
the lives of others with whom we come into contact.

Let us take time to meditate, pray, and put positive thoughts
into our own minds, and beyond, reaching out broadly into the
Universe. We *can* make a difference in healing the planet, guided
continually by the Creator, who knows the Highest and Best for
each of us.

May we live in a state of joyous, continuous expectancy
knowing that the Universe supplies us with positive thought
waves to live each day in the Spirit of the Divine, which naturally
accompanies practical living in a mystical world.

We walk a path of continuous enlightenment, guided by the
Divine thought in how each moment is preciously spent.

Fill your body, mind, and soul with spiritual food.

NUTRITION

April 10

May we give our body, mind, and soul the best nutrition and care that we are capable of.

We all have probably read or heard about good nutrition for the body. It is important to put healthy *fuel* into our bodies in order that they may *run* sufficiently and effectively, not too unlike automobiles using good gasoline. Yet what do we put into our minds? Do we put the premium fuel of loving thoughts, thoughts of service to others, joy, and wholesome humor into our minds? Do we think of God and how the Creator supplies us with health, happiness, and prosperity, or do we throw guilt, self-criticism, and hate in there as well?

Let us begin to call forth nurturing thoughts for our minds as well as thoughts of compassion, well-being, and Divine Love. Although the mystical trinity of the mind/body/soul cannot be separated, let us be kind to the soul's journey, however arduous. It is our birthright to feel good inside and out.

May we use the *supreme fuel* in our vehicle to God.

We feed our soul with the delicacies of the Divine. Peace, poise, happiness, and prosperity are forever ours.

Nothing seems to last but constant change.

GROWTH

April 11

May we intuitively know that we are always in a stage of growth to be more like our Creator.

Everything in the Universe is in a perpetual state of evolution and growth. Humankind cannot be stagnant. Even after death, there is continual growth in a different Light, and in a different realm. On an emotional, spiritual, and physical level, we are always growing, whether we feel like we are accomplishing anything or not.

Let our minds continually be open to new ideas and inspirations from the Heavens. If we feel like we are not growing, moving forward, or learning, we may need to plant a seed in the earth and gain wisdom and insight from the beautiful and incredible natural laws of the Universe. Every few days, with the proper nurturing, can we not see a new leaflet sprouting or a slightly taller stem? Look out the window—is there not progress, movement, and growth everywhere? Even if we cannot *see* growth as it takes place, we can have reassurance that Mother Earth and the Universe are in perfect order according to the Divine Natural Laws.

May we rest assured that we and everything are simultaneously growing toward the Light.

The world evolves at a rapid pace. In calm reassurance, we see all life in the Light of God's perfection.

Nurture yourself in the same way you would nurture a child.

WHAT YOU TELL YOUR SELF

April 12

May we give ourselves loving and accepting messages each day.

Our natural state of being is being God-centered, at peace, and loving. In a world where, sometimes, we have either heard negative messages from parents and teachers, or we have little confidence of feeling adequate, we may have to work a little harder to reprogram our minds into a more positive mode. What messages do you give yourself? Are they chastising and berating, or are they loving, kind, accepting, and nurturing?

Let us reprogram our thinking. This can be accomplished in many ways. For example, in meditation we can align the entire being with the God-self or Higher Self that knows truth, goodness, dignity, and Divine Bliss. In this natural and peaceful state, our God-conscious minds give out loving, positive affirmations to feed the soul. With practice, we will notice a sense of calm self-assurance and a deep sense of well-being with which to proceed in our daily affairs. This centered state stays with us in our relationships to ourselves and others.

May we learn how to tell ourselves "I love you."

Loving ourselves is the same as loving God. Let this stronghold suffice, when our patience wears thin.

We are moving from a "mine/yours" world into
an "our" world.

ALL BELONGS TO THE CREATOR

April 13

May we acknowledge that everything in this world belongs to the Creator.

There are times when we want to take *all* the credit for some job done, or monies made, or any other accomplishment. It is natural to think that *we* did all the work. However, the reality is that the energy produced to do the work is a free gift from the Creator. Where do we think the very breath of life comes from? Where do we think Einstein received his inspirations in physics? The next time we let too much pride overcome us; let us think more deeply as to where the source of our prosperity, health, and happiness lies.

Let us give thanks continually to our Creator for *all* our blessings, hopes, accomplishments, and rewards.

May we live in gratitude to the Creator for all effort, thought, word, deed, and our humble breath of life.

For anything well done, let us give thanks to the Divine Spirit working through us. This Higher Energy is where our love for God shines. This is the direction of the heart.

Life is a balancing act.

WELL-BEING

April 14

May we continually carry within us a sense of well-being.

As we live and experience more, we find what works for us and what does not work for us in our bodies, minds, and souls. The balance and harmony of our lives depends greatly on our attitudes. The more positive thoughts that are in our conscious and subconscious minds, the more successful and fulfilling our daily lives are.

Let us always strive for that harmonium of the Spiritual Trinity and maintain a sense of well-being in our physical, emotional, mental, and spiritual lives. When one of the components of our makeup is out of balance, it can upset all other aspects of our total selves. Therefore, let us ask the Creator for immediate restoration of all the components in order to give others and ourselves the gift of positive balance and peaceful harmony. Most often, when the spiritual aspect is aligned first, then all other aspects will fall into place.

May we continue to be aware of our self in its totality, and to explore all of our physical, emotional, and spiritual aspects for the purpose of harmonizing them into our well-being.

We rejoice in the harmony of our body, mind, and soul. We maintain spiritual gratitude for living a life that is healthy and whole.

What one decides is real, is real for that person. It may differ from another's definition.

WHAT IS REAL

April 15

May we know that our True self is perfect peace, harmony, and love; all else is mostly learned falsehood.

When we reside in deep meditation, we are at peace with ourselves, the world, and our Creator; no obstructions enter our bodies, minds, or souls. This state of Perfect Harmony, where Divine Light fills our every cell and atom, is our True Self. During those times when we feel *any* negativity enter our minds, let us know that this is past conditioning, learned behavior. It is someone else's message we are replaying on the tapes in our minds. There is importance in meditation or trying to calm the mind in whatever ways that benefits us. For when we learn to quiet the mind, we know Peace. Peace of mind is what is real.

In our hurried world and busy schedules, let us take at least five minutes a day to become totally unencumbered by external intrusions. Let us know that we are unconditionally loved by the Creator, the Angels, our Divine Teachers, *and* our students alike.

May we carry the calm and Peace found in our True Self, our God-Self, with us throughout every minute of each day.

Our True Self is innocent, free, and unmoved by external circumstances. The very breath of God flows through us. Heightened awareness enhances our every true thought, word, and deed and we want to work for a better world.

To be in self-doubt is to be in self-debt.

THE TWO SELVES

April 16

May we learn to deeply understand the two selves.

Everyone has within them two selves that are always at work. One self is the personality, our character traits that make us unique and give us individuality. The other self is the God-Self or the Higher Intuition, inspired by God. We find, at times, that we may have an inspired idea, yet the self-doubt of the personality keeps us from taking action on that idea. This is where faith in the Creator comes in—to carry out the idea, in spite of minor complications that may arise along the way.

Let us not let self-doubt come between our Creator-inspired ideas and dreams, and our success and happiness. Let us always ask for inspiration from the Higher Self, and let that Higher Self work out the details and logistics. Then, with Spiritual alignment, the personality-self can take action with unwavering faith.

May we have faith in knowing that our two selves are always working together to bring us new ideas and the power to carry them out.

The two selves battle once in a while. Yet, when acting on faith, the battle ceases.

Tears of gratitude are Angel tears.

CRYING

April 17

May we know that our tears are healing.

Crying is a part of being human. Usually, our tears come from a deep hurt disguised as frustration, anger, rage, sadness, self-pity, grief, depression, fear, or injustice. Let us know that our tears are healing. It is the body/mind/soul's way of expressing pain and grief. Tears can also be felt from a longing to be in the arms of our Creator, free from human strife. Usually, after we cry, we feel better. The salt in our tears is the salt of the earth, nurtured and supported by the feminine Mother Earth—restorer of balance and harmony—who washes away our tears and cleanses our soul, freeing it of sorrow. It is good to reach out to a close friend, teacher, or someone who fully understands our situation. It is also good to seek comfort in knowing that the natural laws are working *for* us, not against us. For in each single tear will also spring forth another Joy in one's life. Perhaps it is a comfort to know that all things change and will pass. It is part of our dynamic human experience, and we may weep tears of gratitude. This is also an emancipation of past sadness, shining forth into the light.

Let us be comforted by thinking of the sun shining its rays on the last of the rain clouds, urging a rainbow. This rainbow is symbolic of the change, the cleansing, that we have experienced by raining down tears from our eyes. The heart is soon soothed, insightful, and eventually grateful.

May we rejoice in our humanness and know that, in actuality, we are truly spiritual beings, feeling what it is like to be human.

Our experiences can be joyful and also painful enough for us to find tears in our eyes. We are reminded that the eyes seldom lie to others.

Have enough faith not only to dream your dreams, but also to bring life to them.

MANIFESTING OUR DREAMS

April 18

May we take action on our Divinely Inspired ideas.

We all have Divinely Inspired ideas that come from the Higher Self, or the God mind. When the Creator guides us in meditation, let us immediately affirm our inspired ideas with the thought that we can make these ideas a reality with faith in that unseen Power. Self-doubt, usually stemming from society's conditioning, keeps us from bringing ideas into fruition.

Let us keep all negativity from our minds by knowing that the Higher Self can and will aid us in bringing all of the details together. When we take action on our ideas, we are reinforcing our faith in a Higher Power. What keeps us from entertaining our dreams and seeing them through into physical manifestation? Is it a time factor? Perhaps we're just too busy to take that painting class. Or is it about what others will think? The truth is that often, others will admire the fact that we took the time and energy for joyful, soul-enriching activities. Our limiting thinking limits our limitless possibilities.

May we let our Higher mind guide us in all that we do, think, and say.

Putting action behind our ideas is having faith in our Creator, for spiritual success and happiness are what our Divine mind thrives on.

True independence is knowing how to take care of ourselves.

TAKING CARE OF OURSELVES

April 19

May we constantly learn ways of taking good care of ourselves.

We have all heard the phrase that we cannot give away what we do not have in ourselves, or that we cannot love others until we learn to love ourselves. There is truth to this, because we have to be fit spiritually, emotionally, physically, and mentally ourselves, in order to help someone else who may be lacking in one or more of these areas. It may *seem* selfish to take good care of ourselves first, before others, yet it is a *healthy* selfishness that we need to establish. As we gain insight into ourselves, we can have more insight into helping others. We are all on this life path together. When we are weak, others who are stronger at that time can help us. The reciprocity quickly comes back in the other direction.

Let us know how to take better care of ourselves in order to meet and overcome *any* obstacle that arises along the path. As we do, we can share with others how to better take care of themselves, so that *they*, too, can overcome their obstacles.

May we know that the Creator gives us the tools to take better care of ourselves every day. In turn, we may then share that caregiving with others.

We love ourselves so that we may love others. We know this by respecting others and ourselves. We can overcome our own trials and help others overcome theirs as well. We know there is a loving Spirit guiding us in all ways, at all times.

Balance the chakras until each rotates in the way that is the most harmonious with the Universe.

BALANCING THE CHAKRAS

April 20

May we return to our center each day by balancing the chakras.

The chakras, the unseen energy wheels of the body, need to be free flowing throughout the body so as not to become blocked with any negative, obstructive energy. In meditation, we can breathe out any imbalances down the legs, out the soles of the feet, down the spinal column into Mother Earth.

Let us then give our thanks to the Divine Mother for transforming this adverse energy into fresh, new unobstructed energy. Then, by calling upon the Divine Spirit within us, we can use Divine Energy to restore each chakra, starting from the first chakra and moving up to health and balance and, ultimately, to Grace. By using the breath, we inhale the restored energy back up into the body, one chakra at a time. By the time all of the chakras are free flowing and we reach the chakra at the top of the head— the Higher Self—we find that we understand what it means to not be identified with the body or the mind. We are without thought; we are resting in Divine Light. We are cleansed of all obstacles that keep us from resting in the white light of the Divine.

May we learn how to balance each chakra daily and use our creative imagination to find a way that transforms any blockages into clarity of motion.

Breathe the chakras clearly through the body. Find a balance to which each can accompany the living, vital centers we all possess. Then draw upon the Light in each center, one by one, until clarity of Divine Mind is found.

*See yourself as a rainbow to understand the complete
spectrum of color.*

COLOR

April 21

May we have lots of color in our life!

Color can have different meanings for people. One may have
a favorite color or one may like all colors. Variety is a good thing.
Color variety helps us to keep flexible and out of dull ruts. Do
you *feel* like a color? Do you wear a specific color on a certain
day to express your mood or your thoughts for that day? We may
do this consciously or unconsciously. One does not have to be an
artist to appreciate colors. Think about how light adds value to
colors. Just look out the window—what colors do you see? How
many shades of green or gray are there? If you want to see more
color than gray buildings, take a drive in the country, or walk in
the park for healing green. Colors can be healing, exciting,
depressing, spiritual, and so on. Each chakra is represented by a
different color:

First: red—located at the base of the spine
Second: orange—located two inches below the navel
Third: yellow—located in the stomach area or solar plexus
Fourth: pink or green—the heart center
Fifth: sky blue—the throat area
Sixth: dark blue or indigo—the point between the eyebrows;
also called the "third eye"
Seventh: violet—at the top of the head; also called the
"crown chakra"

If we put these together, we have all the colors of the
rainbow—a full spectrum—harmonious balance. Black is the
absence of color or light. White is the reflection of all colors.

May we add color in our life by really "seeing" the different hues in all subjects and appreciating the value of *all* God's Creation.

We are opaque. We are pastel. When we use the beauty of color, we feel healthy and happy. Let us see the beauty and variety in this world today and give thanks that we can see one another in a new and different way.

Your Guardian Angels are wise. Take good notes on
what they show you.

ANGELS: FRIENDS FOR ETERNITY

April 22

May we recognize the Angels as our dearest friends.

Angels are our best friends, since they support and guide us in all that we do. Another name for Angels could be spirit guides or Divine Messengers. They do, indeed, exist, and we can reach them in meditation or simply in quiet moments. Angels give us the insights we need to live productive, useful, fulfilling, happy, and successful lives. Spirit guides are of the Divine, the Creator, the Universal Intelligence, or God, whichever term fits your concept. We have all embarked upon a Divine journey, whether we are aware of it or not. Our guides are always and have always been with us.

Let us call upon our guides for guidance, and remember to give thanks to God for placing such healing and Divinely intelligent Angels in our lives. They serve as a link to the Highest Divine Source. And they are extremely helpful.

May we show gratitude to the Creator for living out the mystical practicality of the Angels' direct guidance.

We will hear their voice and give thanks to the Divine Intelligence. We will be guided by the gentle revelations of our intuitive friends.

Goose bumps are electric!

SPIRITUAL GOOSE BUMPS

April 23

May we accept the good energy around us and be uplifted and inspired.

Have you ever been around someone with incredible insight, good, pure energy, and with whom you felt inspired? Did you get goose bumps? Have you ever rested your eyes on something beautiful, like being in the tropics or on a mountaintop with a breathtaking view, and felt those same goose bumps again? Spiritual goose bumps are electrical impulses—a gift from the Universe or God's Creation to you.

When you feel the spiritual connection, the body, mind, and soul feel it all over with you. Goose bumps soon go away. However, if you feel them and are inspired, try expressing your joy—either by talking to and inspiring another person, writing an insightful line or two, intuitively drawing a picture, singing, playing an instrument, meditating, or any other way of expressing your joy to your Creator and others. These impulses are much more than mere coincidence. They have a deeper purpose and a meaningful message.

May we give someone else spiritual goose bumps by our Joy, inspired by the Creator.

Why did our worries disappear when we gazed at the immensity of the ocean or the sky? Because we were totally filled with Spirit, and in that moment we did not need to ask questions.

*Let your conscience lead you to the knowledge of where you
are wrong. To be wrong is to learn with humility.*

ADMITTING WHEN WE ARE WRONG

April 24

May we always remember to promptly admit when we are
wrong.

As we travel along life's path on Earth, we learn the lessons
of being human. There will be times when we may say words or
act inappropriately. We, at times and even unintentionally, give
someone else wrong information, messages, or our hurtful
reactions. When this happens, we need to go back to that person
and admit that we wronged or harmed them, taking mature
responsibility for our words or actions, which we may or may not
have innocently expressed. Admitting when we are wrong fills us
with the integrity that we need to no longer dwell in the problem
and sets us free to live humbly in the solution. No one is *right* all
the time. We all are learning what it means to be human.

Let us be open to more and more lessons about life, learn
from the mistakes, and move on.

May we have the awareness of when we are mistaken and
admit it to ourselves and another, pray for guidance not to repeat
the mistake, and move on to the next lesson.

*We take the responsibility for our part in the problem and we
allow others their part. May we both learn a vital lesson and find
our own integrity in every situation that may present itself as less
than harmonious.*

*Letting the Creator do His or Her job is relinquishing the
control we only "thought" we had in that situation.*

DOING ONE'S PART

April 25

May we maintain discernment in knowing what is our job
and what is the Creator's Job.

At some time in life, we will meet opposition or
confrontation. No one likes this job, yet it is part of our journey—
to learn how to handle confrontation with others. One way is to
avoid; yet the lesson will be prolonged if it is repeatedly avoided.
Another is to have faith that the Creator will give us the wisdom
and the wisest words to say, leaving the results in the hands of
God. Reacting quickly in anger is a lesson as well. We can always
try to have composure, step back, take an honest look at the
reality of the situation, and later, pray for the Creator to bless the
person we are at odds with, and let the Creator do the big work.
Our part is to pray for those whom we may have resentment
toward, leaving God to shower them with the richest blessings.
Our serenity increases and our fears diminish. Soon we will find
that by praying (even if we do not really mean it all of the time)
our resentment turns into compassion and understanding. The
Creator is omnipotent and a reliable problem solver.
    Let us place our problem in God's hands, and let the Divine
do the Divine's work. Meanwhile, we trust in the solution and get
on with our lives.
    May we know when to speak and take action, forever guided
by the Creator.

*We saw another in the dim light of fear, until we felt the love
of God transform that fear into compassion and understanding.*

We are reassured in the Light.

STAND TALL IN THE LIGHT

April 26

May we, no matter what happens or how we feel, stand tall in the Light.

There are those times when we give our power away to others, lose our serenity, and, at times, get the wind knocked out of our sails. When this happens, we need to know that the Creator and our Angels love us unconditionally, even if it appears or *feels* that no one else does. We need to know that we have a Divine Purpose, which may be found through meditation or other healthy means, and that we are greatly appreciated by our Creator and all Divine Beings who help us to continue on and fulfill that Purpose. Divine Intervention helps us to stand tall in the Divine Light in the face of adversity.

Let us hold our heads up in order to receive God's Grace, Wisdom, Peace, Illumination, and Blessing. When we walk with bowed heads and downcast eyes, we just might be inviting more adversity into our lives. If we give ourselves permission to feel *lost* or *down and out* for too long, we could be advertising that we deserve negative treatment from others.

May we know, even when the chips are down, that we have renewed strength and inspiration that is given to us by Spirit. May we walk in Divine Assurance.

The Angels comfort us in our sadness. Let us know that we have a right to our feelings, and that we are immortal children of the Creator's Enlightened Eternity.

Your spirit has a wide range. Direct it with careful discernment.

CALLING YOUR SPIRIT BACK

April 27

May we call our spirit and our power back to us, should we intentionally or unintentionally give it away.

Are there certain people, institutions, or situations in your life that zap your energy, that cause you anxiety and lessen your serenity? To whom do you give your soul? To whom do you give your power? If the answer is another person, then let us call our spirits back to whom they fully and truly belong: to ourselves and our Creator. It is somewhat a paradox when we give our whole selves—body, mind, and soul—to our Creator, we find that what we receive in return is completeness, wholeness, and freedom. The Creator does not exploit us in any way, does not engage in bargaining nor play games.

Let us feel the incredible freedom of giving ourselves to our Higher Power, to feel powerful, strengthened, and strong in spirit in return. Let us begin to place our power where it belongs—in the hands of the Divine.

May we cease the power play with finite humans and receive boundless joy, love, and power of spirit from the Creator.

Let us give of ourselves totally to the omnipotence of the Divine Source where there is no manipulation, sadness, or negativity. Here is where the ultimate Power resides.

If one believes in a Creator, one believes in oneself.

BELIEF IN ONESELF

April 28

May we believe in ourselves enough to accept the Grace of the Creator.

Perhaps we have all been through a phase of disbelief in our lives—disbelief in a Creator, disbelief in humanity, and disbelief in ourselves. This point of despair is usually when the Miracle happens. The Miracle could be blinding bright or subtly disguised. Nevertheless, it is when our total being has a true insight into itself that this discovery finally becomes integrated within us, and we say "A-ha!" If we believe in miracles, we believe in a Creator. With this knowledge, we find that it is much easier to believe in ourselves and, eventually, to restore our belief in the goodness of others and in humanity as a whole. Now it is up to us not only to recognize the Miracle, but also to receive the Grace of the Divine in the spirit in which the Miracle happens. When we believe and accept the Grace, there is no turning back to an old way of belief or disbelief.

Let us incorporate a fresh, new belief system in what we know to be true for ourselves. To believe in oneself is to be true to oneself, to have the confidence to reach one's Highest potential, and to share this gift with others.

May we believe in ourselves enough to give thanks for Grace, accept the Miracle, and share our gifts of the spirit with others.

If we reject ourselves, we reject the Divine within us. Let us receive Grace and realize our full potential.

Do not take the air for granted nor underestimate its power.

AIRING OUT

April 29

May we air out our bodies, minds, and souls.

In good weather, do you ever open the windows to air out your sacred living space? Feels good, doesn't it? With our eyes closed, let us imagine the Creator as a cooling breath. As we relax and breathe in and out, slowly and deeply, feel this Divine air filling and passing through our body, mind, and soul. Each of us is a free spirit, with the ability to make choices in our lives. The freedom that comes from airing out is the Divine Spirit, which we *all* have.

Let us feel the Power and strength that come from simply acknowledging the Creator. Breathe it in and know that you are a part of every molecule and atom in this Universe. We expand our scope, broaden the mind, open the heart, and give thanks to the Great Spirit for allowing itself to move through us.

May we remember, from time to time, to air out our living space and our entire being, clearing the way to allow Divinity in.

We felt closed in and overwhelmed, so we opened our window and our heart to the Highest Spirit, and we felt our soul take flight.

Your Journal is between you and your Creator; use discretion for whom you wish to share it with.

SPIRITUAL JOURNAL

April 30

May we continue to write in a spiritual daily journal any thoughts that help us to grow.

One need not be an author to jot down ideas or inspirational thoughts, to record the significant events of the day or messages received in meditation. By simply keeping a spiritual journal, one can review it every now and again to see spiritual progress. We are born to be full of the Light of our Creator; to keep the spark alive, and to see and feel it grow into a more peaceful, brighter Light is a longing for most.

Keeping a journal of meditation messages can be very useful, as insights come to us when we are quiet and guided by Divine Light. The more insight we have into our own being, the more able we are to help others along their way, in understanding and compassion.

May we keep our journal in order to keep the Divine Spark glowing bright.

If we see ourselves as clay, there is no room to grow. When we see ourselves as Light, we give the Creator room to inspire us.

When one is comforted, there exudes confidence and security.

COMFORT

May 1

May we be comfortable in knowing that we are loved in the Divine Light.

What does comfort mean to you? Does it mean that every one of your physical and financial desires are met? Indeed, this is partially what comfort means; yet there is a deeper meaning. Suppose all of your physical and financial desires were not met. Think of what your attitude and life would be like then. You would rely more on your inner resources and gain tremendous insight into the way the world works. Perhaps, one would rely totally upon faith in the all-providing Creator to fulfill his or her life with internal and external richness. There is comfort in knowing that one will be provided for, that one is unconditionally loved by the Highest Love, and that one is filled with the capacity to love God and others in return.

Let us have the insight that our journey is filled with opportunities for learning; this may be a broader concept of comfort. Let us be comfortable in this knowing.

May we understand that all of our needs are already met, and may we be comforted by knowing that we are deeply loved by the Creator.

Having faith brings nurturing comfort. Placing this in the heart of the Divine, we are freed.

We are all winners in God's eyes.

ADEQUACY

May 2

May we feel adequate in the eyes of our Creator.

In the Greater sense, we all are unique individuals traveling along life's journeys, interacting with others, and learning significant karmic lessons. There will be times when our security will be somewhat threatened and self-doubt will creep in. Let us know that, if in any way, we feel inadequate in relation to others, we may have lost sight of the big picture. Let us constantly remind ourselves that we are more than adequate in the eyes of our Creator and that any problem or obstacle can be overcome by trusting in that Highest Love. The Power of God's Love is stronger than our feelings of inadequacy.

Let us meditate on the lovingness that we are, indeed, perfectly adequate as we are, without having to think that we must change something about ourselves. We are loved and loving right this very moment, even in the face of aridity or adversity. We are human, all with various personalities, feelings, thoughts, and outlooks on life. May we begin to celebrate in the compassionate knowingness that each of us, separately and collectively, are more than enough.

May we go forth confidently and quietly, and realize the power of Spirit.

Perhaps we compared ourselves to someone else today instead of seeing him or her as our sister or brother. When we broadened our perspective, we saw a rainbow overhead that symbolized our Creator's Love for all beings.

Our Guardian Angel always knows exactly what we need.

ANGEL TALK

May 3

When feeling ruffled or confused as to what to do, how to go about certain situations, or how to conduct ourselves, we can always talk it over with the Angels.

If we find ourselves in a state of confusion, sorrow, depression, or worry, let us give these states of mind over fully to those who know exactly what to do. Have a little Angel talk. Close your eyes, take three long, slow, deep belly breaths, and call upon the Angels of Higher Wisdom to gather around you. Talk to them as you would a team of experts who understand your situation and who possess All Intelligence. After you have talked to them, be still and silent to receive your answer. It will come, if you persist. You may want to open your heart to the All-knowing Universe, should your beliefs rest in a comfort other than angels.

Let us gather helpful insight as a result of tapping into our given wisdom. This wisdom may be likened to the Godspark within us all, waiting to be fanned into the Fire of Understanding, Knowledge, and Guidance from the Divine Unseen.

May we pause quietly and breathe in fresh counsel as we see a Light, a helping hand, or hear a Divinely sounding bell.

We are awakened in the knowledge of new beginnings, where we soar upward with our newly found wings.

Critical judgment lessens when we can see ourselves in each and every human being and creature on Earth.

MIRRORING

May 4

May we realize that every living thing we meet is a mirror of ourselves, and is reflected back to us in all ways.

It is important to know that when we criticize another person, we are actually harshly judging ourselves. People are mirrors for us, so are animals and the beauty of nature. Likewise, if we celebrate and love another, we are rejoicing in the love that we have for ourselves. Let us have this realization in mind when we interact with other beings, and try to keep an open, positive frame of thought.

Let us celebrate who we are, wondrous children of the Creator, and in turn, celebrate the joy in our brothers, sisters, animals, and all life. This makes for harmony in the world, as we remember that world peace begins with the individual.

May we love and respect all those who we see in the mirror.

Let us see each other as our comrade, traveling the journey to the Highest Stars. We celebrate each other—for we are all the same—evolving and growing toward the Divine Light of Eternity.

If we were meant to be "there," we would be.

WE ARE RIGHT WHERE WE ARE SUPPOSED TO BE

May 5

May we be free of guilt and fear and remember that, according to the Creator's plan, we are exactly where we are supposed to be in our lives, our healing endeavors, and even in our differences.

Perhaps we are working on ridding ourselves of destructive habits that no longer fit comfortably into our ever-changing lives. Our expectations of ourselves to succeed in the habit-breaking process could undermine our own inner peace if we take the outcome into our own hands. Let us pray to have all of the necessary tools that are supplied by our Divine inner resources readily available. Let us have faith in ourselves and in our Creator, knowing the time to let go becomes as natural as our breathing.

Let us not chastise our failed attempts to break the past habits that stand in the way of our loving perseverance in the present. It may be highly beneficial to free our vocabulary of words such as, "should," "ought to," "supposed to," etc., as those messages are more harmful than helpful. Just as there is an emerging into the different seasons, we are also growing and evolving along our journey. It is possible that learning exists in the various situations in which that we find ourselves, that there is a season and a reason behind our particular placement on the planet at exactly this very moment.

May we love ourselves where we are in our lives, our healing, and our particular chosen spiritual path as much as we possibly can. May we trust the process.

Persevere in your faith and love for your Creator as your Highest aspiration. Seek unity of your ego and spirit in times of quiet desperation, and simply know that all is well.

*If something does not "feel" good to you,
work with yourself a little.*

TRANSFORMING NEGATIVITY INTO BEAUTY

May 6

May we work internally with anything negative, until we have transformed it into something positive, constructive, and beautiful.

Yes, it is true that at some point during the day, week, or month, we must work with a negative thought or emotion. Let us know that this situation is not necessarily about another person, place, or thing, but it is about us and our perspective or opinion. Instead of *stuffing-in* negativity, we can learn to appropriately express it, and then transform it into positive thoughts by using various thought forms or techniques. One way could be a type of meditative visualization programming. There are many books on creative visualization.

Let us allow ourselves to be creative about our visualizations. By using our imagination and meditating, we can transform the object, situation, or person about which we are angry, anxious, or depressed into a constructive way of presenting the particular situations to ourselves. We could use our breath to breathe out negativity and breathe in unconditional love, Divine Healing Light, and forgiveness if our problem is anger at a particular person. We could step back from our subjective mind and objectively see any negative experience as a form of comedy. Humor is one way to dissolve adversity. We could visualize a white or golden mist surrounding the circumstance or person, and watch it vaporize into nothingness.

May we know that by the Power of the Creator, we can transform anything that is toxic into a beautiful work of art, a comedy, or a spiritual experience.

Be for your Self, not against. Breathe in the beauty of your own Spirit.

*The best advice we may ever receive is to go outside and
sit on a tree stump.*

WALKING IN THE WOODS

May 7

May we take a day to walk in the woods and capture the full
energy of the Creator with our breath.

John Muir was a philosopher and naturalist who lived in the
mid-1800s. He explored nature and wrote books on the subject of
humans' relationship to it. The site of one of his expeditions is
known now as Muir Woods in northern California, a place where
the tallest living thing on Earth dwells—the redwood. Being
surrounded by these trees, some of which are over 1,000 years
old, one cannot help but feel the Divine Presence of a Creator.
Just as people have spirits, so do trees, all other vegetation,
animals, and stones.

Let us walk in the woods or any place in nature, and breathe
in the atmosphere of the plants and trees, which give us oxygen
to inhale with the fresh air and take, in turn, the carbon dioxide
that we exhale. Feel the tree spirits and find your favorite tree,
spending a little time giving thanks.

May we learn to appreciate all of nature and the incredible
Universe in which we live.

*Deep within the silence of the woods, we can hear the Divine
Voice. The trees and humans share the same spirit, and we can
feel the total innocence therein.*

Do not place limits upon your mind.

EXPLORING

May 8

May we have the courage to explore the world, our Self, the Universe, and all multi-verses.

It takes courage to look deeply into ourselves with our shadows as well as our light. Exploring the whole self is the most important work we will ever do in our lives. To look inside and see that we, in our natural state, are actually innocent children of the Divine can be truly refreshing. One of the many reasons that keep us from fully exploring the self is society's conditioning, which has been placed upon us. There is a lot of *psychobabble* out there that can frighten us when looking at ourselves. As well as exploring the inner world, we need a balance, so as to not become too focused on ourselves alone. It's a wide world. Let us explore this aspect and try to see how we can relate the insight that we find in ourselves to others and the entire Universe. After all, all humans share the same air and see the same sun and moon.

Let us explore beyond to the unseen, the psychic world, and the world of energy, broadening out to other universes in space outside our atmosphere. Why would we think that our universe is the only one? Let us always try to broaden the scope of how we see our world, within and without, in the deep seas, and above in space.

May we realize that there is no end to what we might explore.

We are infinite because God is infinite. Keep your feet on the ground, yet let your mind explore your sacred spirit, for in that itself, is found an entire Universe.

Simple elegance is natural beauty.

SACRED SPACE, BEAUTY

May 9

May we surround our home, our sacred space, with beauty.

One does not have to be extravagant to surround oneself with beauty—works of art that represent our spirit and soul, perhaps objects from nature, a shell from the beach, or wood shapes from a forest can be displayed artfully in one's sacred space. Your home is your place of rest and serenity. It is your creative space waiting to be filled with your spirit. As you go out from your sacred space, you carry that spiritual *ambiance* with you, so let us make our spaces and their aura as beautiful as possible. Displaying photographs of loved ones is another way to make your space loving and beautiful. When others come into your sacred space, they can *feel* and sense your spirit and all that connects you with it.

Let us Bless those that enter our sacred space and those with whom we can share our spirits of simplistic, original beauty.

May we bless our own sacred space with beauty and the internal richness of our Divine Soul.

We can see our homes as precious and sacred, where the very depths of our souls are interwoven into every single thread of that safe tapestry that surrounds us and maintains our peace of mind.

There is magic in affirmations.

CHANGING SHADOWS INTO LIGHT

May 10

May we use affirmations and meditation to release the negative past in order to look forward to a brighter future.

If we could release everything negative that has taken place up to this moment in our lives, we would find that all that would be left is a positive, goal attaining, bright, successful, and happy future. One way this can be done is by the use of meditation and positive affirmations. We can visualize anything negative as a dark shadow in the mind, body, or soul. By use of the breath, we can then breathe the shadow out of ourselves by seeing only spiritual white or golden light filling every cell of our bodies and our surrounding aura. With persistence and repetition, and with the help of the Power of the Creator within us, we can bring the shadow into the light.

Let us begin to integrate our shadows, bringing it into a whole oneness, whereby the shadow loses its fearful hold on us as something separate from ourselves.

May we identify our shadow first, then either integrate it into our total being or lovingly release it into the Divine Light that constantly surrounds us.

We give thanks for the giving and loving benevolence of the heart, which guides the mind to begin the work of Spirit.

If you get up on the wrong side of the bed,
get back in and try again.

START THE DAY OVER

May 11

May we come to believe that we can start our day over at any time.

We all have those days when trouble seems to just pour over us and attract more of the same as the day progresses. This is where a little attitude adjustment comes in. Instead of simply telling ourselves that it will be a *bad* day all day long, we must remember that with prayer and a little effort on our part, we can start any day over for the better at any time. Also, remember that the Angels are eager to work for us and are always ready to help us in times of need. Perhaps we need to do a little physical exercise to clear our minds, and breathe fresh air, expanding the lungs. A walk or a swim is also refreshing to the spirit. Memorize a positive affirmation and repeat it to yourself throughout the day.

Let us know, in time, we may find that trouble does pass and our attitude and outlook on life is positive once again. This is life with its ebb and flow; stopping for a moment to close our eyes and meditate on our blessings, including the very air we inhale and exhale, can be extremely helpful.

May we know that trouble passes and that we do not have to attract more of it. We are in control of how we relate to our world, with the help of the Creator's Healing Power.

Woe we may have been, yet, like the wind, there is always a change surrounding us, happening within us, moving us toward our highest good.

When you find yourself in the dark, flip on the Light.

MOVING FORWARD AND BEYOND

May 12

May we trust our intuition enough to know when to move on.

At times, we may find ourselves in situations where we would rather not be or we are around someone who is somewhat less than pleasant. Instead of standing in the line of fire, we need to trust when to move on. There are times when we need to confront our fears and walk through them and times when we simply need to walk away.

To walk away from negativity does not mean avoidance. It means that we are taking care of ourselves by moving forward and beyond. If something or someone does not *feel* right to you, then trust your *gut* reaction, and move on. There will be other situations and people who are more positive and uplifting coming into your realm.

May we know when to "get out of Dodge!"

Allow others their feelings, whatever they may be. Yet, keep your heart focused on the Light and the Good, which is the essence of who you truly are.

May we create a pleasant resting place and call it "home."

ROOTS

May 13

May we have roots into earth and an eye on the vastness above us.

Having roots at home inadvertently gives us the freedom to be independent. Also, having a firm belief in the Creator, a dependency as some would call it, gives us the independence we have always longed for. To go *home* is a safe feeling. We may experience a sense of *home* when we are with a loved one, when we return from a trip, or when we meditate—knowing that we can have Heaven right here on Earth.

If our home in childhood was happy, we can recreate that same feeling as adults in our present homes. In contrast, if our childhoods were not filled with all good and positive memories, then, with prayer and the assistance of the Divine, we have another chance to create happy homes. Going *home* can mean feeling at One with the Highest Divine Spirit—a Universal connectedness. We can also view death as a returning *home* to be with loved ones who have passed on, our Angels, and primarily, our Creator. Whatever our view of *home* is, let us make it a safe and beautiful place to dwell.

May we utilize our freedom of independence to project confidently out from a safe, well-rooted home base.

Wherever we are, we have all the comforts of home, because our creative vision is simply a breath away.

Every thought is now a memory.

CREATE NEW MEMORIES

May 14

May we release any old memories that hurt and begin to create new memories of greater joy.

There are those who may be saddened and haunted by past memories. It may be time to release old painful memories into the Light, surrender, and accept a new day to create new memories! The past is ours to learn from, trying not to repeat the old patterns. Let us try something new, uplifting, and life-fulfilling. Think of something that you have always wanted to do or a friend to call and catch up with. What has been holding you back? Fears, old traits, or family ties that were not pleasant can be changed for the better. We clear our minds of old *clutter* in meditation and recognize our progress thus far.

Let us affirm our abilities to move beyond the past with guidance from the Creator as we move into action, creating new memories that are pleasant and happier.

May we take the action necessary to rise above melancholia or anything negative concerning the past and replace the old, outdated traits and fears with new, pleasurable moments as much as possible.

We may have lived with a soft melancholia that deepened and lessened at different times. Some can record the depths with verses that rhyme. Tears and laughter both offer release, which makes the underlying sadness less important, allowing us to find an overall sense of peace.

Inside one tiny seed is found the entire Universe.

PLANT SOMETHING!

May 15

May we take a little time this spring to plant something in good soil, nurture it, and watch it grow.

What an incredible gift from the Creator a seed is! Contained within one seed is the miracle of the universe. It is not unlike our own life, metaphorically speaking, beginning with its male and female components, its roots like an umbilical cord growing into Mother Earth. Following gestation, when the stem shows its face above ground, like all creatures, this new growth needs adequate air, water, nutrients, nighttime to rest, and sunlight for health, further maturation, and eventual blossoming. Healthy nutrients and a good foundation offer beautiful results.

We also grow toward the Light with the rhythm of both natural sunlight and moonlight. This can be an analogous to Spiritual maturation. The seedling is exposed to the elements and sometimes to harsh conditions. This is like our own pain and hardship in life. If the roots are strong—if our spiritual condition is strong—we will survive the harsh winds of change. In time, the plant may bear fruit, provide shade, or produce beautiful flowers or food. Plants utilize our exhaled carbon dioxide and provide us oxygen in return. Have you ever thought about the fact that human beings would perish from Earth without the oxygen freely given to us by plants, trees, algae, plankton, herbs, and the entire plant kingdom, thereby creating a vital, wonderful reciprocity? Think about this for a few moments...breathe deeply, pause, and give thanks to our green friends.

May we nurture ourselves and other living things and rejoice in the growth therein.

We, along with everything in the Universe, are growing slowly but surely toward the Light. We allow for rest inside the darkness, blessing both in awe and wonder.

It is interesting to think that we may have opportunities over many, many lifetimes to evolve into Pure Peace.

REINCARNATION: ONE SCHOOL OF THOUGHT

May 16

May we have the courage to explore other philosophies of the afterlife.

Perhaps you were raised in a Christian home, or have come to believe in a certain way about the afterlife. Some Christians may not believe in reincarnation, because it is not in their Bible. While it is good to have an inspired book to follow, let us begin to broaden our scope to other religious philosophies. Reincarnation is a belief held by most of the Eastern religions. One philosophy is this: when a person dies, they go to "Heaven school" where they study lessons not yet learned previously on Earth, depending on how evolved they were spiritually. The Soul in the spiritual realm chooses its next life with guidance from the Divine. Together they choose the soul's new parents and its path in order to best learn the lessons it needs to have. Karma, the law of cause and effect, plays a part here. We may encounter certain people from a past life with whom we have unfinished business. Just as we meet them again and again in each lifetime, they too have their paths, their karma, their unfinished business with us.

We are responsible for following our spiritual paths back to God and into the Spiritual world to reunite with our Creator. When all lessons are learned, we do not have to come back to Earth to learn any more lessons here. We then reincarnate in other spiritual realms, perhaps to assist others on Earth in their spiritual growth back to the Ultimate Life of Peace. Such is the wheel of life, according to some.

May we take responsibility at every given opportunity to better learn our spiritual lessons on Earth.

We may have lived on Earth many different times and in different lands. We know the Creator guides us in our learning.

We all vibrate at different frequencies, as well as emit
different colors in our astral bodies.

AURAS

May 17

May we project an aura of loving and spiritual Light.

An aura is an emanation surrounding a person. Some people can see the aura that another person emanates. Auras have different colors found in the rainbow spectrum. The halo we see in art curving around the head of a Saint, the Christ, and the Madonna is usually depicted as gold or white, suggesting a very High Spiritual Quality. We can create our own auras of spiritual growth by visualizing the color we wish to project and using deep breathing to surround ourselves in any color of Light we choose. Usually, metaphysically speaking, an aura of gold or white can be projected for protection around a person or for using the Higher God-Self in thought, word, and deed. Auras may also change colors with each emanated vision or exhale.

Let us create a gentle aura around ourselves before we go about our daily activities, and in so doing, emanate more Peace.

May we learn to create the Highest Color in our aura when greeting the day.

Perhaps we forgave an old resentment and the aura became pink—a gift of a rose in contentment. While we breathed in unconditional Love and Healing Divine Light, our aura changed in Love to Golden Sparks amid the All Spiritual White.

All healing is Spiritual in nature.

DIVINE HEALING LIGHT

May 18

May we bathe our mind, body, and soul in Divine Healing Light.

There will always be those times when some aspect of our body/mind/soul needs to heal. Should times of fear or insecurity arise in one's life, remember that strength and peace are ours for the asking. Taking the time to close our eyes, breathing deeply, and asking the Creator for the courage to meet any problem, not only increases our faith, but also could save our lives. We can visualize this Divine Peace enveloping us and flowing through us by seeing our mind and body being bathed in Divine Healing Light. This is helpful for any and all types of problems, whether physical, medical, financial, interpersonal, or emotional.

Remember that the more Light we carry within our minds, our bodies, and our auras, the more we are able to share that Light of Hope, Peace, and Love with others. It is when we can see and feel the healing in our own lives that we can be an inspiration for someone else to heal. We have the experience and evidence to assist or teach others who still may be afflicted with similar maladies of some sort. When this happens, we are better able to understand that all things in life are working together for the Greatest Good.

May we continually cleanse and bathe in the Loving Light of the Divine, and experience Peace in knowing that it is our God-given right to heal.

God is greater than any obstacle in our path. We can feel the Source near, as we conquer our greatest challenges, helping others to do the same.

If we are good to ourselves, others will be good to us in return.

BE GOOD TO YOURSELF

May 19

May we always remember to be good to ourselves in all ways that we are able to be at the time.

Being good to ourselves involves taking good care of ourselves in many areas, including physically, emotionally, mentally, and spiritually. Any effort we make to try and improve the quality of our lives in these areas is progress and growth on our part. Another way that we can be good to ourselves is to surround ourselves with uplifting, supportive people whenever possible—those with whom, most importantly, we have a strong heart connection. This is another way that we can nurture ourselves. Humor and creativity also are extremely healing and soothing and may add meaning to our life and to our soul.

Let us give ourselves permission to be good to ourselves. We are giving others permission to be good to us, as well. With our efforts in this area, we may also inspire others to be good to themselves.

May we be more aware of the messages that we are sending to ourselves and to others.

We are aware that even the smallest effort on our part to feel more connected with both Mother Earth and the Divine Spirit that created us, allows us to rejoice in the sunlight of the Heavens.

When Ego calls, take a message.

EGO

May 20

May we realize that while the ego has its attributes, spiritual wholeness may be more essential to human growth and harmony.

The ego is defined as the self and is considered as the consciousness of the individual, distinct from other selves. The ego has a self-assertive and self-preserving tendency. We need the ego to stand up for ourselves, in certain situations, and for our basic survival. Yet, when the ego declares, for example, "I am right," a touch of self-righteousness could step in and can somehow seem to take over our entire being. When the ego is inflamed, spirituality is lessened. Perhaps it would be better if the order were reversed. When we consider our Divine true Self, we have more of a connectiveness with all other selves. Therefore, there is a lessened need to be so unique and separate from all others. All beings possess different qualities and personalities that create a whole world of variety. Although this in itself can be stimulating and inspiring, deep down, each of us is searching for the same thing. We all have a longing to be loved and accepted, to give love, and to fill any emptiness we may feel. We long for a connection to what we believe to be spiritual to us in the context of love, forgiveness and goodness.

Let us, during any day, find that by saying to ourselves or aloud the name that we give to our Higher Power or Source, that our heart and mind are immediately tuned in to a more spiritual flow of thoughts that can remind us of Universal Truths.

May we be ever reminded of our trues selves and that a higher nature of order is working in our lives.

Our ego swelled and we simply forgot who we were. The ego made too much noise—a busy buzz. Then we remembered our true nature, whole and benevolent, a child of the omnipotent Creator.

Power is Grace made manifest.

THE POWER OF OUR CREATOR

May 21

May we always remember that the Power of our Creator is stronger than any weakness, any problem, and anything on Earth and beyond.

Life, indeed, presents us with challenges at times. During these times, harmful, overwhelming stress may be at the forefront. When difficulty arises, let us call upon the immeasurable Power of our Creator. If, for example, we are exerting too much effort to overcome addictions, we can ask for that Divine Power to be in control of our minds, bodies, and souls. We, as humans, tend to have various weaknesses and addictions, that we may need to keep in check for our overall well-being. When we are ready to let go of an addiction or weakness, let us remember the Grace of the Divine, the Mercy of Christ, or the wise teachings of Saints and sages throughout the world.

Let us rest assured that if we call upon the Divine, we will receive guidance and wisdom to undertake any problem, worry, or weakness. When we have mastered the overcoming of any weakness, including letting go of excess stress, let us give credit to the omnipotence of the Creator and rest in Divine Grace.

May we knock upon the door of the Creator in order to receive direction and become open to new ways of living a happier, healthier life.

We knocked and the Divine responded. Grace healed us with the mystery of God's Love.

A flower doesn't force itself to bloom.

EVERYTHING IN ITS TIME

May 22

May we keep the wisdom of the winds, that everything in life has its time and place.

Let us know the wisdom of refraining from using our self-motivated will to try to force *reality* to happen. Everything has its time and place. When we try to control a situation, it usually backfires on us.

Let us clear our minds of forcefulness and control and remember the peace found when we go deep within. If we complicate situations, driven by unhealthy motives, we can make ourselves frenzied and almost dizzy! If we try to control another person, we are saying that we all know better than God, or that we can control Universal and Spiritual laws. In the process of misusing force or self-will to a means to our own end, we usually become hard and bitter people. As a result, we push our true, heartfelt feelings down further into the empty, dark abyss where our souls once flourished. If we listen to our inner voice, we will know when the time and place are right for us to undertake whatever is at hand to do.

May we be still and listen to the natural and Universal Laws of the spirit within.

We went into the woods alone to think. Ideas were manifested and our problems became more manageable.

The Light has always been there. It is our own eyes
that have dimmed it.

STAND IN THE LIGHT OF THE CHRIST

May 23

May we stand tall in the Light of the Christ and feel the loving mercy of such a wonderful being.

There are many times in our lives when we feel low in spirits. A message directly given to me from my Angel, "Stand Ye tall in the Light of the Christ!" was wise advice. At one point in my life, when I heard this powerful message, I felt my strength returning. In addition, I felt the confidence one feels when they are unconditionally loved. We are meant to be secure and sound in our understanding of the Divine. It is a fallacy to believe that we do *anything* by ourselves. We are guided by the Intelligence of the Creator in all things. We are always loved by the Divine, however and whomever we choose to believe that Divine Power to be. Christ is loved by people worldwide. The Christ stands for Love and Forgiveness.

Let us all over the world embrace His teachings and try to carry them through to the best of our ability. By simply thinking about the compassion that Christ had, our souls can be soothed.

When we feel low in spirits, let us call upon the Creator's Love and Light and be uplifted.

May we always look *up* and be uplifted in the eyes of the Christ, as we contemplate the truth of His message.

We stood upon a white rock with a light blinding bright.
'Twas the Love of the Christ that helped us stand tall.

Forgetting who we think we are, is when we remember
who we truly are.

PRACTICAL PATH

May 24

May we walk a practical path with an ethereal air.

When we reach out into the Higher Etherics, we always need to remember that we walk on the Earth and deal with day-to-day human issues. We have heard it said that we need to have our heads in the clouds and our feet on the ground. This go-between within Heaven and Earth can be a little tricky if a healthy balance is not sought and found. Let us ask to be guided by the Creator in our endeavors to live life on this Earth. Few are called to renounce the world and live in Himalayan mountaintops, in caves, or in Monasteries.

Let us be realistic about our callings and act accordingly. The Divine Purpose shall be revealed if we sincerely ask, seek, and put one practical foot in front of the other.

May we be willing to work with what we have been Divinely inspired to do in this life.

A trek to the Mountain's arduous summit may be just that—a trek. The learning is in which particular path we take.

The quickest way to be peaceful in any given situation is to be grateful for the lesson found within it.

CREATE YOUR OWN PEACE

May 25

May we create peace, internally and externally, no matter what the circumstance.

Peace is like truth—it is an individual's understanding of what it means to them in their own lives. Everyone also has their own truth as a result of their circumstances and experiences in life. Such is the way of Peace. One may be influenced by spiritual teachers or inspired by religion, yet one must find and create their own Peace within their outward daily lives. Peace may be found in helping others or in meditation or working with animals or walking in the woods. However you find your Peace is up to you. One may ask, "How does one have peace while in an argument or when the car breaks down?" Try to transform your problems into opportunities for learning.

Let us prepare for the day with a quiet mind and notice the reactions we receive from others and vice versa. If one is met with adversity, there exists a lesson. No other person, situation, place, or thing has the right to interfere with our inner and outer peace, unless we allow it. If we are being true to others and ourselves no harm comes to us, unless we interpret it as so. With a spiritual focus, we realize that everything that happens in the world has its purpose. All is interwoven into the Divine Tapestry.

May Peace always be with us.

When we thanked our opposition for the lesson, we knew that our true Peace lay in the arms of Divine Creation.

*Our life on the spiritual path can be likened to a mountain trail.
There may be more than one trail to ascend to the top
of the mountain.*

ENJOY THE CLIMB

May 26

May we enjoy who we are and what we do while walking upon our spiritual path.

We all have *shadows* and light. Although we do not ignore or deny the shadow side, let us transform this shadow into light. To shed light onto the shadow, we accept all of who we are and where we are on our particular spiritual paths. Instead of downgrading ourselves for not being farther along on the path, let us enjoy the scenery of the path at different levels as we walk upward toward the summit.

Let us take time to smell a flower or examine a fern or hug a tree while we catch our breath. The trail does not have to be impossibly steep, unless we make it so. We can take the *loop* that is not as strenuous and still reach the top of the mountain. If your climb is not enjoyable, rest and wait for further guidance from the Divine.

May we enjoy the climb as well as the view, knowing that eventually we will get to the mountain summit.

Taking one step at a time lets us enjoy the climb.

One need not be solely idealistic to reach his or her potential,
yet they must be willing to meet all given obstacles
as well as joys.

POTENTIAL

May 27

May we recognize our potential and use that extra effort to achieve it.

The potential in all beings is actually unfathomable. We can, each and every one of us, reach our highest potentials and beyond. It is the ego's fear and society's conditioning that says we must be limited. Most people do not reach their potential because they do not believe that they deserve to make their dreams into realities. If we align our goals with the will of the Divine, the entire Universe works for us to help us reach that goal. When we reach one goal, we expand our potential to reach still another and another. It is endless.

Let us set realistic goals in the beginning. With prayer and effort on our parts, we will reach those goals, step by step. We keep reaching goals until, before we know it, we have reached our full potential. It means that we work diligently, guided by the Creator every step of the way.

May we reach our full potential and always reach beyond even that.

We are all moving upward. Nothing that has life is stagnant.
Never be satisfied with yourself so much that the seeds sown in
the mind seem unimportant.

*Some people do not try to forgive, because they are afraid
that it might work!*

RECONCILIATION

May 28

May we reconcile any differences with others in the Spirit of
the Divine's Highest Good for all concerned.

In the *Desiderata*, a beautiful script for a peaceful life by an
anonymous author, there is a line that suggests we to try to be on
as good terms as possible with all people. There may be someone
with whom you would deeply like to be on good terms yet, an
old, familiar, stubborn ego and resentment is preventing you from
settling the differences in a new Light.

Try to do this reconciliation when you are ready. To be *ready*
is to find forgiveness in your heart of hearts. Try closing your
eyes, take some deep breaths, and visualize this person in an aura
of pink light. Try to bring this person into your heart and forgive
that person, just as you would like to be forgiven for your faults,
hasty words, or actions. Ask for Divine guidance, and align your
entire being with your Higher Self, and then forgive yourself.
Once we begin to forgive ourselves, we will find it easier to
forgive others. In the name of the Creator anything is possible.
Just try it.

May we be reconciled with ourselves and others today. If we
are not ready, then let us forgive ourselves for not tending to this
today; yet keep it in the back of our minds and our hearts for the
earliest possible opportunity.

*How can we blame others when we are equally at fault? Most
often, it is stubbornness and fear that traps us.*

Fear narrows, Love expands.

LOVE AND FEAR

May 29

May we always act, think, and speak out of love and not out of unfounded fear.

Much is written that the only two emotions in one's life are Love and Fear. The two cannot coexist. When we are able to step out of ourselves and see ourselves as we truly are, then we are better able to distinguish if we are acting or talking out of Love or fear. We can simplify this concept by understanding that when the ego is in control, we are acting out of fear.

We think something is threatening our ego's basic survival, yet take a deeper look. Something or someone is threatening who you *think* you are; that person you have worked so hard to define as yourself and your personality. In contrast, walking in Spiritual confidence, when we are in the Spirit of Love, lets the ego take a breather, and we are flowing securely in the limitless arms of the Divine. We talk, think, and act effortlessly. This is who we truly are—One with the Universe and the Creator. We are Light, vibrating with the natural and spiritual laws of the Universe.

May we feel the Lightness of Love.

Fear is heavy. Love is Light. All is well in the Divine Plan. We do, indeed, have a choice as to which path we choose to walk upon.

Pausing is composure and poise in action.

PAUSE

May 30

May we, when moving, thinking, or speaking too hurriedly, pause and give thanks to the Creator.

When agitated or when thoughts get ahead of what the body is capable of doing, take a few moments to pause—a little time out to gather your thoughts and place them where they belong. Before you go to a gathering or begin your day, try a little deep breathing, surrounding yourself with Spiritual white light, and give thanks to the Creator for your breath. This changes the vibration of what could be hectic encounters or an *off day*.

This simple exercise can make for a more joyful day.

May we always remember to pause for a moment and feel blessed by the Divine.

We are blessed, each and every one, each flower, tree, rock, animal, all of creation.

The Creator reveals only that which we are fit to receive.

REVELATIONS

May 31

May we allow our Creator to work through us, revealing insights about others and ourselves, as we are ready to receive them.

Sometimes, we can become so bogged down trying to figure everything out! What unnecessary burdens we place upon ourselves when, ultimately, the Creator is in control. Whatever our concept of a Creator is, we can pray that this Highly Intelligent Energy Force reveals to us that which is necessary for our and others well-being at the time.

Let us remember that when faced with a problem, sometimes we must simply *be* with that confusion or difficulty without having the concrete solutions revealed to us at that time. As difficult as it is to do at times, we must be patient and trust that our concept of God has our situation perfectly under control and that we will eventually understand the problem, hopefully learn from it, and move on. There is a season for all creatures and creations to grow and flourish.

May we learn from the revelations given to us by our Creator and realize that the God-given insights are a gift from the Light of Goodness.

We can manifest revelations, as well as inspirations. This happens when we align our energies with the All Intelligent One.

*You are a bright star and you have your own place
in the Universe.*

STAR PEOPLE

June 1

May we see our life and the lives of others as special and wonderful in this Universe.

Imagine yourself as a star in the worldly sense, with all the finer aspects life has to offer, glittering, shining, enthusiastically applauded, and well-respected for your unique talent. This is you. In a sense, we all have our splendid wonderfulness that deserves appreciation. Now imagine yourself as a natural star in the sky, beautifully shining in the Heavens among billions of other stars, brilliant and twinkling day and night. From our Earth's perspective, we can see these stars in groups or configurations making up what we call constellations. Perhaps this could be symbolic of our lives consisting of each unique and bright person living in harmony with all other unique beings. In meditation, we can visualize the intelligence and brilliance from the Creator's illumination coming in through the tops of our heads, filtering down to include every cell and atom in our bodies.

We are all Light vibrations and have the capability of turning on the *Light* within. Remember, when using this meditation technique, to firmly ground yourself in Mother Earth, so as to be able to bring the star-energy down into your body while you are surrounded by God's Grace and White Light.

May we choose to vibrate at a brighter and higher frequency with the totality of God's incredible creations.

Benevolent is our Universe, shining Divine Light upon one and all.

Emotional blocks come from trying to dam the flow.

FLUIDITY

June 2

May we realize that all life, including ourselves, is fluid and in motion.

Nothing in life is stagnant. There is always motion. Think of the atoms, molecules, and cells that you studied about in science class. A fifty-story building looks solid and, by the law of gravity, is sturdy. The atoms, protons, and electrons in the steel, iron, wood, and sheet rock have their own particular makeup of the minute elements, which are the same as those found in organic life forms. They are simply arranged differently for individualization. We are all moving toward the Light of the Creator. It is a comfort to know, psychologically speaking, that no emotion is permanent. If we feel irritable, low in spirits, or sad, these feelings will change.

Let us rest in the truth that everything eventually passes. We will take ourselves a little more lightly. We can remove ourselves from fear-based negativity by shape-shifting our attitudes. We simply identify and acknowledge the feeling and let it go through prayer, meditation, breathing, physical exercise, sharing with another person, or any means and tools that reside in us as a well of positive resources.

May we learn to flow in and out of moods and situations and know that the Creator is alive and flowing through us.

The Earth we stand upon is in motion. We move Gracefully, with the natural rhythms of the seas and the mountains. Our bodies are fluid and changing, and it is our intuitive heart that the Creator transforms.

Independence is having firmly planted roots.

TRADITION AND GROWTH

June 3

May we be fully grounded into Mother Earth by our roots of tradition in order to experience our limitless mind.

What do you think of when you think of tradition? Family traits, your country, your religious beliefs, or ancestors? It is true that all of these elements involve tradition. Roots give us the strength and endurance to grow and bloom independently. When we *outgrow* the family traditions that no longer serve us for our good, and when we mature and begin to make choices for ourselves, we may evolve beyond tradition's limits.

Let us feel physically and firmly grounded by our roots, yet have the courage to blossom in our own unique way, to experience fully the limitless power of the Creator within. When our feet are on the ground, we have the opportunity to make our own decisions as guided by the Divine will of Heaven.

May we walk surefootedly, with a boundless, open mind.

Just as a flower sets roots and grows upon the strong stem, let us unfold into our own form and color, regardless of outdated traditions.

We are all psychic. Some people are just more finely tuned.

PSYCHIC ENERGY

June 4

May we take in and broadcast out only positive vibrations.

The brain is a large energy center—what we put into it, we give out to the world. Therefore, let us fill ourselves with positive energy in order to give out positive energy. Do you think television and movies broadcast positive energy? Do you watch violent shows or heightened sensationalism news? How do you think this kind of information can help you? Perhaps it helps you to live a fear-based existence, which is the opposite of a loving existence. Everything you do, think, feel, and say matters! It is recorded in the atmosphere's ether and in our subconscious minds.

Let us be very careful about what we put into our minds, as it also goes out, whether we are conscious of it or not. We can even change negative psychic energy into positive energy by lighting incense and candles or by going outside and looking at the sky and nature, remembering the spiritual aspects of life. Clearly, these are more important than the trivia of the day.

May we notice what fills our thoughts, and, if negative, may we use the spiritual tools to change it into positive vibrations.

We nurture our minds with kind and loving thoughts and gentle vibrations. We are incisive and conscious about all that we let into our hearts and minds.

*Helping is staying in the present moment and being as positive
as possible in all situations.*

HELPING

June 5

May we, in any given circumstance, always ask the question,
"How can we help?"

We do not have to be ostentatious about our gifts to others or
make huge contributions to organizations or volunteer all our
time to meaningful causes to be helpful. It is the little ways in
which we offer our kindness that really counts. Throughout the
day, ask yourself, "How can I help this person or situation?" Try
to remember to ask yourself, "How can I be a part of the solution
now and less part of the problem?" We are not to rob others of
feeling their pain or confusion. They need to be with that feeling
in order to arrive at the space beyond it. We can, and always do,
have inside us the resources to make someone else's burden a
little lighter.

Let us learn to be more giving in our gestures, all the while
remaining as loving and giving to ourselves, as well.

May we be helpful to others and extend ourselves in kindness
to brighten up a day.

*When another is agitated, do not try to fix them. Simply ask
yourself in silence, "What is the Highest Good for all concerned
here and how can I be part of attaining that aspiration?"*

*If every day were an extra-productive day, then we would not
have an "off" day to compare it to.*

OFF DAYS

June 6

May we know that some days may be less productive and let
that be okay.

Sometimes our Creator and our Angels give us little signs to
slow down. This may come as a slight headache, a tummy ache,
or irritability due to lack of rest. Our bodies talk to us. We need
to listen and then pray for the next right move. Sometimes the
next right move is not to move. It is indeed a lesson in life to go
through the *off days*, consciously calling them just what they
are—not a particularly productive or great day. With this insight
we can use healthy means of changing our attitudes, even though
we may not be able to change certain given situations.

Perhaps a cup of hot tea, easy music, or a little nap is what
we need. A tummy ache, for example, is an integral part of the
entire Universe. Maybe we need to learn to live in the ebb and
flow accordingly. We are not under any illusion of a darkened
curse. When we feel better, we feel like exerting and extending
ourselves a little more. By the end of the day, we may thank God
for giving us the knowledge of how to heal ourselves. We sleep
soundly and begin a new day tomorrow, rested and with new life-
giving enjoyments. Our country is very achievement-oriented.
We do not have to paint a masterpiece every day. Let us let that
be okay.

May we do what we can each day and know that every *off
day* is filled with the hope of an even brighter tomorrow.

*We cannot always be "on." Sometimes we need to pause and
nurture ourselves for the Greater Cause.*

Being loving is natural. Hostility is learned behavior.

NATURAL STATE

June 7

May we enjoy our natural state, given as a Blessing from the Creator.

Our natural state is Innocent, Pure, and Loving. This is how we came into the world. As we grow, there may be family or social conditioning, peer pressure, or trauma that unfortunately can make us turn to alcohol, drugs, or other disheartening habits later in life. Our natural God-state is still there, however, yet the Light is dimmed for a while. At times, we can feel like lost souls.

Let us remember that our souls belong to the Creator and that we long to be close to this Divine Light, the flame of that Light burns brightly again, and we *go home*. Home is our natural state, resting securely in the arms of the Creator, surrounded by our Special Angels' Protection and Goodness. One way we can *go home* to this natural state in our daily lives is with the practice of meditation and remembering our innocence as an infant in the world. The Creator Loved us dearly then, and still does, just as much, now.

May we feel God's Presence at all times by understanding that our natural state is a sense of comfort within our heart and mind.

Thank you, dear God, for our life. We breathe in your Love and Light.

See mistakes as your classroom.

BENEFITS OF HARD TIMES

June 8

May we understand that every difficult time we have truly has positive benefits in the long run.

The above statement is not written from the hand of a *Pollyanna*. It is written as fact. When we go through rough and rocky times, it is usually the Creator and our Guiding Angels who are trying to teach us something for our benefit. Every low thought or act of suffering is a way to "weed out the old" and make room for the new, positive thoughts coming into our minds to make for a better future. This could be like a tree losing its leaves in the fall and budding out again in the spring.

Let us consider the negative times as our periods of semi-dormancy, for there is still much life and activity within the trees' roots, as there is in our bodies, minds, and souls. Instead of frantically trying to eliminate negative aspects and situations in our lives, we simply try to handle them differently and in a new spiritual way, shedding Light into our hearts and minds from all that we have learned from life's experiences thus far.

May we continue to meditate during our difficult times, resting our active mind within the quiet Light and Peace of the Creator.

The Christ and Buddha suffered bitterly during their lives, as we do at times. Simply because we are spiritual does not mean we are exempt from life's darkness. Perhaps our perception of darkness is merely finding our way into the clarity of Light and Inspiration.

Singing creates endorphins.

SING YOUR LITTLE HEART OUT

June 9

May we remember that singing transforms the heart and mind.

When we were children, we may have learned some songs from our parents, or in school, or from our friends. We will be surprised how, at any given time, the little tunes can spontaneously pop into our adult minds. Have we grown so far away from those innocent and happy children that we dare not sing or even hum those tunes that speak just to us? Everyone has his or her favorite songs. We may not be Pavarottis, but we can still "get in the groove" and "let our hearts move."

Try singing along with the radio or your favorite CD. See how singing can transform a broken heart or brighten a day. Don't worry about being on key, for the Creator hears the feeling.

May we just sing our little hearts out and feel close to God and our happy times in childhood. Or sing simply because we want to.

We sang until our blues whirled away. Maybe we even made up our own little tune. When we are totally in the moment, expression is such a gift.

God is in charge! Why get all worked up?

EASY HEART

June 10

May we take care of our heart the light and easy way.

We know that heart disease is America's number one cause of death, yet do we stop and ask ourselves why? We scurry around trying to overfill ourselves with what we think will make us happy. At times we wear ourselves out on it, feeling empty, unhappy, and depressed. We are a culture that is dying of a broken heart, an uneasy heart. Let us remember that what is broken can be fixed. This does not mean running frantically to the next sex partner, or breaking our backs trying to be wealthy, or taking more alcohol, or finding another drug that *works*. It means being easy on ourselves, less critical and judgmental, while honestly examining our behavior. The emptiness we feel can be filled up with the Love of our Creator.

Let us experience communion with God in meditation, so we can carry this fulfilling Love gently into our loving relationships and relax the mind in order for creative thoughts to enter. Creativity is God-given intuition, to utilize for our own benefits and for the benefit of the whole. If we need to be fanatic about something, then let it be Peace, Health, and Goodness filling our hearts and minds.

May we let go of the toxic thoughts, emotions, and substances that stand in the way of our easy hearts.

Open your heart and love all mankind. Let peace flow in and remove all dis-ease.

*Gratitude is humbly witnessing our own progress
on our lives' journey.*

.

SUBTLE CHANGES

June 11

May we be aware of the subtle changes in our lives which
have helped us grow into healthier and whole persons.

Every little change we make for our health in body, mind, or
soul may seem as if it makes such a small difference, that we may
abandon that effort after a little while. Let us remember to stay
with a healthy change long enough for the subtle changes to have
a great effect. We may not notice such a minute difference, yet
our body's cells may be healing by leaps and bounds. For
example, drinking more fresh water, which our body needs to
function properly, flushes out toxins. The change can seem a little
awkward or different for a while, yet as we see positive responses
in the body; it could well become a new healthy habit.

Let us remember that when we heal on a physical level,
we heal in mind and soul, too. The system works together on a
collective basis—all in unity. When we heal emotionally and
mentally, the soul is better able to walk steadfastly on its spiritual
path back to the Creator. Maybe we can look for ways to create
more health in our daily lives!

May we be proud of the changes we allow ourselves to make
for improvement of the spiritual trinity—body/mind/soul.

*Our souls are happy. Our minds are clear. Our bodies are
healthy. We can walk with our heads up, as we create a little more
health, little by little.*

Thinking good thoughts can alter an entire belief system.

OCCUPYING GOOD THOUGHTS

June 12

May we fill any idle time with thoughts of goodness.

We hear all sorts of negative things about idle time. This is just another opinion. Idle time can be extremely beneficial, if we fill our hearts and minds with goodwill toward all humanity, thinking of ways to be of service, and meditating to feel closer to the Divine Source. The mind is usually like a workaholic—little rest or peace is found by just letting it roam wild. Let us control our minds by taming the thousands of runaway thoughts with peaceful and simple thoughts.

Let us simply enjoy relaxing from a busy day, trying to stay in the moment by watching the breath flow in and out of our bodies for a period of well-used time. Remember—we do have charge over our thoughts and emotions. If we do not like them, we can change them. By the assistance of the unseen Spirit, we can turn useless, idle time into a creative, intuitive situation by remembering the Good of all concerned.

May we occupy our busy minds with helpful and beneficial thoughts—making for a more pleasant and joyful future.

We observe the moment, both joyful and otherwise. Our thoughts unfold into a new season with each breath.

Sleep is merely a different awareness.

HEALING SLEEP

June 13

May we remember to state our intention, before going to sleep, in order to rest peacefully, breathing the breath of God.

What do you do before going to sleep? Do you carry any negativity, fear, or worry into your dreams? Let us remember that we can have deep, restful sleep and a pleasant dream-time, awakening refreshed and rejuvenated, if we rid our minds, bodies, and souls of anything troubling before retiring. We can do this by reading the inspirational literature of our choice to accumulate good thoughts. We can use breathing to inhale positive attributes, exhaling the negative. If we find pain or discomfort in the body, we can use deep breathing to exhale that as well.

Let us remember that, as we sleep, God breathes us. We are safe in the night with Divine comfort to restore us.

When we state our intentions before falling asleep, we ask that our rest be healing for the body, mind, and soul. We set a biological time to awaken and ask that our dreams be pleasant and rich with healing messages.

May we "sleep with the Angels tonight," as the old Spanish expression goes, and give ourselves the quiet rest we deserve.

When we sleep, God cuddles our soul. We rest deeply; arising healed, refreshed, and rejuvenated.

*Stay vigilant. Exercise all of your muscles just in case
you may someday need them.*

USING MUSCLES

June 14

May we exercise our physical body, our emotional healing
tools, our mental abilities, and our spiritual peace of mind for our
total well-being.

When we use different muscles in the body, like in working
out at the gym, we may *feel* them the next day. Usually this is a
good soreness, as we know that we have done something
productive and for our benefit. When we use other muscles to
exercise good habits for our mental, emotional, and spiritual
good, we may find that something *feels* different about our
healthier lifestyle.

Using different muscles may seem a little awkward at first,
yet we can be assured that our continued use of these new
muscles for our Highest Good can become good habits for the
benefit of ourselves and others. After continued use, and without
overexertion, our muscles are not sore anymore. They simply
work for our betterment. And remember: the healthier we are, the
more we exude a light and healthy Peace to others.

May we exercise all of our muscles to strengthen us against
any hardship.

*Meditation strengthens the Spiritual muscle. Physical
exercise—the body's muscles. Positive thoughts—the mental
muscle. Nurturing ourselves—the emotional muscles. Put these
together and we have life's miracles.*

One can touch another with a loving thought.

TOUCH

June 15

May we understand our need for being touched, not only by the Light of our Creator, but also by the warm hand of a human being.

We know that babies need to be held and be given the appropriate and sufficient nutrients to sustain their life in infancy. As we grow and mature, developing personalities, we still need a human touch to keep a healthy physical balance and to know that we are loved. Some of us may live alone or have a significant other or be married with a family. We still need that tender touch by someone close, someone with whom we can not only give back, but also accept that nurturing in return. We may have had unhappy childhoods or have been through traumatic divorces, leaving our levels of trust diminished. When we can trust in ourselves to *feel* again, we learn new and healthy meanings of intimacy. The Divine Spark of Love touches us all.

Let us not solely contain that spark for ourselves, but share it with others. If you are alone, you can schedule a professional massage or some other type of healing bodywork; being touched appropriately and receiving the healthy benefits of touching.

May we know the importance of being touched.

When we are touched with a loving thought, we can feel Divine Energy running through us.

Commitment is exercising integrity.

COMMITMENTS

June 16

May we be true to others and ourselves in keeping our commitments.

What are the priorities in life to which you are committed? Do your values reflect your commitments? To *whatever* it is in life that we are committed, let us periodically stop and ask ourselves if we are doing our best to keep those commitments. Where there is a true desire to have someone or something in our lives—a cause, a career, or a friend, let us dedicate ourselves to those values or people where the outcome of our efforts are in the hands of the Divine. If we have chosen a solitary spiritual life, then let us devote ourselves to God and to helping others in prayer. Half performed tasks or vaguely spoken words do not usually achieve our desired results.

Let us commit ourselves with enthusiasm, which is inspiration from the Divine. It is a good feeling to see ourselves through to the end in any undertaking. This thoroughness also builds character and strength in times when we may need both of these qualities the most.

May we be thorough and persevere until we see our task through, keeping the commitments that we have made.

Always persevere. Never give up. The result will be the overflowing love of the Angels.

Joy cannot be hidden.

SHARE YOUR JOY

June 17

May we share the joy that we have found through the Light of the Divine within.

Have you ever had a favorite song that you wanted to share with someone else? Or a book or a new idea? A personal success? Sharing joy is natural, fun, and healing. This sharing is common among all people. To experience positive energies together enhances the positive even more, as well as the White Light of the Divine. Let us inspire as we share our Light.

Let us be sincerely joyous for others' successes. Through meditation let us wish goodwill for others. The Divine Light cannot help but shine from and through us onto others. Most often, spiritually, words are not even needed to communicate with others who are sensitive enough to *feel* our Peace projecting forth.

May we be inspired by meditating on the Divine and share our lasting Peace and Light with all whom we come in contact.

I found two seashells and gave you one. How symbolic of the Creator's endless Love for all! To live fully is to give fully.

Identify the problem. Heal the cause.

IDENTIFYING THE PROBLEM

June 18

May we use our thinking skills to separate issues in our life, identify the problems, and ask our Creator for assistance in our healing process.

Sometimes our thinking may become imbalanced. When some aspect of our life is out of balance, we may become totally consumed with that negative aspect and allow it to grow, making room for further negativity. Then we may become depressed about our entire lives. We blame God, others, or ourselves and allow a *benign* problem to become a *malignant* one, simply by our distorted thinking. In metaphysical science, we learn to change our thinking, understanding the immense power of thought. We can more easily recognize a problem and nip it in the bud before it blooms. This is done by giving ourselves positive affirmations, keeping our perspective, and meditating deeply to maintain Peace of mind through the Loving Light of our Creator. Our answers are within; waiting for the appropriate questions to be asked to the Divine Spirit that exists in all persons. The metaphysical student realizes that a *negative* can be changed into a *positive* by a God-centered mind state.

Let us avoid fanning the fire of any problem with more negative thinking.

May we look within for positive and creative solutions, with the intuition generously given by the Primary Divine Intelligence.

All problems have solutions. Look within for your answers.

Who cares if it rhymes? Expression is perfect in God's eyes.

POETRY

June 19

May we realize that, with the inspiration of the Divine, there is a poet in all of us.

When we reached out to the Higher Etherics,
our purpose on Earth began to unfold.
Our suffering has not been unlike that of others,
much of it has remained untold.

Yet through the darkest journeys,
there has always been a Light
Sometimes dim, yet bright enough to lead us to greener
valleys
where we have continued to be refreshed by cool waters
Our burdens are laid to rest.

It is a place where all darkness takes flight,
and our souls know beyond a shadow of a doubt
that each of us has a purpose to be revealed
by the loving Creator within us.

In our persistent search for that Creator,
the light brightens,
emotions lighten,
and the Spirit is healed.

May the poet in each of our souls live on and continue to be compassionate to all, understanding humanity's dilemma and striving to be of service to those in need.

Always have a project.

PURSUE YOUR INTERESTS

June 20

May we make the time to pursue our interests.

If our days stream along with work, over-responsibility, and stress, we know that there may be something wrong with that picture. One way to reduce stress is to pursue our interests. If we feel that we do not have time for doing what we most enjoy, we may have some trouble living life to its fullest. In fact, we are not living at all, we are merely surviving. Life does not always have to be a grind, or a struggle, or filled with pain. Perhaps we can find jobs that incorporate our interests or take an overdue vacation. Just something as simple as visiting a good bookstore to find books on subjects in which we are interested can help. The same goes for our favorite kinds of music. Does watching depressing news and violent shows on television help people to develop their interests?

Let us take time to pursue joyfully our God-given interests, providing they are healthy, wholesome, and in the spirit of goodness.

May we do what we love and love what we do.

A spiritual path can be pursued with joy and humor. For a job everlasting, let the Creator be the Grand Employer.

To understand the cycles of seasons is to understand ourselves.

SUMMER

June 21

May we enjoy the summer months.

In the Northern Hemisphere, June 21 is the first day of summer and is also the longest day of the year. Beginning with this day, the amount of Light will be diminishing slowly until December 21, the first day of winter and the shortest day of the year. Let us celebrate the longest day of the year by giving thanks for the Light, which can be symbolic of our Creator. Long ago, some civilizations worshipped the sun as a god. The sun grew their food, provided warmth, and gave their bodies the necessary amount of light to carry them through the upcoming darkest seasons. Today, we know that the sun gives us vitamin D, an essential nutrient in keeping our bodies healthy.

If summer is *our season*, we are usually more active. There are people who suffer from Seasonal Affective Disorder; moods are affected by the amount of Light they receive. They usually function better in the warmer months, where there is more sunlight and when their moods are more cheery. If summer is not *our season*, at least we can thank God for air conditioning, refrigerators, and freezers for ice!

May we celebrate summer and roll with the flow of all of the seasons.

Seasons change. All is necessary for Earth's balance. All is necessary for balance of all of God's creations.

Study yourself thoroughly and know freedom.

BE YOURSELF

June 22

May we always be ourselves.

Although there are adjustments to be made in dealing with different people, we can always simply be who our Creator made us to be when we are around any person or when by ourselves. It is healthy to have wholesome heroes and heroines in our lives and to fantasize about accomplishing different feats. Our heroes and heroines may change over the course of our lifetimes, depending on where we stand on different issues, as well as our taste in music, and our values. Yet we must get to know ourselves well enough to realize our limitations as well as our strengths. If we are in a 12-step recovery program, we understand abstinence, limitations, growth, and the importance of a Higher Power. We can strive to be the best we can be with our given limitations, while we rely more on our strengths.

Let us, in our self-discovery, always be who our Creator intended us to be—loving, creative, peaceful, dealing with others in the Spirit of the Highest Good for all concerned.

May we be all of who we are to the best of our ability.

We are all traveling on the road that leads back to the Purest Peace of the Divine. Learning the necessary lessons with every unique personality, the Creator teaches us with the breadth of Spirit.

Our darkest hour passes in time, and the dawn awaits us there.

DARKEST HOUR

June 23

May we be filled with Light and be uplifted in our darkest hour.

There are those times when we may have to go through almost unbearable suffering. I believe that we all have known these moments. Although we may not see it at the time, we are going through a transformation of some sort. We are letting go of something and perhaps experiencing grief, excruciating turmoil, or physical illness. It is in our deepest, darkest hour that the Angels are the nearest and the Light of the Divine is the closest. When we call out in our darkness, "God, help me," our Creator hears us. This is when the miracle happens.

Let us ask the Creator for the strength to go on with our lives, knowing that the dark times will pass eventually.

May we reach out to the Light in our darkest hour to our Creator and feel the nearness of our protective Guardian Angel.

We are led by the Light within our soul. This Spark of the Divine is like a bell tolling, which sheds the old and makes room for the new. Soon will come the courage to move forward.

Trust in the Will of Heaven.

INDIRECT PRAYER

June 24

May we learn the Highest Meaning of our Prayers.

Although there is actually no right or wrong way to pray, when we pray for, "the Highest Good for all concerned," one could say that this beautiful prayer shows much concern and love for the afflicted. There are two kinds of prayer—direct and indirect. Direct prayer is where we have a specific purpose, like "God, please, heal this person's cancer." Indirect prayer is a more global and spacious prayer, allowing God to be God. Whatever is intended is asked in a way that is in the Highest Good for all Concerned. There is much grace involved in letting God do what God does best. The saying, "Thy will, not mine, be done," assists us in relieving the burden of how God does, or does not answer our prayers. There may be many unseen reasons for what happens in our world. People are not actually responsible for *any* outcomes, speaking in spiritual terms. We know the power of all well-intended prayers, yet we can see a larger picture of the world by the resistance of trying to tell the Universe what to do. Nature is doing its job, perfectly.

Let us let our prayers be in accordance to the Will of God, for what will be most harmonious for the entire Universe, and the Highest Good for all concerned.

May we see the benefit of indirect prayer.

When we let God be God, we transform the output of Loving Energy to include the entirety of Heaven and Earth.

*Far too much energy is spent in our resistance of what
needs to be done.*

RESISTANCE

June 25

May we reduce our energy of resistance.

One definition of resistance is to strive against something, or to exert oneself to counteract, defeat, or frustrate. When we resist a disease or physical ailment, this definition works for our benefit. Yet, psychologically speaking, to resist an idea for our learning benefit does what the definition constitutes—it frustrates us. The mind is meant to be peaceful, yet we complicate situations at times, creating confusion. Usually, the confusion lies in our resisting peace, goodness, or any other constructive means to live a happier, healthier life. The opposite of resistance would be to surrender ourselves to that which we are resisting. This does not mean to give in and accept an idea or action that contradicts our moral or value judgment. Instead, it means to be open to new, creative ways of looking at ideas, situations, or our own thoughts, and to use wise discernment. Usually, what we resist, we give a lot of energy to. Why not spend energy for constructive and positive uses? We know that what we fear attracts more of the same.

When we free our minds of the paralyzing fear, and allow constructive and loving thoughts to expand our awareness, we are receptive to more workable solutions to our various problems and stresses.

May we surrender to and simply accept situations, people, and ideas and not strive so hard to repel them. The world is as it is.

Let us not resist the Love of our benevolent Creator, but rather bask in the sunlight of Divine Spirit.

Our daily strength comes from spiritual maintenance.

GOD'S INSURANCE POLICY

June 26

May we keep spiritually fit to insure a good, healthy, well-balanced life.

To insure is to make certain, or to guarantee one's well-being against loss. We have all experienced loss in our lives and have felt the repercussions as sadness, grief, depression, and emptiness. Let us take out a policy against losses and trauma by *paying* faithfully our spiritual premiums. These are our fortifications of prayer, meditation, healing work, and being of wholesome service to others. By our efforts in persevering against life's bumps and bruises, we actually are getting paid back 100-fold from our conscious contract with the Creator. What a deal! Everyone benefits and, globally speaking, people who pay their spiritual premiums become healthier, wealthier, in a sense, and wiser by the karmic action upon the entire Universe.

We know that if one person is healing, this positively affects the rest of the world to be a more wholesome planet of a Higher Consciousness. How about subscribing to God's Multi-Level Insurance Policy!

May we remember to pay our premium on the Creator's *Can't Miss* Insurance Deal.

All is simply well in the world. We trust that the Creator is healing all people and situations. We are pioneers in the purest sense, protecting our families, all nations, and ourselves when we buy God's Insurance Policies.

There are as many ways to interpret the Creator,
as there are humans in the world.

UNIVERSAL PARENTS

June 27

May we realize that we have a Spiritual Mother and Father from whom we are in direct lineage.

Think of the beautiful concept of each being on Earth as having God and the Divine Mother as parents. It is true that this way of thinking supplies us with masculine and feminine aspects of ourselves and the Divine in Holy Balance. God needs a feminine counterpart for this Holy Balance to take place in Heaven as well as on Earth. The Creator can be anything we can conceive, as long as we believe that this Creator or Higher Power is more intelligent, powerful, loving, forgiving, and Holy than our human egos. The Native American culture gives thanks to Mother Earth and Father Sky, appreciating the sacredness of nature. The expanded consciousness beyond human beings may well be helpful in our remembrance of our True Family—our Holy Ancestry. Our thinking shifts in the Light of the Divine presence, where fresh perspectives can be healing and comforting.

My spiritual teacher tells us that we are simply, "Tadpoles of Light, swimming in the Sea of Love." In other words, we are all little *godlings* of our universal parents. Let us consult the Holy Council of our Divine Parents when needed and give thanks for their Presence in our lives.

May we show love, joy, and gratitude to God and the Divine Mother and celebrate in the Holy Union.

Our worldly parents are less than perfect. Let us entertain the thought that we have Holy Parents who shed unconditional Love, Wisdom, and Protection.

What one sees in life is but an interpretation
of one's inner attitude.

OPTIMISM

June 28

May we be optimistic as well as realistic.

To be optimistic means to think and hope for the best in a person or a situation. This does not mean being a Pollyanna, whereby the entire spectrum of a given situation is not viewed. It means being realistic about life, seeing the pain as well as the pleasure, the dark as well as the Light, while still maintaining a positive attitude. As grim as things may look on the surface, let us go to another deeper level and see that the Creator has everything running smoothly according to the Divine Plan.

Let us trust the perfection of the learning process that the Universe is trying to teach us and be grateful for the gift of the Divine Teacher. Seeing life in this manner restores our optimism, our innate knowing that all things must pass, the hard times as well as the good times. Yet balance is maintained in the recognition that this is the way life is. It is not always what we *want* it to be, but the way it *needs* to be to keep the Divine Status Quo. All things work together for the Universal Good.

May we persevere in our optimistic attitude toward ourselves, others, and life.

It was the intuitive Light of our Angel intervening. Just when it seemed like our life was falling apart, the Creator allowed us to see the deeper meaning. In our meditation, a larger picture was revealed and we suddenly felt more connected and fully healed.

Do not take a sunny day for granted.

LIGHT: THE PINEAL BODY

June 29

May we utilize natural sunlight to stimulate the sensitive and resourceful pineal body, which our Creator gave us to regulate many different functions in our bodies.

Modern science did not recognize the special pineal body, once called a gland, in our brains as being useful to us until rather recently. The gland is centered about one inch behind the eyes. It is spoken of spiritually as, "the third eye." It was thought to be activated in animals only during the mating season. Now, the body is known to receive incoming light, regulating our sleep/wake cycle and hormones. The combination of natural and spiritual Light is important to the body's natural opiate activators—beta-endorphins. When the pineal body is functioning properly, one usually feels healthy and balanced, and filled with Spiritual Light, even if less natural light is provided. Science and technology have made it possible to recreate natural light. Full spectrum light bulbs are available in stores. When used indoors, these special bulbs simulate natural sunlight. These bulbs also provide assistance for those who suffer from Seasonal Affective Disorder, which can cause depression for some people in winter months when less natural light is available.

One way to have access to the Light is to meditate by visualizing the pineal body being activated by the Divine's Healing Light, streaming down into the top of the head. Feel the warmth of imagined sunlight draping over the entire body and entering into all cells of the body. Let us then give thanks to the Creator for the relaxing warmth of the inner Spiritual Light, and the imagined external sunlight, when our precious daylight sun is less available.

May we learn to appreciate both spiritual and natural Light, while concentrating on the activity created by the pineal body.

Our bodies are truly magnificent in their abilities to utilize Nature's most simple resources.

Fan the inner spark of the Divine, and heal in body, mind, and soul.

Celebrate your life every single day.

GOODWILL

June 30

May we have goodwill toward ourselves, others, and the entire planet.

We may think of goodwill in our Western culture only during a holiday like Christmas or Easter. At these times we may attend a church, a meditation retreat, or have meetings or meals with friends or family. These times of demonstrating goodwill toward others are always beneficial. What would our world feel like if we began to incorporate this feeling of wishing others the very best in our every breath, action, word, and thought. By creating Peace and Love first in ourselves, we can fortify our well-being with good, Divine Energy. Then prayer can then be sent to the rest of the world. May we make this a daily practice in our loving, kind meditations. We also wish goodwill toward those we may resent or have adverse feelings towards. By doing this, we are forgiving others and ourselves by praying for our wrongdoers to have Peace and Harmony in their lives as well.

After cherishing such good thoughts, notice how you feel. Your thoughts have already accelerated the positive in your life, attracting more of the same. Imagine if every being practiced this method every day! We may now begin to see how world peace begins in the heart of each individual.

May we always be in the spirit of goodwill toward all.

What we give boomerangs back to us. As we open our hearts, we receive bounteous gifts.

Be diligent about something pure and wholesome.

DILIGENCE

July 1

May we be diligent in our spiritual quest, as well as in our everyday encounters.

To be diligent is to be perseveringly attentive and painstaking about something. As we diligently search for spiritual truths that speak to us, we become devoted to such quests or paths, following our hearts with diligence. One may simply be devoted to the Creator, accepting all paths, knowing viscerally that they all lead to the same Divine Source.

Let us allow the diligence that we place in worldly affairs to be equal to the attentiveness of our spiritual concerns, therein creating a balance spiritually, emotionally, mentally, and physically.

May we be assiduous and balanced in our pursuits to achieve health in all areas of our life.

Diligently we search. Eventually we find. As we discover our new self, we release the old.

What power there is in a mere thought form!

SPIRITUAL HEALING TREATMENT

July 2

May we believe in the Power of the Creator and the power of the Creator within ourselves to totally heal any physical, emotional, mental, or spiritual ailment.

With the Power and Spirit of the Creator in mind, we can assist in healing ourselves and others. This is called Metaphysical Treatment, whereby we enter into a state of meditation and program the subconscious with healing affirmations, without any trace of doubt. We declare a healing by the Power of the Creator within us and give thanks for the healing. All doubts are removed in the mind. This can also be done by self-hypnosis and creative visualization, whereby we relax the mind and body, allowing the Presence of God to enter our awareness.

Let us literally visualize the ailment leaving our bodies on a cellular level, filling our cells with Unconditional Love and Divine Healing Light. Of course, in the event of a disease and other major afflictions, we seek medical help, as well as utilizing the healing affirmations. Metaphysical treatment complements medical remedies. The two are not thought of as opposites, but compatible.

May we use meditation to heal.

The healing power within is the spirit of God present in our body, soul, and mind. As we acknowledge this Power and its Divine Source, we are assisted in our quest to heal.

*Our peace of mind is in direct proportion to our
level of acceptance.*

PEACE IN ALL SITUATIONS

July 3

May we make our goal Peace in all situations, regardless of the situation.

The book, *A Course in Miracles,* speaks much of Peace when we are in conflict, as opposed to trying to find detailed solutions to our problems. Humans can sometimes *work* a problem too much, creating more worry and confusion. We humans, with our egos leading the way, can make for a complicated set of wants and desires, blocking out the Spiritual Light that shines within our souls. Let us take the time for Peace, whether it is in pausing before we speak or reacting in ways that we will later regret. Meditation is a simple and beautiful way to rekindle the Divine Spark within, allowing us to know the Eternal Peace of the Creator in our hearts and minds. We then can ask ourselves, "Does this little conflict really have any meaning in the entire scheme of the soul's journey to the Light?" With an expanded awareness, our problems may be somewhat reduced in the light of what is really important in this life.

Let us not get bogged down in details of conflict, but rather see the big picture, which is Peace for all concerned, Peace for the welfare of ourselves and others and Peace as the Highest Good in all situations.

The teachings of the Dalai Lama may be a wonderful guide for us in our resolution of problems.

Peace is the way to resolve conflict. Violence in speech, action, or thought can only restrict us.

Most people benefit much more from empathy
rather than sympathy.

EMPATHY

July 4

May we always be empathetic with others.

Empathy means an imaginative projection of one's own consciousness into another being. When we truly listen to another's feelings, usually we can find a similar experience to our own, to better understand what exactly the other is going through. If we have not had the same experience as the other, we project our imaginations. Sometimes, our minds can put us in the other's place in order to feel closer to that which is being related. The Great Philosopher Plato said, "Be kind, for everyone you meet is fighting a hard battle." Surely, this is a wise statement of empathetic concern backed by Spiritual principal.

When we realize that all souls are journeying toward the Light, we will find that even death is a coming home—to a place common to each and every one of us. Some people are fortunate to have their *Heaven* on Earth, being in the world, yet not be of the world. All people vibrate at different energy frequencies, at different times and are on their own evolutionary paths to another place. Let us be patient and tolerant of others, realizing their internal struggle as well as the joy they feel at different times.

May we rest deeply within the protective wings of Angels who are the most loving empathics.

It is such a comfort to have a loving friend, Angels and/or Creator(s) as our consolation.

Be passionate about life even in your stillness.

BEING STILL

July 5

May we learn the art of being still, listening to our inner soul, our mind, and body.

Do you sometimes find the need to be busy and moving at all times to create a sense of productivity and self-worth? There are times when it is beneficial to slow down a little in order to really listen to the voice of your own soul. Some people have a lot of natural energy, while others have a more sedentary nature. There is a happy medium between the two. Although it is good to exercise the body, to be responsible for our health, and to relax when we feel the need, being still is not the same as laziness, unless we enter into procrastination. Being still is to be fully present in the moment, attentive to the body, mind, and soul. The best way to be still is in quiet meditation, where we let the Love and Light of the Creator enter into our hearts and minds.

How we choose to meditate is up to us, yet it is important that we relax and take the time for it. There is no one way to meditate; yet all includes the quietness of mind that is necessary for rejuvenation. Simply sitting still and noticing our inhale and exhale of breath for five minutes a day can be extremely beneficial for our minds' rejuvenation. Afterwards, let us give thanks to spirit for the precious breath of life.

May we refine the art of meditation each day, stilling our mind and body, and experience the immense joy of our Creator's Love for us.

We paused and looked inward. We saw the spark of our own soul being fanned into the Love and Light that was intended for us all to have.

Be discreet, yet spontaneous in your actions.

USEFUL ACTION

July 6

May we take action wherever necessary in life, provided it is in the best interest of all concerned.

Have you ever wished that you had taken some sort of action in a given circumstance, after the fact? Although it is true that pausing to think before we act is best, there are certain situations that call for immediate action. This could be called re-action, for example, in a life-threatening emergency. However, it could save our life or someone else's. Taking action on constructive ideas is equally important and adds a positive effect to goal-oriented plans. Taking action of this sort is taking responsibility. We indeed have an active, responsible part to play in filling in the missing pieces of our planet. We may not think that our small actions count, yet the Creator allows this Earth to work in harmony.

Let our actions have an impact in their own way, contributing to the world in a positive way.

May our actions count for the goodness and harmony for all concerned.

We fed a bird some seed and experienced harmony. Wherever there is a need, may we choose to remedy it gracefully.

God can readily enter a soft heart.

SOFT HEART

July 7

May we maintain a soft and gentle heart.

There are those times when we close our hearts to certain people, places, or things. How does this make us feel? A hard-hearted person can neither let Love in nor give it away. Having a soft heart is knowing how to be empathetic to all living creatures—letting Love flow through the heart naturally from one to another. One can be softhearted to animals, children, and those in need. Some people may feel the need to disguise their soft heart for defense purposes, yet, it still shines through in one form or another. How one *seems* to relate to the world on the outside is not necessarily how they really feel on the inside.

Let us note that being softhearted does not mean we let others take advantage of us or abuse us in any way. It means we develop sensitivity to all creation while maintaining our values, sense of morality, and spiritual principals.

May we develop a soft and sensitive heart, attending to our needs, and then giving sincerely to others.

One can develop tremendous strength in being softhearted. The lessons therein are the most valuable.

*When you are victimized, simply remember the times when
you may have been a perpetrator.*

DE-VICTIMIZATION

July 8

May we surrender up our role as victim in this life, take
responsibility, and move forward with our life purpose.

So many of us choose to look at ourselves as victims in life.
Perhaps we were victimized to different degrees as children, and
even on into our teenage and adult years. Another way to view
this tragic situation is to take responsibility, on a soul level, for
choosing our lessons with spiritual counsel in this lifetime even
before we were born. We chose these lessons to learn how to
overcome them, to remove hate, guilt, and self-pity, etc., from our
lives in order for our souls to live out our chosen scenario and
move beyond obstacles. We journey ahead on the road of
recovery and live our life's purpose.

We do not have to play the victim anymore, which breeds
self-pity and other negative, toxic emotions. We can overcome
these obstacles in our lives and move on in a positive light. When
we can look at all situations from a soul level, we can truly begin
to live the lives we were born to live.

May we always look at life from a soul level.

*Our insight deepens as our lessons persist. The struggle
comes from our own reactions and resistance. Yet, hidden in the
mist is the Light of Hope, wherein lies our refuge.*

Tone of voice can make or break communication.

COMMUNICATION

July 9

May we communicate clearly to convey and express ourselves according to our own needs and to help with the needs of others.

Communication is how we relate to ourselves and others. This can be done in many ways, both verbal and non-verbal, as in our body language or when we are alone or with others. What messages are we giving ourselves and others by the sound of our voice or by the way we hold our body? Are we able to look at people in the eye when we speak to them? Are we telling the truth? It may be advantageous in situations to become aware of how we are communicating. It is important, as well, to notice what we tell ourselves at times. Do we love and support ourselves as we would our friends in the same situation?

One way to communicate clearly, keeping in mind the Highest Good for all Concerned, is to first communicate with the Creator. Before we speak, we pause briefly and say silently to ourselves, "My Creator, please speak through me." In this way, we are confident that it is the Creator who is guiding our speech. Notice the tone of our voice. If there is miscommunication, then we are not critical of ourselves. We simply ask for guidance again.

Let us affirm that we are communicating clearly and with intuition. In this way, communication becomes easier the next time.

May we be direct and loving in all of our sharing on this planet.

The words we speak can have great impact upon others. Therefore let us be kind to our brothers and sisters on this planet.

*Amidst immense suffering, there is equally much beauty
in this world.*

NATURE AND GOD

July 10

May we surround ourselves with nature and feel the closeness of God.

Sometimes, when we have the opportunity to immerse ourselves in nature, we usually, automatically and naturally, feel closer to our Creator. Is it any wonder? In nature, miracles are everywhere among the flora and fauna. We, as humans, also feel a sense of belonging there with the trees, plants, flowers, and all the creatures. We feel the warm sun or the pull of the moon. We breathe fresh air—the vast amounts of oxygen given by the flora in our relationship of exhaling carbon dioxide for the trees and vegetation to use. Perhaps there are edible plants or herbs that can be utilized medicinally and in cooking. Maybe we simply choose to sit quietly and absorb the natural life that surrounds us.

If it has been a while since you have been in nature, treat yourself to a little trip in the country or to the beach or mountains and feel your vital relationship therein. We are all one harmonious Universe, radiating the oneness with the Creator's Love for all living things. We are growing and blossoming according to the Will of God, just like the little wildflower that we see out there.

May we feel at one with the miracles that occur all around us in this beautiful world.

We feel the freedom of the weaned fawn. What a glorious picture of nature God has made!

Those who have an inner knowing about God usually walk with more confidence.

RELIANCE UPON A HIGHER POWER

July 11

May we rely upon our Higher Power in all ways, each and every day.

There are those days when we need a little extra support, encouragement, acknowledgment, and recognition. All persons need this to a degree, some more than others. Yet, what if one is alienated and isolated? A sense of Self must come from inner strength and courage. We rely totally on the Higher Self that is in harmony with the Higher Power, the Creator, however we may name this supreme Power. In meditation, we can intuit and distinguish the ego from the spiritual self. Higher Wisdom holds all of life's answers and solutions to everyday problems.

Let us work with what we are given. If we do not like what we see, we quietly go within and ask the Higher Power to change our perspectives. Total dependence upon a Higher Power paradoxically creates more independence in daily life. When we realize that no one knows us better than ourselves, and that we have all the answers inside of us, we then understand the importance of a conscious contact with a Higher Power or our wise inner selves. These are gifts from the Creator. Let us use them to the best of our ability.

May we feel the joys that life has to offer, even in the midst of our pain.

There is a Power greater than us waiting to be a part of our life. We can make contact with this Creator and experience joy and peacefulness that are our actual birthright.

It is a virtue to meet obstructions with Grace.

OBSTRUCTION

July 12

May we accomplish all that we need to do today with confidence and ease.

Emerging out of difficult times can be enlightening, providing we choose healthy means for dealing with obstructions. Sometimes obstacles blur our way, and we may feel that it is impossible to make any kind of headway. Without times of darkness, how could we ever know that which is True Light? Let us rely on the Creator during these times, keeping in mind that they do indeed pass. Life is never free of problems. Even when we know our life's purpose, many obstacles present themselves in order for us to persevere through them. Should we begin to doubt our path in life, that is the time to ask our Angels or the Creator for the strength to move forward. Our confidence comes from the spirit within, illuminated by the Will of Heaven.

Let us speak with the clarity of truth and act calmly, even in the face of obstruction, always keeping in mind and in heart the closeness of Spirit.

May we know, even in the heat of obstruction, that Grace is ours. It is there by asking for it from a Higher Power.

Partaking of our share of Spirit, we drink from the natural springs of life and weave all into Health, Truth, and Purity.

Now surely, today has produced something to be grateful for.
We are alive, aren't we?

SEARCH FOR THE JOY

July 13

May we find the joy in our life today, however persistent we must be.

Some days are better than others. At the end of the day, on those off days, it may be wise to take an objective inventory of the entire day. If we are truly honest, we can find at least one thing that we are grateful for and adjust our attitude accordingly. Let us take the time to change a negative outlook, asking for the assistance of the Creator. We usually notice that the change happens within ourselves, rather than other people, places, and situations, which we do not have control over. We may be taking a lot of goodness for granted! Not all is doom and gloom, even though we may feel that way.

Let us simply let our mouth curve into a smile to give a stranger whose life may be far less fortunate than ours. One may never know that they may have restored another's faith in humanity with a simple gesture of kindness.

May we be the sunrays in someone else's rainy day, even in the face of our own aridity.

All is never totally lost, no matter what feeling dominates.
For we are a product of our experiences, weaving our sunshine
and our thunderstorms into magnificent rainbows of promise.

Just as we wish to be forgiven, let us forgive others
as well as ourselves.

TRUSTING IN GOODNESS

July 14

May we trust the inner goodness in ourselves and in all others today.

If we are weary and somewhat agitated with ourselves and others, it may be to our benefit to abstain from the impulse to internalize any bitterness or to spew irritation onto anyone in thought, word, or deed. Perhaps we need to air out our worldly concerns with someone we trust such as a therapist, a friend, our Creator, or by writing down our thoughts. By talking or writing it out, we can relieve some of the pressure and find the necessary solutions. Even on days when it seems impossible to maintain our composure or our sense of gratitude, the Creator continues to keep this Universe in balance.

Let us, before we go to sleep tonight, be thankful that all is virtually well in this Universe. We are not in control of what happens or the purpose of it, which sometimes is not revealed to us. We can control our reactions to any given person or situation. It may be helpful to simply surrender to our Higher Power the events of a pressing day. This letting go of problems can bring such a sense of peace to us, if we allow it to.

May we look for the innocent Love within our hearts and give ourselves the gift of compassion and, in turn, exude this compassion to all others.

A beautiful, fragrant rose has harsh thorns, yet its aroma takes us back to Eden. It reminds us to simply breathe in the sweetness of Divine innocence.

One way to view the big picture is to fill ourselves with Love and Light and then spread that Love and Light to others.

SHADOWS

July 15

May we have courage and strength to face our deep-seated fears today.

We all have the shadow side of ourselves. This side may be revealed to us in our dreams or many other ways. In actuality, it is an aspect of ourselves that is calling out for love, healing, and compassion. The shadow side could also be residue of a past life experience, which needs to come out into the light in this lifetime in order for us to learn lessons therein. It may be more helpful to not deny the shadow-side, yet learn to integrate it into a balanced whole of who we are. When we take the courage to look at the shadows, we have already begun to heal any fear. No one is all good or all bad. We all have goodness as well as darker sides within. How wonderful it would be if each person could accept all aspects of themselves and others. We most likely would see that we are all human creatures; we are more alike than we formerly believed we were.

Let us incorporate Unconditional Love and Healing Light into our heart and have the courage to embrace each and every aspect of ourselves. If we notice certain aspects that are harmful to others and ourselves, it may be helpful to pray for the strength to change them.

May we see our truths, take honesty as our shield, and be uplifted.

As we grow and evolve, we shed old belief systems that block our true Spirit.

Is it any wonder that gratitude and humility go hand in hand?

GRATITUDE

July 16

May we consciously give thanks to our Creator, who has blessed us with the gift of life.

Gratitude is humility in action. How often do we take the beauty of people and this planet for granted? When we realize that we are interrelated to flora, fauna, earth, sky, and basically every single molecule around us, we are truly free. As we honor the Creator and the God-part of all beings, creatures, and everything else in the Universe, we begin to honor and respect ourselves.

Let us give our thanks for the breath of life and for the wisdom and power that each soul has within themselves to heal and to create a healing world. We go to our Higher Power in meditation, to quietly touch that primary Source, and to give thanks for all opportunities and challenges in our lives, however painful and difficult they may be. Some schools of thought suggest that all things happen in God's world for a reason. The power of Spirit allows us to live our lives with open hearts of grace and wisdom. This world of ours may not be a perfect world, yet if we have the willingness to appreciate the good and beauty that really does exist in all beings and in nature, it makes our lives easier.

May we forever maintain a sense of gratitude.

In the stillness of meditation, we find refuge in our God, who completely understands us. The gifts we have received from our true Source are to be celebrated in gratitude and humility.

I am...! I can...! Yes!

POSITIVE ATTITUDE

July 17

May our attitude be healthy and positive today.

We can train our mind to be more positive by having joyful expectations instead of being filled with negative thoughts. Every day, may we have something to look forward to, even the smallest task, or perhaps a self-care-taking pleasure, like a warm bath or eating healthy foods. When we treat ourselves with respect, health, and positive thoughts, this world is a gracious place in which to live.

It takes a lot less energy to create a positive attitude than a negative one. One can almost feel the weight of a negative attitude. Do you wonder why some people drain you completely? A positive attitude creates a more positive atmosphere in which to express oneself freely and spontaneously, a true gift from God.

May we always choose the positive, as best we can.

The cobwebs and dark caverns where we used to dwell do not hold us anymore, for we have swept clear the debris of old patterns and now joyfully wait to see what life has in store for us.

Creativity is to be open for inspiration.

OPEN CHANNELS

July 18

May we learn to open ourselves to new possibilities that bring fulfillment into our lives today.

We can open our hearts and minds to all of the Creator's goodness as it freely flows to us. When the intuition is aligned with our Highest Self and Highest Intention, the process is a simple step—merely asking for Spiritual guidance. When calling on Divine Inspiration, notice what happens either immediately or over the course of the day. The creative thought process evolves; sometimes inspiration may manifest itself into productive projects or ideas express themselves in a dream of revelation.

How easy it is to ask for God's inspiration. Our lives are unfolding exactly in the way and at the pace they are supposed to. With love in our hearts and laughter on our lips, we awaken to our Light within.

May we align ourselves with uplifting people, inspirational thoughts, and new ideas of how to better ourselves and enrich our lives. When we are Spiritually aligned, we can more easily be an inspiration to others.

We are not a stagnant pool, but rather a life-giving river that flows freely and easily. We gently move toward our Highest Source.

Priorities help us to "walk our talk."

PRIORITIES

July 19

May we prioritize our life today, placing all ideas in order according to those that most benefit our well-being and the well-being of others.

Suppose we were in a Twelve-Step program, recovering from alcohol addiction. Our first priority would be to ask the Creator to let us live clean and sober that day. After our first priority is established, it seems to follow that all others will fall into place. By establishing priorities, whatever the day looks like, we have more of a sense of purpose, organization, and direction.

Our days flow more smoothly when we allow our Creator to guide us in all ways. Any stress or sense of being overwhelmed leaves our mind when we obtain that deep, heartfelt sense that all is well, and will be accomplished with ease and calm.

May we learn to prioritize our needs and live accordingly.

We are organized and at peace, with the belief that Spirit is guiding us. For nothing today is more important than our peace of mind, which is our first priority.

Those who live in the present have tired of reliving the past and worrying about the future.

LIVING IN THE PRESENT

July 20

May we shed any old and outdated belief structures from the past that inhibit our joy of living fully in the present.

May we love ourselves as our Creator loves us— unconditionally—and release the need of being right and perfect, for we are perfect in our imperfections, in the eyes of our benevolent Creator. When we can finally come to the point of accepting any past suffering and move to a realm of forgiveness, we are truly free to live in the present. When we do not try to control or project outcomes in the future, we will also find more peace in the present moment.

Let us be the best we can be for this day—respecting ourselves and all other beings, as we breathe in the peace of this present moment.

May we give away to others the unconditional love that we may have found within ourselves, realizing that acceptance is the primary key to happiness and life-giving awareness.

When we expand our awareness of others and ourselves we learn more how to love and cherish all of the different parts that make us human beings. That understanding alone can assist us in every other aspect of life.

Focus is a disciplined skill that takes practice.

FOCUS

July 21

May we train our erratic minds to better focus on what is most important today.

Usually taught as a meditation practice in some of the Buddhist traditions, mindfulness assists one in being fully conscious in each particular moment of life. The hectic pace usually found today in most major countries and cities may seem to curb the practice of this ancient art. The average mind thinks about 60,000 thoughts a day, 95% being those same thoughts we had yesterday and the ones we will have again tomorrow. Let us try to tame our runaway minds to focus a little more on prioritizing our day.

Let us be open to intuitive thought and Divine Inspiration, seeking to have them flow into our tired, predictable thought machines and all of the energy spent on that day's thought, word, or deed. Even a short time spent in meditation can help us to focus better on what it is we need to do.

May we take a little extra time today in mindfulness and meditation, centering ourselves so that we may enjoy the fruits of life.

Let our hearts be uplifted in the joy of knowing that there exists a Power greater than ourselves that we can call upon at any time, to enrich each moment of our day.

To laugh at oneself is to laugh with the world!

LAUGHTER

July 22

May we look for the humor in all situations today.

It has been proven that laughter, literally and physically, massages the heart, thus relaxing it and freeing up hardened areas. True, there is a time to be serious and a time to giggle and a balance between the two is living in harmony with this world. Let us be uplifted and lighthearted in our journey toward balance and wholeness, realizing that there are really more things to laugh about than we most likely consider. Let us look for the humor. One way to find humor is by surrounding ourselves with those people who bring smiles and laughter into our life. Even in the face of fear or low times, today let us find one thing to laugh about. The healing occurs when there is laughter at oneself, for the Angels laugh with us. Angels love a sense of humor and possess one as well.

Let us not take personally what people do or say, as it is not their responsibility to cater to our emotional needs at all times. Plus, they may need the healing of laughter themselves.

May we try to look at ourselves and our situations more objectively and celebrate life with a smile.

The gift of humor comes from the Angels. Laughter can place us all in the realm of Light and Love.

Lying deep within solitude and quiet are the secrets
of the Universe.

PEACE

July 23

May we seek peace in all situations today and find calmness in our souls. Whether alone or involved with others, may we exude this peace to all beings.

Peace begins with compassion, whether we are talking about individual peace of mind or world peace. If an individual exudes peace, it will fall upon all other creatures, situations, and places that our souls come in contact with. Think about this kind of energy emanating from all beings—world peace then becomes more than merely a vision. It becomes a reality, because it is the reality of each and every human being. See how this works?

Let us strive for peace within ourselves and express it outwardly to the world. Peace of mind can be habit-forming. This does not mean we are saints and dress in a white robes. This simply means that we maintain composure and grace on all occasions. We breathe in Peace from our Higher Power. The synergetic energy helps in uniting all creatures, for world peace begins with one person finding inner peace.

When one being heals, the Universe can readily feel the impact.

We can learn to be more peaceful in all areas of our life. We can find peace even in the midst of stressful or unhappy situations.

Loving ourselves is a gift of Grace from a Higher Power
to be eventually expressed to others.

NURTURANCE

July 24

May we nurture ourselves gently today, so that we may in turn nurture others who may be in need.

There are so many ways to nurture others and ourselves. Nurturance is a quality innate to most creatures, humans and animals alike. Most of us probably have ways that we nurture or care for others, yet there are times when we need to nurture and support our own selves. It is much easier to be there for others if we know how to be there for ourselves. Taking time for ourselves is a time to gather our thoughts, re-energize, give ourselves a gift and feel good about it, removing any sense of guilt for doing so. Pamper yourself today.

Let us give away, freely, the gifts we receive from parenting ourselves with wholesome goodness.

May we bloom today and grow into our full potential by loving ourselves enough to respond to our emotional needs.

May we learn to re-parent ourselves according to our own needs and then give this nurturance to others who will, most likely, pass this good quality on to another.

Trust is not naïve—it is reverence for the Divine,
ourselves, and others.

TRUST

July 25

May we place all Trust in our Higher Power today to guide us in our every thought, word, and deed.

Early in life, some of us learned not to trust people or ourselves to help us along the way. If this is the case, let us trust in a Power greater than ourselves to reveal ways to deal with situations and people in life. The Higher Power is just an asking away and is ready to be there for us. We must trust in God before we can trust ourselves, and we must trust ourselves before we can trust others. When it comes to people, we do not blindly trust everyone. We must use beneficial judgment. God places people in our lives that guide us, help us, and love us, whether we are aware of it or not.

When we learn to trust in the goodness of the Universe, we will more readily trust in ourselves, and by using Divine discernment, we can more easily trust others.

May we *know* deep within our souls that we are not alone in this world, and may we utilize our intuition to know whom to trust.

Guidance comes from both within and outside us from our
Source. We rely on our Higher Power, which is always available
to lead us.

To share both laughter and tears with a friend
is an eternal bond.

FRIENDS

July 26

May we celebrate the joy of being with friends today—old friends or new.

In the winds of time, true friends are an important part of our lives. We are social beings and we do need other people; for human beings are not meant to be isolated and alone all of the time. Most people choose to surround themselves with supportive and positive friends. Time does indeed tell our true and loyal friends. Friends can bring joy when we think that there is none left. Usually, we find that we can confide freely with a friend, and will be accepted unconditionally.

We are blessed if we have one good friend, realizing the true gift of God that they are to us.

May we make the effort to surround ourselves with loving, caring friends today or to call someone who is of like mind and heart to establish closer communication.

Like an oasis in the desert, we seek the company of a good friend. For we are always willing to gratefully give the warmth of a handshake or a hug.

Enjoyment is an attitude.

JOY

July 27

May we enjoy our plans today with a deep sense of knowing that our Higher Power is not only in control of things, but also has our best interests at heart.

Have we gotten so far away from simplicity and nature that we fail to find the joy in witnessing a promising rainbow or feeling the morning dew on our bare feet on an early summer morn? The more joy we can find in life, the more joy finds us to appreciate it. There is excitement hidden in life and in all that we do.

Let us discover the joyful purpose in all things today. Our Higher Power takes care of us, and we feel, beyond a shadow of a doubt, that all is well—this is the knowing of deep joy.

May we find the joy in living our life to its fullest today, letting our innocence and spontaneity lead the way.

Our spirits are free, and we enjoy all of Earth's creations with our open hearts.

Pain is a calling for deeper understanding of ourselves

PAIN

July 28

May we learn to grieve our hurt and pain, remembering that grieving is a necessary part of letting go of the pain.

We all feel the pain of life's experiences at times. There is an emotional process to pain that can motivate us to take a different course, or adopt a new attitude or perspective. Eventually we let go of the suffering, yet we need to actually feel the pain and grieve accordingly to finally reach a point of acceptance. We can feel the fear of pain vanish into the Light when we take our Higher Power by the hand. Physical pain can also be a message directly from the body. If we listen to the body, perhaps we can find the source of the pain and begin to heal it there. Emotional pain can also manifest in our bodies, becoming lodged and toxic to our health. It can produce anxiety, depression, and other maladies. Perhaps we seek out therapists to help us work through emotional pain and relieve some of the pressure and confusion. It is our right to heal.

Let us find the source, nurture the hurt and pain, and begin to heal on all levels—physical, emotional, mental, and spiritual. To find the source of pain takes willingness and rigorous honesty and is not always easy to do. Our prayer to do so can be of use here. We may find that our best resource is to take our Creator as a partner.

May we always know that our pain will pass.

We all have known pain to different degrees, and have felt it deep within. In the Spiritual world, our tears do not go unseen, nor do our prayers go unheard.

With rest, the mind and body heal.

REST

July 29

May we take time today to rest our mind and our body.

Rest in any form is healing and refreshing to our minds, bodies, and spirit. In most Western cultures, the emphasis seems always to be on doing and producing something rather than just being present to ourselves or with others. Our eyes like to close and feel rested periodically. This is not to say that we need to sleep our lives away. It simply means that in order for optimum potential to be reached, rest is necessary.

Let us find enough necessary rest in deep meditation or in sleeping at night or with a catnap during the afternoon. If we are too busy to rest well, we may want to look at the source of our unrest, and begin our healing there.

May we feel the healing within our spirit when we rest our mind and body.

We are content to rest and listen to what our mind and body are trying to tell us. We are refreshed and renewed in those precious moments when we relax completely.

When we do not expect anything in life, we just may be
pleasantly surprised at what we are given.

EXPECTATIONS

July 30

May we have fewer expectations of ourselves and others today.

Life is just what it is. If we have too many expectations of people, places, and situations to be only the way we wish them to be, we live in a delusional world, which could eventually lead to a world of despair and extremes. High, unrealistic expectations of our ourselves or others will leave us with many disappointments in life. We cannot expect others to think, talk, or act the way we do or would want them to in any given situation. In contrast, if our expectation of ourselves and others is too low, we may build a world of pessimism, paralyzing ourselves into being even remotely motivated to succeed anywhere, fearing to be happy for those who succeed. The Creator is ultimately in control.

The more we simply accept people and situations as they are, the more serenity we shall have.

May we accept life on life's terms, relinquishing our fears of success or failure.

We balance our expectations and feel more content with ourselves and others.

If one is dissatisfied with any part of their life, that can realistically be changed, they have, with the help of the Creator, the power to transform that area.

TRANSFORMATIONS

July 31

May we find wisdom to learn from our past fear and suffering, and transform our life accordingly.

Humans are on earth to evolve and grow through loving and learning, according to our experiences. Through the learning process, we may need to work through some of our rough spots, in order to cleanse ourselves, and make room for new transformations. If there is an area in our lives that needs tending to, we can begin this transition period with an intention to the Creator that we release our perceived negative aspect and replace it with a positive one. With our willingness, the Creator can work through us on those areas of our lives that may need transforming. Whether it is a lifestyle change or an aspect of ourselves we want to improve upon, willingness involves a type of total surrender and trust in the Creator. Miracles are indeed possible with God's help, as long as we remember that all transformations happen when the soul is ready to grow and, at last, we find peace within ourselves.

Let us let our Higher Self or the intuitive part of ourselves guide us in all ways this day to look beyond what seems to be on the outside.

May we choose to evolve and grow toward the Unconditional Love and Divine Healing Light.

Change within ourselves takes courage. When we ask for God's help, change is possible.

Fear narrows; Love expands.

PERSPECTIVE

August 1

May we have the power to step back and look at ourselves and our life from new perspectives, taking a more objective view of situations.

When we are in fear, our mind narrows, and we lose our view. When we can see the Love, our love and our minds expand. Let us constantly look for ways to expand awareness of ourselves and our present situations. When fear shortens the view, we have fewer options and choices. No one likes to feel as if they have no other viable choices or to feel locked into one way of thinking with no other options. We can broaden our perspectives in meditation by opening our channels to God's good, as we protect ourselves with Spiritual White Light.

When we relax with God, our Creativity unlocks to let us see other ways of viewing ourselves, others and situations. New, inspired avenues open, and we naturally feel more free—which is what life is all about—total freedom for body, mind, and soul.

May we always broaden our scope, so as not to feel trapped within our own minds or in any given circumstance.

The spirit is free when we can change our focus. To expand into the Love-center is a truly gracious gift.

Humility is being grateful for every precious breath we take.

HUMILITY

August 2

May we walk humbly with steps guided by our Creator, acknowledging our assets as well as our liabilities, all together in harmony of who we are.

Let us always remain teachable in the learning of life's incredible mysteries, including the lessons found in soul searching. Everyone has gifts in certain areas. Everyone has certain limitations, if they are honest. Humility is not degrading to the self. Humility is the balance of self-knowledge achieved by those who realize their potential and are totally accepting of their imperfections, striving to reach their desired goals through discipline and improvement.

Let us take our greatest weaknesses and, by God's Grace, turn them into our greatest strengths. Humility is strength and is coupled with healthy self-esteem. Humble people are secure in their capabilities while acknowledging the need for improvement.

May we be grateful for our talents and patient with our imperfections. We are a whole person—body, mind, and soul, just as our Higher Power created us, with the realization that our potential and our strengths can lead us to the realm of the Divine.

We rejoice in our humanness. We are grateful to be alive, and we walk with dignity and respect.

There have never been, and never will be,
two days exactly alike.

CHANGE

August 3

May we accept and adapt to changes in our life with ease and a sense of inner security.

Change can be exciting, full of new opportunities to learn and grow. Humanity is not stagnant; this is impossible. Resistance to change can produce physical illness, confused thoughts, or unpleasant emotions. We evolve and take in stride all different aspects of life while making attempts in personal growth. Usually it is not change that we fear. Rather, we are stuck in our resistance to the changes. Indecision is destructive and unprofitable. Once we make the decision to change, we take faith, and find ourselves in new cognitive action. From that point on, change is easier.

Let us not allow our resistance to contaminate us to the point of staying stuck in old ideas about ourselves, situations, places, things, and others. Unhappiness and low self-esteem result from the unwillingness to change. Therefore, let us pray for the willingness to grow, evolve, and change according to the present situations in our life

May we release old habits or belief structures that do not work for us anymore and remain open to new possibilities that do work for our benefit and the benefit of others.

The spirit within urges us to change and grow in order to be
fully alive.

Healing is an art—be an artist in your own right. You are more talented than you think you are.

HEALTH

August 4

May we listen to what our body, intuitive mind, and spirit are telling us and act accordingly for the healing to occur.

Our Creator designed a marvelous instrument for us—the body/mind/soul trinity. When a person is healthy, the physical, emotional, and spiritual aspects are well-balanced. When one aspect is out of balance, it will throw the others off, too. For a sense of well-being, we need to be mindful of what is nourishing for the body, the mind, the emotions, and the spirit. In meditation, if we listen for messages given by all aspects of the self with assistance from the Creator, we can detect any problem and begin the healing process.

There are times when we may need medical advice, psychotherapy, or a spiritual teacher to lead us back to balance. The Creator places other qualified people in our lives for a purpose. Let us utilize them when necessary.

May we use our intuition and all of the resources available to us to heal our body, mind, and spirit.

Healing occurs when thought, emotion, and spirits are aligned. Self-healing is truly an art form.

Do not judge your judgments.

JUDGMENTS

August 5

May we simply allow our judgments to be there as they cross our minds throughout the day, realizing that they, too, are a part of who we are.

We all have judgments, some beneficial, some overly critical. If we judge ourselves for having ill judgments, this empowers the critical self and perhaps guilt. We need to know that there is a difference between judgment and discernment. Discernment is a preference. Judgment is thinking that something must be right or wrong, good or bad. Many judgments usually come from society's or long-standing family conditioning. Do you ever hear yourself using judgments similar to those of your parents? Let us not be like a blind flock of sheep, all headed for the steep cliff at a dead run.

Let us think for ourselves and make use of our minds' potential. Surely, judgments can also result from one's personal experience. Instead of getting trapped in likes and dislikes or good versus evil, let us simply use our preference-sense as a measuring stick, taking responsibility for these preferences, rather than exerting outward criticism of others or situations.

May we transform our judging into discernment, realizing that judging is a part of our humanness and is universal.

As we evolve from judgmental to discernment, we are gentler with others and ourselves.

Spirituality is being fully human.

SPIRITUALITY

August 6

May we fully understand that we are, each, a spiritual being who is simply experiencing the lessons of being human.

Each person is made of Love and Light. We are on a journey in life to learn to Love, which triggers the memory that we are indeed One with our Creator. Unity with the Primary Source can be found in many ways—laughter, joyous moments, intimacy, and quiet communion, even when we are emotionally moved to tears in our grief or sadness. We are neither separated from our Primal Source, nor are we separated from All That Is. When we are in sync with the Universal Flow, we notice effortlessly that we are happy, joyous, and free. It is the outdated perspective of separateness that precludes unhappiness. When we realize the Main Pulse of Life and Spirit as One Universal Intelligence, we know no separateness. This Source is Love and Light, Unconditional Love and Divine Healing Light.

We all originated from this sphere of Love and Light. How can we conceive of ourselves as anything else? We all possess the Love, Wisdom, and Power of the Divine.

May we seek a path that allows us to be fully human, evoking the confidence that we are already, by our birthright, highly spiritual.

It is in the remembering that we are moved to seek our Creator—the memory that we are a part of the Source and so much more. The journey home can be filled with obstacles that we must overcome, yet it is deep within our souls that we find the pure and truthful kingdom.

If you like to be appreciated, show appreciation to others.

APPRECIATION

August 7

May we appreciate the beauty around us today.

Beauty may be found in natural surroundings, nicely decorated homes, people, and in many, many situations. Beauty is creative perception. Everyone has a personal concept of what is beautiful. Our spirits are also beautiful. When we appreciate the beauty in our own spirits, we see this beauty in others. We need to acknowledge this beauty as often as possible. Should we lose sight of this beauty, may we simply look into the mirror and love all of what we see in ourselves, including our imperfections. An exercise to increase our appreciativeness is to simply think of what we are grateful for and give thanks accordingly.

Let us not take our universe for granted. When we acknowledge our goodness instead of our unworthiness, we are better able to see goodness in others and in all things. When we are moved to show appreciation for someone or something, let us do so in humility and sincerity.

May we learn to appreciate our inner beauty and our uniqueness and to accept and appreciate the beauty of others and all creatures, situations, and places.

Our spirits are made of Love and Light wrapped into an individual personality. The beauty we see in others is a mirror of the beauty within ourselves.

*Recovery is holding on long enough to receive the Grace
of the miracle.*

RECOVERY

August 8

May we allow the time to recover from any given illness.

Recovery is Grace from our Creator. If we give ourselves a
chance to grow and change in the miracle of a new way of life, our
personal circumstances are greatly enhanced. On the days or in the
moments when we feel like we are paddling upstream, let us not lose
sight of the entire process of recovery in whatever form it chooses to
come. Let us be grateful that we live in an age where we can address
our addictions or maladies, and that we have the most current
medical technology and breakthroughs in alternative techniques
available to us for so many different kinds of support. Should one of
our illnesses be an addiction to alcohol, mood altering drugs,
gambling, or other obsessive-compulsive behaviors, it is recognized
that the Twelve-Step recovery movement is the most spiritual
movement in the world today. Not only does it give people freedom
from entrapment; it offers a way of life that utilizes all of the spiritual
principals. Twelve-Step recovery programs pave the way for self-
discovery, ultimately leading to a successful, empowered, joyous life
of total freedom from a life threatening illness.

Patience is necessary in any form of healing. Self-forgive-
ness also comes into play in recovery, whether it is forgiving our
body for letting us down in illness or forgiving our reaction to
life's stresses that could manifest itself in emotional, mental, or
spiritual discomfort.

May we have the strength and courage to face what obstacles
come our way, one day at a time. Prayer aids our choice to remain
in recovery of *any* kind. It is a free choice from our Creator and
a precious gift to our soul.

*The Grace of our Creator has shielded our mind/body/soul.
May we receive the miracle in day-by-day humble prayer.*

When one releases something negative, it needs to be replaced immediately with something positive.

RELEASING

August 9

May we release any negativity with total acceptance and love, in order to find peace today.

Problematic issues gone by, whatever they may be, have actually urged us to grow and to be healed. Recovery from addictions, abusive people, and bad memories of places and situations all drift into a time now gone. What is important is our attitude toward ourselves and our own life today. When we release the negative past, we are more open to the inspiration of a positive future. Letting go is not always easy, yet is a systematic process. When we turn our troubles over to the All Loving Creator, we are freer to be guided into a more positive place in life.

Let us release any old resentments and take responsibility for our lives today. We can then begin to surround ourselves with creative, supportive, loving people who nurture and facilitate positive growth. In prayer and meditation, we lift our problems up and give them to God.

May we take an attitude of gratitude for leaving unpleasant things behind.

Our Creator urges us to grow and evolve into the Light. Love surrounds us with arms of Truth that enhances our spiritual progress.

Do a spiritual house cleaning.

CLEANSING

August 10

May we wash our body and mind of any toxins that may have been building up for some time, in order to create a healthier spiritual flow throughout our being.

There are many ways to cleanse the body of toxins: flushing with fresh juices, body massage, water, meditation, exercise, rest, crying, or by other health-oriented means. We give our mind and body a cleansing vacation today, including new, healthy attitudes that lighten our outlook on life. We celebrate the mind-body instrument that our Creator gave us, treating it with honor and respect. We feel clean and fresh from the inside out, as we incorporate this cleansing into all aspects of life.

Spiritual house cleaning can be done in several ways. One can recite an uplifting, spiritual prayer, while carrying rose-scented incense or a white candle throughout the home or office. This dispels any negative psychic energy that may be present within or around the one who is in need of this type of cleansing. We can also use breathing techniques to cleanse the cells. We can also cleanse our thoughts by feeding them with positive and inspirational material, thinking, acting, and speaking with a sense of well-being toward oneself and others.

May we air out our mind, body, and spirit today.

We can breathe in the Purity of Spirit to reclaim our God-centered self.

Some people have to work a little harder to overcome
their wounded shadows.

RISING OUT OF DEPRESSION

August 11

May we comfort ourselves today, if we feel depressed or are in low spirits.

The first step from relieving ourselves from depression is to acknowledge that we are *in* a depression to begin with. Then take extremely gentle steps forward into the Light of a more positive perspective in life. We nurture ourselves by making the attempt not to isolate from others or to create any more globally negative thoughts. We realize that our depression is internalized anger sprouting from a deep, deep wound, past or current. To appropriately express the anger, without creating more harm to others or ourselves, will help release the "boogieman." After identifying the culprit, then perhaps we can integrate it into the whole of who we are. Talking to a professional therapist or a trusted friend can supply the needed support and offer a more objective view of many situations. A friend just may need to be needed today, and could offer an empathetic ear. Meditation on a nurturing Angel may also help soothe the hurt.

Let us remember that God and the Angels of Mercy are always near and are only an asking away. A few words that may help the severely depressed are, "Don't give up five minutes before the miracle happens." This inspirational phrase can be found in a Twelve-Step recovery program.

May we seek the comfort of our Creator either through other people or in quiet meditation, realizing that the depression will eventually pass.

Our Creator nurtures us when we feel low. Tears are our soul's Angel-chimes.

Independence is a freedom found in the heart.

INDEPENDENCE

August 12

May we celebrate our independence today, knowing that we can be whole and content on our own, either apart from a significant relationship or while remaining in one that may nurture and support us.

Let us allow our sense of freedom to echo from the Creator, with a deep sense of knowing that we are safe, that we are loved, and that all is well. We are each our own person, unique and special in the eyes of the Creator. Whether or not we are in a relationship should have nothing to do with our honest sense of independence. There can be as much freedom in relationships as there is being solo.

Independence is an attitude of grace and poise in any given situation. It can help in carrying oneself with the kind of confidence given only by the Grace of the Divine. Much false confidence is short-lived, egocentric, arrogant, or just a cover-up for how inadequate some people feel deep inside. Independence is inspiration and Divine intuition drawing us to the places where we need to be in order to act, speak, and think in the Highest Good for all concerned. Independence is trusting in the creative flow of the Universe. It is a knowing that there is a Divine Plan that involves all of God's creation, working toward a balance of essential goodness.

May we give thanks for our individuality and our creativity. All beings are creative in their own way, and all have their special gifts. We choose to utilize our gifts to create our independence.

Deep inside our soul, we know that we are not alone. For we have seen many miracles that prove otherwise.

She is the Great Mother who nourishes all.

MOTHER EARTH

August 13

May we take the time today to relish in and upon our Mother Earth.

The earth supports and nurtures us. If one dwells in a city, take the time to go to a park or drive out into the country as often as possible. Feel the earth beneath your feet, and look at the trees and flowers, inhaling their beauty. If one lives in the country, breathe in the fresh air. Notice the animals, woods, beach, and mountains.

Let us try to appreciate all of Earth, giver of life; perhaps plant a little garden wherever you are, and take delight in the growing of seeds. Wear green. Celebrate the oxygen given by the trees. Maybe Mother Earth needs a hug today. Have you ever hugged a plant or a tree? Both the tree and the person benefit!

May we honor and respect Mother Earth and contemplate her vastness, her richness, her fertility, and her beauty, as we live our life in gratitude of the Great Mother.

Smell the richness of the land. Touch the wings of a butterfly. See beauty all around you. Taste the morning dew. Hear the dove at dawn. Feel the Creator in all things. Live!

It is the <u>way</u> we approach life that is insurmountable.

GENTLENESS

August 14

May we be gentle with who we are and, in turn, be gentle to all others, as much as possible.

While in a conversation, collecting our thoughts, or using our bodies and hands in performing even the smallest task, let us do so in a gentle way. One can use tact in dealing with others, without sacrificing one's own values or position. We can utilize our intelligence with calmness, clarity, and ease. We balance our nurturing energy with performing energy, creating our unique way of living one day at a time. In a hurried world, sometimes we act in ways contrary to gentleness. Just the tone of voice of someone making a request can make all the difference in the energetic ambiance.

The next time you wish to be overtly demanding, remember your little Angel's voice of gentleness. Our world could use a dose of gentleness. By simply taking a moment or two to take some deep breaths before we think, speak, or act can give us the power of love and consideration needed in most given circumstances.

May we bathe others and ourselves in gentleness, for all are our sisters and brothers.

In a world that may seem so harsh at times, we can soften the way we conduct ourselves throughout each day.

Closure is a beginning.

CLOSURE

August 15

May we take the time to say good-bye to people, places, and things in our life that no longer coincide with our inner belief structures.

There are people, places, and things that have served a purpose in our life, and we feel a sense of gratitude for their being a part of what has made us who we are today. Actually, there are no permanent good-byes, for everything is fluid and temporary in this world. If closure seems to be overwhelming, we can ask our Creator to remind us that when a door is closed, another opens. This is significant and beneficial to us in the whole scheme of life. When Love begins to awaken the consciousness, and we see a broader view, we see and understand the cycles or wheels of life.

To every completion, there is a new beginning. Just as rebirth is necessary, so is closure, as we are all growing and evolving toward the Unconditional Love in the Highest Good of our Creator.

May we intuit when closure is necessary for us to move on.

We are comforted in knowing that nothing is truly over. It is merely outdated and its usefulness to us has been somewhat diminished.

Be truthful and honest with yourself first.
Integrity will follow.

TRUTH

August 16

May we seek true wisdom today in all of our affairs.

To find truth, we must know ourselves well enough to be discerning. Studying spirituality or ourselves is a choice where an immense freedom can be found. What may be true for oneself is not necessarily true for another. In searching for our own truths, we are guided gently into a Universal Truth, which allows us to feel safe within our own universe and able to live comfortably in our own skins. To see Truth in people is to first know oneself well. What knowing oneself means is to have the clear intuition of what our positive and negative traits are. Values, morals, standards, spiritual principals, and truths all fit in with who we really are.

Let us remember that our true nature is love, joy, peace, wisdom, beauty, freedom, innocence, creativity, spontaneity, and humor. This is how we came into this world. Rediscovering these attributes may take us a lifetime yet is, indeed, achievable.

May we match our insides with our outsides.

Seeking Truth can be a double-edged sword. Yet the beauty within rings Universal.

*Lying deep within the solitude and quiet are the secrets
of the Universe.*

MEDITATION

August 17

May we take the time today in meditation to become still and quiet, listening to our inner knowing.

May we clear our mind of worries, disappointments, fears, and noise and let these thoughts drift upward like smoke, eventually dissolving. Void of fear, we let the pure Love of our Creator enter our body, mind, and soul. We feel the Love surrounding us, and our entire essence becomes Peace. One way to meditate (and there are many) is to simply watch the breath. The point in the body where air is inhaled may be the tip of the nostrils. On the in breath silently say the word "in." With relaxed breathing, on exhaling silently say the word "out." Another way to watch breath is to say silently, "rising," as we feel our chest rise with the in breath. Then on the out breath say silently, "falling." While saying "in, out, rising, falling," our eyes are closed, yet are focused on either the tip of the nostrils or the upper chest.

When thoughts come into our mind, as they will, we simply let them pass, like ships on the ocean, and gently return our attention to the breath. At first, try this meditation for five minutes only. Then eventually increase the time. Once a day is fine at first, then gradually increase to twice per day or more, whenever the need to clear the mind arises.

May we love ourselves enough to allow this Peace to envelop us, letting our meditations be an oasis in our day.

*Our soul knows Peace, for this is what it is made of. We listen
to the quiet and find serenity therein.*

*Self-healing may be as simple as breathing deeply
and consciously.*

STRESS

August 18

May we release any stress from our mind and body today.

At times, when perhaps there are too many situations to deal with, and we feel we need to take care of all situations immediately, we may become overwhelmed. When this happens, we can prioritize, take care of things little by little, chip away at tasks, and then congratulate ourselves for handling all we possibly could in one day. We remember to breathe deeply, releasing any stress in our body on each exhale. Stress can undermine a person's physical, mental, emotional, and spiritual well-being. Even if stress in daily life is unavoidable, we can learn to deal with it as it comes up. Yoga, Tai Chi, breathing exercises, working out, swimming, meditation, and many other tools may be used to deal with stress.

Let us not be slaves to stress. Let us take the initiative to make our lives as stress-free as possible.

May we rest, eat healthy foods, and comfort ourselves with thoughts that all is well and that stressful situations will all pass in time.

The next time stress comes knocking, tell the Creator that you do not need it anymore.

*If there were no chaos, how could one understand the true
meaning of organization.*

CHAOS

August 19

May we remain calm and organized in the midst of total chaos.

A crisis will pass in time, yet the height of the crisis is the time to have a talk with the Creator, asking for guidance as to what the next step will be. Sometimes the content of that talk will be only "Help!" We may be amazed at our abilities to handle chaos and keep our cool.

We can maintain dignity and keep centered even in the midst of total confusion. If we are led to give assistance, and if we could be a part of the solution, then we may want to do so. Let us always try to be a part of the solution instead of part of the problem. We can keep sure-footed in the journey, acknowledge the chaos, do what we can to help it dissipate, and have a deep sense that all will be well. Ironically, organization and chaos can actually exist at the same time. The school of thought in many Eastern philosophies is termed, "yin and yang," where complementary opposites can abide in perfect balance. Sometimes, this way of thinking may be somewhat comforting to anyone who finds themselves in the midst of chaos.

May we intuitively find organization in chaos.

*Inner peace can be ours in the tumultuous storm. Divine
guidance is found by asking.*

Respect is shared dignity.

RESPECT

August 20

May we treat ourselves and others with respect today, acknowledging the dignity in all.

If we are overcritical of ourselves, we will, in turn, be critical of others. A Loving Creator helps us to look for our strong points and embellish upon them without being arrogant, which is merely a gross insecurity.

With newfound self-respect, we are able to bring out the strong points in others. A creative energy is shared, and inspiration results. Most people have been hurt enough in their lives. May we be a source of healing.

May we be uplifting—to ourselves and others.

Shared inspiration urges the Angels to smile broadly.

Did you tell us to meditate? We couldn't hear you!

NOISE

August 21

May we learn to find inner peace and maintain calmness even in the midst of external noise or the noisy internal dialogue inside of our head.

Quiet meditation, at some point during the day or evening, can give us the peace of soul necessary to confront the fears that we may experience in a given day or throughout the night. When we are centered, we are calm. Meditation helps our mind and body maintain health, and our soul is happy and giving.

It is very soothing to the soul to be outside with nature, without the sound of traffic, air conditioners, radios, televisions, and all other noise present indoors or in a city. Even the sound of the refrigerator running can add to daily stress. We can learn, however, to tune these noises out and listen to the music of the Divine and the silence of Peace or the heartbeat of Pure Love.

May we live within this Realm of Peace, even when our world is upside down.

Our mind is made quiet by the healing of meditation. With inner calm, we can more easily handle any situation.

Angels are very real—they reside close to us.

ANGEL COMFORT

August 22

May we feel the presence of our Angel today, knowing that we are never totally alone.

We can talk to our Angels or our Guides. If we want them to reveal themselves to us, all we have to do is ask and then listen with our hearts. With the comfort of our Angels, we may, in turn, help someone else this day. We could, without even knowing it, be the calm in the midst of their storm.

If we feel stressed or lonely, let us call upon our Angels. Angels are only as far away as the asking. The Creator is as close as our next breath.

May we have a deep sense of knowing that all difficulty passes in time, coupled with the insight that all is well in the grand scheme of this Universe.

May we look within to feel the Love of our Angels. We ride upon the wings of seven white Doves.

*We need not be anything or anyone special in order
to be loved by the Creator.*

FRUSTRATION

August 23

May we learn healthy ways to release our frustration.

When our world gets clouded over and stressful, we tend to lose our perspective on life. Some ways to deal with frustration are praying, laughing, crying, meditating on letting it go, resting, going to a Twelve-Step meeting, moderate exercise, talking about it with a trusted person, taking it out on a pillow, or going off by oneself and screaming. These are a few of the many ways to release tension in body, mind, and spirit.

Let us use healthy, constructive means of releasing frustration.

May we turn our sour attitude into one of kindness, using frustration as an opportunity to utilize our strengths of character.

When we uplift others and ourselves with positive actions and prayer, we find the hidden Love of Spirit. It is always, always within us.

Hope is the courage to change our perspective on life.

HOPE

August 24

May we always carry hope in our hearts.

As long as there is breath in our bodies, there is hope. Despair is temporary, and in the midst of that feeling, we still can have the hope that we will be all right. Our Creator designed our minds and bodies to be resilient. Deep meditation gives us the insight that we are well taken care of at all times by a Loving Universal Intelligence, or whatever name one wishes to call God.

We are responsible for some footwork, yet upon surrendering mind/body/soul to an All Loving and Forgiving Creator, we are uplifted and transported into a Spiritual Realm and a new way of thinking.

May we know, without a shadow of a doubt, that our Creator will take care of us, as long as we do our part to help ourselves. Hope is universally available.

Oh, Great Spirit, may we be blessed with hope today. After the storm, may a rainbow appear to seal our promise.

Inner resources are more valuable than gold.

INNER RESOURCES

August 25

May we utilize our inner resources to make for a more fulfilling day.

Each person has the potential to be rich in character. We have our own strengths and abilities to call upon to sharpen awareness, learn, or create. When we take care of our personal needs, we have a wealth of energy to share with others and to devote to other worthwhile causes such as work, family, and friends or recreation.

Inner resources are those qualities that we can call upon in times of need or simply to enrich ourselves more, to *push* just a little harder, to go that extra mile when we have no idea from where the energy comes to do so. The energy is God within, manifesting itself through our being. Like a muscle, inner resources work better for us the more we call upon them.

May we be grateful for our inner resources, which are gifts from our Creator.

Awareness of inner strength is always available, because our Creator continually replenishes the source.

Fear breeds more fear. Love and Light embrace the darkness.
Ultimately, we choose how to live.

FEAR

August 26

May we acknowledge our fears and try to be as compassionate with ourselves as possible. Then let them go.

Fears may be founded or unfounded, and at times we need to separate the realistic from the imaginative ones and act accordingly. We can take the necessary precautions for founded fears and then leave the rest in the hands of the Creator. As far as imagined fears, we can be grateful for a creative mind.

Let us remember to turn on the light, and the darkness fades into a sense of relief and comfort. Remember to look for the Light and Love in all situations. We have probably read and heard much about there being only two basic human perspectives—Fear and Love. When we arrive at a place where we see fear as an illusion and Love as the only reality, we have indeed embarked upon a spiritual path.

May we always choose Love, as the fear dissipates into the void of illusion from whence it came.

Because Fear and Love are not compatible, we have a choice to live our life loving or fearful.

Grace is merely a prayer away.

GRACE

August 27

May we be open to receive the Grace of our Creator today.

Grace is a free gift from the Spiritual World and is extremely healing. It brings harmony, peace, and gratitude and allows us to feel the joys of life. Grace can also be like the calm after the storm. We may feel overwhelmed and stressed at times, but it passes, sometimes quickly, sometimes slowly. When we allow ourselves to feel our feelings, we know that the fears and negativity will pass, and by the Grace of our Creator, Love and Peace will follow. All is within the Universal Balance. Grace is not something that is bestowed only to a select few. It is a free gift from God. We can witness Grace in answered prayers and manifested dreams. Grace can also be associated with poise. It is felt by all those who come into contact with a graceful person. To be graceful is an art that can be learned from the Great Teacher.
May we accept the benevolence of Grace.

The promise of Grace may be compared to a rainbow. When the thunderstorm passes, we are left with God's colorful Halo.

Ask yourself—why do we even want to relive a painful memory?

LETTING GO OF RESENTMENTS

August 28

May we gather our strength and courage to let go of resentments of any person, place, or thing today.

First of all, we can consciously free ourselves from this disabling malady by simply acknowledging the fact that we actually *are* harboring a resentment. Then we can express the anger appropriately, either directly or indirectly, if the resentment is against one who has caused injustice or harm. Let us not repress the anger or act it out inappropriately, but instead pray to be delivered from the negative feeling that the resentment brings. We ask, in prayer and meditation, that the resentment be removed at once from heart and mind, to feel free to be filled with love and compassion, and to get on with life as serenely as possible.

Let us pray or ask for a new perspective of the situation; we will see direct changes in our way of looking at the particular person, place, or thing, as well as feel a softening in the heart. Always ask yourself when you experience resentment, "Will it *really* matter in three months?"

May we gain a new outlook on resentments today.

Love fills our heart again, where darkness used to dwell. We release negativity and smile again because we are now free.

What may seem like an ending is actually a beginning.

CYCLES

August 29

May we accept the cycles of each season naturally, as they occur in nature and within ourselves.

As we witness the change of season from summer into fall, we can also acknowledge the changes that occur within ourselves. We are a little older and have had much more experience. We can take the Light of Summer with us into the fall, as the days grow shorter, little by little. We may welcome the cooler breezes of autumn as a gift from our Creator. As each new season unfolds, so does wisdom unfold gently within us. In some cultures, the symbol for ongoing cycles is an image of the serpent swallowing his tail. We can see that, really, there is no ending and no beginning.

By simply noticing the life cycle of a tree as it loses its leaves in the fall, then buds out again in springtime, we are witness to our ever-growing life. All is a gradual awakening. We keep evolving into Light Beings, as we become close to our Creator.

May we know, according to natural laws, that each of us goes through cycles and patterns just as there are different seasons in the year.

Our Creator reveals wisdom whenever a new transition occurs.

We are all perfect in our imperfection.

PERFECTIONISM

August 30

May we let go of any compulsive need to be perfect today.

While it is all right to strive for higher ideals or goals, care is needed to avoid pushing ourselves so hard that we find ourselves discontented in frustration. When we actually sit down and think about it, we really have nothing to prove to anyone. What we can be content with is doing whatever it is we need to do, to the best of our ability at the time.

Usually, a need to be perfect comes handed down from others in their unrealistic expectations of us. We each are already perfect just as we were created. We each are fulfilling our soul's purpose on Earth and are already guided by our Creator. Perfection has an insidious way of perpetrating itself into over-responsibility and, in turn, we expect it from others.

May we relax in the knowing that our Creator is in control and that we are Loved.

We are doing the best we can with our given awareness. We are the children of our Creator. In this very breath, we are already a perfect success.

If you have difficulty filling your lungs with air,
try breathing through your heart.

OXYGEN

August 31

May we give thanks to the plants and trees for creating oxygen for us.

Breathing is so automatic for us that we hardly think about it. Every time we exhale, we are giving our carbon dioxide to the Earth's vegetation. In the relationship of reciprocity, they are giving us fresh air and oxygen. Also, ozonated water as well as oxygen supplements can help provide the oxygen we need to remain healthy and balanced. Let us be grateful for the tiny plankton and algae in the vast oceans, lakes, and seas, for they, as well, give sweet oxygen so that we may live and breathe.

Let us surround ourselves with green, perhaps by using houseplants, and making trips to the sea or to the countryside whenever possible. Remember that it is by God's Grace that we have breath in our bodies.

May we always remember to be grateful for oxygen.

There is balance in the Universe, and we know we are safe.
Our hearts stay happier when we breathe fresh air.

Funny —when we allow ourselves to love,
little else seems to matter.

LOVE

September 1

May we experience love today and bask in that feeling of Divine essence.

The word *love* can mean so many different things to each of us. It is one of the most difficult emotions to describe in words. Some will say that it is simply a wonderful feeling. Others may use *love* as a verb, as in, "I love to dance." Whatever our use of this word is, it is a reflection of the God-part in each sentient being. One way we love is by opening our hearts to others, to friends, to flowers, or to a sunset, opening to the Good in the world. Let us travel throughout this day knowing that the Creator is near and is lending a hand in all we do. This same Creator sends Angels to help us to open our hearts even more. We give and receive love simultaneously.

Let us see a glimpse of Love in all people, in all we do, and in all situations just for today. Love is always within, waiting to be tapped into and given away freely. In return, we are able to receive it equally as freely.

May we be in the spirit of Love, and feel the genuine warmth that it brings.

Love is always available. It is not bound by any schedule or limitation.

May we find our inner Light.

SUNSHINE

September 2

May we enjoy and be energized by the sun's rays today.

Despite all the bad press about skin cancer today, the sun has many beneficial properties including Vitamin D, energizing effects, soothing and relaxing muscles, and many other healing qualities. If possible, try to take in some sunshine today while taking the necessary precautions. The days are becoming a little shorter now. We relish the Healing Light, which will not be quite as strong in late fall and winter in our hemisphere. We see the joy that the sunshine brings and welcome it wholeheartedly as a new day begins or as it peeks through clouds after a rain.

Let us treat God's creation, the sun, as an intelligent and loving friend—not as an enemy. Being aware of the sun in the sky can make us aware of our own transformations and transitions, which manifest themselves throughout a day or over the course of a lifetime.

May we watch a sunrise or sunset today, in gratitude for the sun, another day, and for our life.

The sun is with us for good reason. May we be aware of its healing power throughout the year.

In our downtime we are actually being lifted up.

TREATS

September 3

May we treat ourselves to something constructively good today.
.

We all deserve a break at times, during a workday and on days off. We can treat ourselves to good food, bubble baths, naps, buying something special, laughter, going to the beach or taking a drive in the country, an inspirational book, exercise, music, or whatever we can think of as a good thing for ourselves. In the rapidly changing pace of our world, we can take a creative breather as often as we like.

Let us take a break in our demanding schedules. Taking a break is taking care of ourselves, as we are resting our minds and bodies in order to return to work more fulfilled, relaxed, and rejuvenated.

May we know when we need a treat, a break, or timeout for ourselves. May we be good to ourselves today.

Angels love creative breaks during a hard day. They encourage us to treat ourselves with their blessings.

Integration is inner harmony, peace of mind, and a constant balance between our multi-dimensional selves.

INTEGRATION

September 4

May we realize today that all parts of our multidimensional self work together in making up the whole of who we are.

We are body/mind/spirit. We can work on integrating all of these aspects of ourselves to feel healthy, vibrant, and whole. When one of these parts is out of balance, it, in turn, causes the others to malfunction. We realize that we are actually a spiritual being that happens to have a human body, mind, and emotion-center. Our human experiences and journeys are predetermined by our never-dying Spirits, according to the work the soul came here to do.

The kindest thing we can do for ourselves is to integrate all aspects of who we are into a loving, balanced, and healthy being.

May we take the time today to reflect on our soul and the integration of all aspects of our humanness.

Awaken, Oh soul, and remember that you alone hold the great answer.

Awareness is Precious.

DIFFERENCES

September 5

May we learn to appreciate the differences in people, nature, and all that our Creator has made.

Let us try to honor the individuality in others and ourselves. Today it could be extremely profitable to delight in the uniqueness of each flower, animal, and rock, in awe that there are no exact duplicates. As in nature, so it is in human beings. We all have our own different personalities, traits, styles, beliefs, and ideas. Joy abounds when we learn to accept and appreciate these differences.

Let us come to a point where we are able to find common traits among the differences, instead of comparing idiosyncrasies.

May we remember to judge ourselves and others less, and to accept and appreciate our varying characteristics.

Beauty lies within all Creation. We see the immeasurable manifestation of our Creator everywhere.

Come to know the Earth. The wisdom therein is immeasurable.

EARTH

September 6

May we be conscious of the Earth that we dwell upon today.

In nature we can surmise there are four elements—Earth, Air, Water, and Fire. They are our life givers. The Earth supports us, nurtures us with food, supplies us with beauty as in flowers and trees, and is constant, as we contemplate the law of gravity. The Earth keeps us grounded and enveloped in the arms of the Universe's security. Mother Earth may be able to nurture us even more than human beings can in certain circumstances. Billions of years old, our Earth has survived under the most dire of situations and evolutions. Perhaps, for these reasons, there exists a large amount of substantiality in the trusting of its solidarity. All four of these basic elements stated above work together to create a balance for us. These four elements are those recognized by North America's Native Americans.

Let us give thanks to the support and beauty of Earth today. It sustains us well even in the midst of our mistreatment of it. This indeed, is an endurable example of Unconditional Love.

May we trust that the Earth will always support us and supply our needs.

Oh, Mother Earth, giver of life and constant rebirth, we acknowledge and appreciate you.

Air is all-encompassing and sustains all Life.

AIR

September 7

May we take time today to give thanks for the air we breathe, the sustainer of Life.

Although we live in a rapidly changing world where, in certain places, the air may not be completely fresh, we can still be grateful for breathing, inhaling and exhaling in a rhythm that nurtures the whole body. Also, we can be outside on a warm day and enjoy a fresh breeze as a refuge. We pause today and are grateful for the air that we breathe, whatever its condition may be. Upon inhaling, we breathe in Love and Light that surrounds us. Upon exhaling, we breathe out Peace and Gratitude.

A simple exercise that we can employ during times of stress is to close our eyes and take some deep breaths, imagining our most ready concerns floating off into the distance, like birds soaring by above us from high in the sky. Sometimes the Magic that happens is only one deep, slow breath away.

May we feel the involuntary rhythm of life-giving air. Our breathing is precious to us. We do not take it for granted.

Birds of the air, we applaud your Lightness. We readily access your trust and courage.

Some futurists say that one can be totally healed by water
and a faith-filled heart, mind and spirit.

WATER

September 8

May we learn to appreciate the essence of water today.

An element of fluidity, refreshment, and creativity, water is essential for life and well-being. Our bodies are composed mostly of water. We may seem dense, but we are actually flowing and in constant motion with the balances of nature. We can celebrate the healing properties of water in our lives today by drinking fresh water, swimming, walking by a creek or the beach, or simply contemplating the necessity of water for survival. Being near a waterfall or a fountain usually can help us to feel good, not only for the beauty, but also because water creates and releases negative ions into the nearby area. Negative ions work by creating more positive, uplifting, and clean air for us to breath into our lungs.

Today, many people are placing small fountains in their homes or yards to create a more serene and peaceful environment. Water is the symbol of our emotions—forever ebbing and flowing in a perfect, Divine rhythm. Water is also extremely cleansing and purifying to our mind/body/spirit.

May we give thanks for this precious element, a gift from the Creator.

We went to the wishing well to draw water, and we witnessed a miracle from our Creator.

We all have fire within ourselves. Let us be
passionate about life.

FIRE

September 9

May we welcome today the warmth, light, and comfort of
fire, the fourth universal element of the Native American world.

Let us be drawn to think of all the uses of fire and realize its
importance. We can think of electricity as a small spark of fire,
running through currents to create convenience in our lives. Now,
as the nights become a little cooler, we may begin to think of a
warming fire for the months to come. We fuel our bodies for the
winter, perhaps eating more than in summer for the body's
insulation. Fire allows us to cook our food.

Let us give thanks to the ancients for discovering fire. As we
know, any of these four basic elements can become hazardous or
out of control at times. This is simply Mother Earth trying to
balance herself with our everchanging planet. Unfortunately, the
Mother can claim lives, which is also a part of the Divine Plan in
a much greater sense. We try to handle these four elements with
conscious caution, which is found innately within each of us.

May we allow ourselves to realize the importance of fire,
even for mesmerizing our mind, as we watch the red-gold flames.
May we be purified by fire to return to our true essence.

We built a fire simply for the comfort, and we noticed that
relaxed thoughts came without effort.

By smiling, one can communicate brilliantly in any language.

SMILING

September 10

May we simply offer a smile today to ourselves or to someone else.

There are those times when we may not feel like smiling. Instead, we feel like crying or are simply in a less than happy mood. Even if we do not want to do it, let us offer a smile to ourselves or to someone else today, someone who could be a total stranger in passing. This is not an act of disguising our true feelings or being false. This is practicing the art of giving.

Think of how you feel when someone smiles at you, perhaps when you feel low in energy. Instead of being suspicious or cynical, simply accept the smile as a gift, and, in turn, try to give that gift to another.

May we practice the art of smiling.

Regardless of how we feel, we allow ourselves to smile at something or someone this day, and perhaps feel more gentleness in the way we handle ourselves in those darker times.

Use doubt as a relearning process.

DOUBTS

September 11

May we allow ourselves to have doubts today, and fill the emptiness with faith and perseverance.

At times, we may experience self-doubts, doubts of our own existence, doubts of a Creator, doubts of our own or others' integrity, and countless other doubts about life's meaning. These skepticisms are not altogether negative, as we learn to relearn. This is a process by which we discard what is no longer true for us and rebuild our thoughts as to what is actually important for us and in life.

It is important for us to understand the difference between doubts and facts. Sometimes our doubts simply need reality checks to be cleared away in order for us to move forward in our journeys. Doubt and faith cannot coexist. Let us remember this.

May the light bulb go on in our imagination to always reconsider our values and beliefs, and to have the faith to live our life in accordance with them.

What is important for us now may not have been ten years ago. As we change and evolve, it is our essence that will decide.

All life prepares for the oncoming season.

FALL CLEANING

September 12

May we keep in mind today what is truly important to us and what is not.

As we prepare for fall and winter, we go through our *things*, throwing out or giving away that which is not useful or important to us anymore. We do this with our thoughts as well. What is actually *useful* to us on our life's journey? We become extremely clear about what we will need to take with us into the coming months ahead: the more contemplative and introspective months.

This is a time for preparation, to weed out the clutter and chatter, and to take what is most important on the spiritual path.

May we have the clarity to understand what is useful and important.

Teach us, Oh Creator, about the necessities of mind/ body/spirit, and help us to quiet ourselves down peacefully enough to listen to your voice.

Our Creator Loves and Accepts us unconditionally.

COMFORT

September 13

May we come to the realization that our Creator loves us.

There is great comfort in knowing that the One who created this Universe and all beings Loves us, Accepts us as we are, and is always available to offer assistance to our every need. In this hurried world, we can find comfort in feeling that we do, indeed, have a place of belonging here, even if our purpose is not totally clear to us.

Perhaps it is enough to know that we are here for the lesson that simply living life has for us to learn.

May we feel loved by our Creator and have a deep sense of belonging in the world.

We breathe in: "We are enough" and "We are learning."

We breathe out: "We are finding that which our souls seek."

*However a spiritual awakening may come, let us not
ignore nor minimize it.*

SPIRITUAL AWAKENING

September 14

May we always look forward to spiritual awakenings in our
life.

Usually, there is one major spiritual awakening in life that
opens the door to our connection with our Creator, and we can
have more and more *mini* awakenings thereafter. As our
awareness grows and our hearts open, we can expect such
awakenings. Some may call these *awareness miracles.* As we
grow to believe in a Power greater than ourselves and make
efforts to commune with this Power, we can be guaranteed the
miracle of a spiritual awakening. Try to listen for messages—
sometimes they come grandly, sometimes subtly. If our highest
intention is for the greatest good for all concerned, we are
protected from anything that is less than for that Highest Good
for all. In our daily meditations we are all awakening to the
consciousness of our inner Truth.

Let us open our eyes and ears to the beauty of awareness, go
within, heal, grow, and manifest in the Light of who we Truly
are—Unconditional Love, Beauty, Peace, and Wisdom.

May we be open to the wonders of our Creator.

*Let us open our senses to Heaven and Earth in order to
witness the vitally necessary rebirth of our soul.*

Clarity comes after muddling through the fog.

CLARITY

September 15

May we celebrate the clarity that comes from the hints of the autumn air today, as the heat of summer is lessening.

In the Northern Hemisphere, clear, crisp air begins to replace warmer skies of summer. Acorns are falling, harvest will soon be at hand, and leaves are beginning to mature, sighing with relief from summer's glow. Like the harvest, we also gather our thoughts and energies to feed our souls, remembering those aspects of ourselves that are important to us.

Let us remember others in the harvest and feed their souls as well. With clarity in the air and in our minds, we go forth with humble hearts into the oncoming season, in gratitude for the bountiful gifts our Creator bestows upon us.

May we give thanks for clarity in mind/body/spirit.

White clouds in a blue sky pass like our thoughts. And above those clouds is the wisdom of the ages smiling upon the Earth.

Music is math in motion.

MUSIC

September 16

May we listen to the music that quenches our thirst for goodness today.

There are so many types of music, and usually we favor the ones that speak to our souls. Music can enhance emotion, set a mood, energize us, soothe us, and give us lyrics that we can identify with, as we go through certain phases of life's journey. Our taste for music can change as we evolve and change. When young and impressionable, we can be extremely influenced by lyrics and music. As we grow and obtain a set of values, becoming more centered, we may be more selective of what reaches our ears. Sometimes we do not need lyrics to identify with a song—merely intonations that resonate with our own spirit's vibrations.

Music is one way to celebrate life. Even our heart beats exactly with the music we are listening to. Music can excite us or help in making ourselves calmer, creating a more serene atmosphere. Every culture has its own unique music, using their own types of instruments. Simple drumming is music. All sounds can be written down in mathematical notes that contain a plethora of sounds and blends.

May we rejoice in the music of the soul and spirit, appreciating the creativity and quality involved therein.

Music speaks to our spirit, heart, and mind. Music soothes our soul.

Let us be mindful of this very day.

PROJECTION

September 17

May we do our best in all things without projecting the outcomes of our effort.

To live one day at a time is to be the best we can be for this day only. Tomorrow is not necessarily promised to us. This entails releasing the past to our Creator and leaving the future to our Creator, as well. Perhaps a prayer in the morning to be guided by our Creator in thought, word, and deed is a way to live fulfilled for that day. We can always take credit for the effort, while we leave the results to our Creator. This way of thinking simplifies our lives and reduces our fears and worries. We cannot change the past nor can we predict the exact future. What we can do is to try to come to a place of acceptance of our past, learning from our mistakes. We can let go of old resentments and come to forgive ourselves and others. This will most certainly bring more peace of mind to our present state of being. If we can change anything in ourselves and in our life, then we do so.

If we cannot change certain things, then it behooves us to accept those people or things as best as possible. As far as the future goes, we can make plans and have goals, yet we will work under less pressure today if we trust that the outcomes are in God's hands. This process is similar to the Serenity Prayer used in Twelve-Step programs. It states:

God, grant us the serenity to accept the things we cannot change.
The courage to change the things we can.
And the wisdom to know the difference.

(Anonymous)

May we always do what is in front of us and leave the outcome to God, who does a perfect job as *Commander-In-Chief* of the Universe. No will or worry of our own can change the will of Heaven.

Peace is ours when we know that our Creator is in control. We loosen our grip and find a sense of lightness in our souls.

To overcome one's own self is truly masterful
in the eyes of the Creator.

MASTERY OVER THE SELF

September 18

May we exert the discipline that it takes to become master of ourselves with the guidance of our Creator.

We are not powerless over our thoughts, words, actions, and emotions. When we ask for guidance from the omnipotent Creator, we can overcome obstacles in our lives, whatever they may be. We do not have to be victims of our emotions and busy minds. We can ask for support from professionals and friends. We can meditate and learn to catch ourselves when we feel we are enslaved to thoughts and feelings. Let us learn to view this life-dream, this melodrama, with healthy detachment so as to keep our spirits free, fresh, and uncluttered.

In the Eastern philosophies and sciences, as in yoga and meditation, there are enlightened souls who have mastered their bodies, minds and spirits by following certain disciplines. For some, this takes a lifetime to achieve. For others, perhaps not as long. We may experience phases in our life where we are more disciplined in body/mind/spirit. If, in other times, disciplines fall away, we are still perfect in the eyes of our Creator. We are doing the best we can at the time. We can still conduct ourselves with poise and dignity.

May we become master of our body/mind/spirit with the assistance of the Great Master.

Let it be our conviction that, no matter how narrow the path, we will be God-centered, even in the midst of worldly strife. For it is the lesson of each soul to remember their true identity and that they are children of the Creator's essence—perfect divinity in human form.

Our soul is a perfect rose forever budding, forever opening,
forever revealing perfect innocent Love.

ROSES

September 19

May we be aware of the beauty of roses today, as well as the beauty of the self inside and out.

Roses, in their variety of colors and fragrances, remind us of the beauty on this Earth, as well as our unfolding beauty within. Like the rose, we are in different stages of growing, budding and opening to share our inner beauty with the world. We cannot force the rose to open, just as we cannot force ourselves to be anyplace on our life's journey other than where we are.

Let us give ourselves the adequate care of the sunlight and nourishment of the Spirit to gently open to Love and Light. We grow in beauty inside that which is reflected on the outside, especially in the eyes. They are our outer connection with the inner world. Let us encompass today the feeling of being the eye of the rose.

May we see a rose today as a symbol of the Beauty and Love within us and within all other beings.

We saw a rose today and were taken back to Eden. The color and fragrance was a mirror for our spirit.

A person unto himself cannot create new life.

DIVINE MOTHER

September 20

May we consciously be aware of the Divine Mother of all Creation.

For many, many years in Western culture, we have envisioned God as a masculine entity. As we know, the patriarchal society in this country is shifting—not totally over to feminine reign, but more to a feeling of androgyny. In the East, especially in India, some religions have worshipped the Highest Order of Intelligent Creation as the Divine Mother. This is a beautiful concept of the Highest Form of Divine Nurturance and Life Force that, if we honestly think about it, is desperately needed in the world today. Earth needs Understanding, Compassion, Love, Balance, and Harmony in both genders to restore its Equilibrium.

With the acknowledgment of the Feminine in both sexes, it would only stand to reason that the Divine Mother would once again become a major force of the sacred arts, including the revival of ancient ritual. During these times in our modern world of trial and commotion, we need a mother figure more than ever. We need the balance of the Heavenly Father and the Divine Mother as our *Universal Parents* for Sacred Protection and nurturance. Let us come to respect the feminine both inside and outside.

May we give thanks to our all-loving Divine Mother.

The deepest seeds are planted and nurtured in the womb. This is where we find consolation and inspiration.

Abandon not your dreams; make your vivid imagination a reality.

CONSCIOUS DREAMS

September 21

May we always acknowledge our God-given imagination, and may we dare to dream.

We can create our own realities in a spiritual sense. They begin with ideas, imagination, dreams, hopes, and beliefs. These ingredients, coupled with faith in a loving Creator, form the basis of great thinking and great deeds. No dream we have is impossible to Manifest, if it entails that which is in the Highest Good for all concerned.

Prayer aligns our endeavors with our Higher selves or our God-selves and assists us in creating peaceful realities of goodness and Grace, wherein we are doing what we love and love what we are doing. It is only our self-doubt that stands in the way of our creating and living out our dream. Usually self-doubt comes from inside ourselves because of old, outdated beliefs and social conditioning that limited us in our childhood. Outside circumstances or negative opinions of others may also try to "burst our bubble."

May we use our imagination today to raise our own level of consciousness, which in turn will help our efforts toward world peace and healing.

Dreams are Holy inspiration from the Divine that shape our reality inside and out. They are an example of a sublime and Unconditional Love from our Higher Power.

*Rain can be as nurturing to our souls as it is in the
nourishing of the Earth.*

RAIN

September 22

May we celebrate the quenching of the Earth's thirst today.

Rain is necessary for the Earth to grow and flourish. Without
it, we could not exist. Perhaps at times, rainy days seem dreary
and filled with melancholia. We can change our perspective on
this and see the rain as a gift from our Creator to nourish and
sustain us. In the native Hawaiian tradition, rain is sent as a
blessing. Rain is necessary for our Green Earth's reproduction,
keeping our soul and seeds fertile and full of abundant life. In
many other cultures, the entire community's existence depends
on rainfall, as in dry climates in Africa. For eons, civilizations
have had to learn how to contain rainwater and fresh water areas
and distribute it throughout their people. We can even walk in the
rain and feel the full sensation.

Let us look for the rainbow after the rain as God's promise to
all beings. The rainbow is the promise of new Life. The rain can
be symbolic of the dark night of the soul. The thunder and
turbulence of our being are actually having cleansing and
positive effects on a deeper level. When the rain subsides, and it
always does, we emerge from the depths with more awareness of
self, even down to a cellular level.

May we learn to cherish the rain and let it quench our
spiritual thirst as well as our bodies.

*All is well and balanced with sun and rain, and we sing a
song of joy with the Angels.*

Broaden your perspective. Look up!

FATHER SKY

September 23

May we notice the sky this fall day and be grateful for its vastness.

In the Native American tradition, Father Sky fills the people with wisdom, vision, and illumination. Try imagining going through a day without natural light. Let us not take our sky for granted. At night, we may witness a silver moon and brilliant stars. We give thanks to Father Sky for the perpetual rising and setting of the sun, and for the waxing and waning of the moon. It is a blessing to have such natural consistency in this vast, ever-changing world. Our sky becomes vital for every breath of oxygen that we need for sustenance. On a hot summer's day, when a cloud covers the sun momentarily, we can usually feel a small breeze come up with the relief of shade.

It is, indeed, a paradox to find so much consistency of every day's sun, moon, clouds, stars, and the movement into each season with the countless amount of change in every cloud, sunrise, sunset and, aspect of weather.

May we look to the sky today in deep gratitude.

Thank you, Father Sky, for illuminating us today. Through you, we hear the voice of the Great Spirit.

Not one living soul is without a Guardian Angel.

WE ARE NEVER ALONE

September 24

May we have the internal knowledge and understanding that we are never truly alone.

Although we need solitude and alone-time to regroup and process our thoughts, at times, we may sometimes feel lonely and alienated. We need to know that the Creator and the Angels are always near, even though we may not be able to see them.

In meditation, we can ask that the Creator and the Angels reveal themselves to us in some way. They can be sensed by a warm feeling, loving thoughts, profound gratitude, a color, a sound, or a light whispering of Grace. The comfort will come. If we persevere in our prayer and meditation time, the feeling of loneliness will disappear.

May we be comforted in the loving arms of the Angels, who are benevolent messengers from the Creator.

Guardian Angel, we know that we are not alone, because of all the Divine miracles that you have shown us.

Trust the healing. Look for peace.

GOODNESS

September 25

May we have comfort and a deep sense of peace that our Creator is of Universal Goodness, supporting us and continuously uplifting this world.

The consciousness of humanity is forever being raised to higher and higher levels of awareness. Our Creator is allowing us to heal totally on a deep level, and we can rest assured in the profound goodness of this entire Universe. It is such a comfort to relinquish self-will into the hands and heart of the Spirit of the Divine. Many fears are dissipated in the knowing that there is a Supreme Light guiding all beings and global changes.

To completely surrender to the Goodness of the Universe does not mean that we will be without direction or identity. It simply means that we trust in a Divine process, which is in Accordance with the Highest Good for all concerned. It means we are no longer slaves to our self-will running riot, but instead intuitively instructed by the Will of Heaven.

May we feel the Goodness of a benevolent and forgiving Creator who only has our best interest at heart and in mind at all times.

The spark of goodness is within all beings and in all of Creation awaiting the awakened potential to be discovered and uplifted.

One can rationalize a motive quicker than any other thought.

MOTIVES

September 26

May our motives always be congruent with what is the Highest Good for all concerned.

We are all motivated by various impulses, drives, feelings, thoughts, words, and actions. It is good to check out our motives with the Creator and the Angels and to be totally honest about them. This calls for some soul-searching and perceptive self-awareness. We can fine-tune our perceptions by prayer and meditation.

Let us be relieved of any guilt attached to our more selfish motives in our quest to act in such a way that is the most harmonious with the Universe, our Creator, and all beings. Let us become aware of impure motives and make the necessary shift for the betterment of our lives and others, and act accordingly.

May we be motivated by the Love of our Creator and ourselves and always reach for the Highest Good in our pursuit to assist others.

The soul will remember its true home. We can travel our journey, matching thought and action in harmonious rhyme.

Many parts make up the whole.

WHOLENESS

September 27

May we appreciate the many aspects of ourselves that make our whole person.

At times, we may feel identified by one single emotion. We think, for example, we are just anger. We then become trapped into thinking that this one aspect of ourselves is who we totally are. We must realize that the whole self is composed of many parts, and all parts work together into fashioning a self, which is a very whole self that is Loved and accepted unconditionally by a Loving, Forgiving Creator. We cannot love only one part of ourselves and dislike another for the true healing to occur.

Let us learn to integrate any shadows or more negative emotions into ourselves and *tame* the "demons," as some call them. With God's help we are able to do many things we once thought were impossible. It is a real possibility to Love ourselves totally and unconditionally.

May we come to respect our shadows as an integral part of who we are, shedding light upon the less valued parts of ourselves.

Standing in front of a mirror, we looked into our eyes and saw Love. We looked into our eyes and saw hate. We folded our hands and asked for Divine Acceptance. We forgave ourselves and saw the wholeness of God in us.

If we want to know what makes us tick, observe the animals.

ANIMALS

September 28

May we observe and appreciate all creatures our Creator has given to this Earth.

Animals are gifts from our Creator. They roam this Earth freely in some areas and are pets in other areas. Let us observe the animals today, their intuition, their instincts, and their habits in order to learn more about ourselves. Some of their basic needs are the same as ours—to be loved and accepted. I have observed wild animals and have noticed that some of their problems are similar to ours—romance, finance (food), and illness. When we feel warmed by holding a cat or petting a dog, we realize what wonderful companions they can be.

Our pets are able to intuitively change the energy in their owners. It is like they almost know, on an instinctive level, what we are feeling like or going through. If we are sad, usually they will nestle up near us, as if they do not want us to feel so bad. Animals are the *smile* of the Creator to humans. As we honor and respect God's creatures, we learn to honor and respect ourselves.

May we feel the connectedness to animals today and respect their right to be upon this Earth.

We held the gaze of the eyes of a deer, and we saw the gentleness within ourselves.

Contemplate your source.

CONTEMPLATION

September 29

May we be contemplative today and touch our Highest Source.

Autumn is a time to review the months that proceeded this season. In reflecting, we may find it necessary to let go of the people, places, and things that no longer serve our needs. We can shed our old belief structures and begin to find new ones that work better for us. We are in the process of a molting, in a way shedding the old, preparing for the new. As we reflect on the past and apply it as a learning experience to live peacefully in the present, we ask our Creator for the strength and courage to change as needed.

Contemplation is necessary for a healthy balance of the body/mind/soul trinity, and is not to be limited to just the fall and winter seasons. Let us take the time each day for contemplation and reflection upon our own health and restoration, as well as for the needs of others.

May we rest assured that any difficulties we may be experiencing will pass and open new doors for us.

The power of prayer is phenomenal, even if the intent behind it is subtle. The clearer the intent, the more profound the results.

True love is effortless.

LIGHTENING UP

September 30

May we travel *light* today, leaving any cares or troubles in the hands of the Angels.

Let us totally be ourselves today. It makes the Angels smile. Let us be uplifted. We have worked on ourselves and in our jobs. We have prayed, and meditated, taken care of others, and possibly have become too solemn and serious. All is well!

Let us take the opportunity today to feel good about ourselves, leaving judgments behind and feeling good about living! If we are in recovery in any form, we have certain limitations, yet we can also be spontaneous, joyful, creative, and fun-loving folks. As we feel the joy life has to offer, let us laugh at ourselves and have some fun, making the Angels laugh with us. We would not want to get a furrowed brow! Fun is as much a part of living as is eating and sleeping. When we don't get enough of any of these basic needs, we can become edgy, nervous, and lifeless. Laughing and having good, creative fun is today's goal.

May we know that our Guardian Angel will always be with us and wants true joy for us.

Love as the Angels Love us—and really live. For they teach us how to enjoy life, express ourselves, and give with joy.

*Worrying is trying to control outcomes over which
we really have no control.*

WORRY

October 1

May we be at ease about our worries today and place them in the hands of the Creator and our Angels.

When we are worried about certain problems in our lives, let us be aware that these are lessons to be learned. We ask our Creator, "what is the lesson?" We may wish to pray that our Creator will guide us in ways to remedy the situation, and when we have done all we can do to alleviate the problem, we need to let go of the results. This is an opportunity to trust the Creator's Omnipotent Intelligence and to trust the Angels' mercy upon us. With a little patience and prayer, we can be free of worry and get on with life. Releasing our worries is offering up to the Creator what we, as humans, may not be equipped to handle ourselves with our finite minds.

Many people find it difficult to ask for help of any kind in their lives. Although self-reliance is healthy to a point, it is all right to ask for assistance from others at times. Sometimes we find out that others may like or need to be needed. We do not have to carry all of our troubles alone. A simple pause in the day or night is all we actually need to do to ask for God's help when we find ourselves burdened with worries, where human helpfulness may evade us.

May we trust that there is a benevolent Creator who is forever watching over us, teaching us, and loving us.

We offered our worries up to our Angels, and we received peace of mind.

The most important part of a circle is what is in the center.

CENTERING

October 2

May we remain balanced and centered today in the midst of life's sometimes chaotic world.

There are those times when insignificant details and disruptions in life can throw us *off center*. The *center* is our birthright to peace of mind and serenity. Amidst the confusion of outer or inner calamity, we can reaffirm the *God-center*. Try taking a few deep breaths and close the eyes, visualizing the heart-center as calm and peaceful; that our hearts are beating with the natural rhythm of the Universe and that All is essentially in Divine order.

Coming back to *center* can be an inspirational experience and can bring awareness into a keener light. Centering is also extremely grounding in the throes of our having to think about so many different aspects of our busy lives.

May we always remember to come back to *center* during those times when we feel disrupted, distracted, or lost.

We were lost and tossed in this busy life, until we remembered the word: God. Then all at once, we remembered how peaceful we could be in this world.

*Overcast clouds can be a symbol of balance and harmony
applied to our well-being.*

GRAY AREA

October 3

May we acknowledge and appreciate the *gray days* as a
balance between our shadows and light.

Many people in North America are accustomed to living in
the extremities of life, mentally, physically, emotionally, and
even spiritually. Some can find the *gray area* dull and boring—
no excitement, no deadlines, no crisis, no tears, no brainstorms,
no outbursts of laughter. We can learn to live peacefully in the
gray area and become accustomed to simply *being* or living in the
moment, without neglecting our responsibilities or losing sight of
our goals. Giving ourselves permission for "downtime," as some
call it, relieves us from the pressure and exhaustion of our higher
stressed days. It is so important and necessary to give our bodies
and minds a break, in order to refresh and nourish ourselves.
Living in the *gray area* once in a while allows us to reflect on
what is *really* meaningful in life. It is the quality of life, not the
quantity than can most help us to remember our spiritual nature.

Let us go peacefully about this day, keeping the Highest
Good for all concerned in mind, while gently pursuing our
affairs.

May we calmly walk through this day and be grateful for the
gift of non-extremity.

*Our prayer is for inner peace and harmony—for ourselves
and the entire world. We find balance and serenity.*

To express our Highest Love is a free gift of Spirit.

EXPRESSION

October 4

May we express all of the Love we have inside today for our Creator and others, as well as to ourselves.

The expression of Love has a healing effect on oneself as well as on others. We can express ourselves in so many different ways. Creative expression opens pathways of the body/mind/spirit and can fill us with a more positive attitude and an illumination of ideas. Love for our Creator can also be expressed in countless ways—a grateful attitude, a prayer of thanks for all our many blessings.

Let us find ways to express the Highest Love in all we think, say, and do. When we express the Highest Love for the self, enormous channels of inspiration and creativity open for us to express this Love to another.

May we give of ourselves to our Creator and to our loved ones. May we give our own special expression of Highest Love.

A smile can express our Love, saying so many words directly from our hearts. Now is the time for the gifts to pour out of us.

*Positive and negative aspects combined create the
necessary energy for living life fully.*

INTEGRATION

October 5

May we integrate both our shadow and our Light today.

How multidimensional we are! We have an enlightened side
and a shadow side. Some call it the "negative," or dark aspect of
the mind, body, and soul. If we become aware of the shadow and
learn to embrace it, then we can have a balance of positive and
negative forces all working toward the Universal Good. The
more we deny our shadow side, the more it will persist to work
against us in some form or fashion. This does not mean that we
act on the less than desirable impulses. We simply accept them
and perhaps improve on them as necessary. If aspects that make
up our entirety are *split off* from us, we could possibly suffer
emotional fragmentation or serious illness. At times, counseling
could be helpful, should we find our shadows too troublesome to
deal with on our own. When we pray or meditate, we can
visualize every cell of the body alive with Light and Love—love
for our strengths and love for our weaknesses. When we integrate
all aspects of ourselves, the healing transformation occurs.

Let us Love and Accept ourselves unconditionally, just as the
Creator Loves and Accepts us.

May we integrate every aspect of ourselves today on a
unified, cellular level to transform into a being of Love and Light.

*In order to be effective, a battery must have both positive and
negative charges. Both create the spark of Light where our
potential for self opens and begins to grow.*

Awaken! And know yourself in all of your Goodness.

NEW DAY

October 6

May we restore our faith in an unseen Creator and start fresh this day.

We may have a daily routine that may seem unchanged, yet in reality, we never know exactly how our day will go. Because every day is a new and different one, let us begin it with spirituality, asking the All Intelligent and Loving Creator to guide us.

Let us go to God in many ways and for countless reasons. Simply in the asking, we shall be confident that no matter what happens, God will be by our side, uplifting us and gently leading us through this new day. As we give the day to God, we will usually be amazed at how much more smoothly it goes and how quickly we can meet the unexpected and more challenging events that may arise.

May we know that we are uplifted, Divinely lead, and totally Loved today.

We feel the gentle Presence of God leading us, and we witness the clarity in all we do, think, and say.

Listen behind the sound: Listen to the air.

AUTUMN HUSH

October 7

May we listen to the quietness of autumn in the air today.

In the fall, many trees will lose their leaves. In a sense, they die before they drop. Because there is less life activity in the leaves, trees are not as much of a *sound buffer* as they were in the summer when they were full and dense. With this concept in mind, let us be aware of the *sound* of autumn. The air is not as *heavy* as it was in the summer. We notice the crisp stillness. Even behind the city's traffic or a slight breeze, there is a hush.

Let us notice this season of less activity in nature and in ourselves. We are entering into the more restful seasons after all of last spring's and summer's more rapid energy.

May we notice the quieter aspects of autumn and those same aspects of our own soul.

We still our mind and enter into the quiet bliss. We receive an Angel's touch and the Blessing of our Creator.

You may have more than just one soul mate.

SOUL MATE

October 8

May we realize today that all souls are our soul mates.

There is much written and discussed about soul mates in this day and time. Although we may have found our primary soul mates, there is a belief that every person we make eye contact with is also a soul mate. This concept considers some cultures' beliefs in reincarnation. Whatever our belief may be, we know deep down that our souls connect with other souls, not just one soul now and forever, but a Universal Soul in wholeness. Some say that they have danced this Earthly dance many times and with many different partners, most of whom they again recognize, especially by their eyes.

Usually, intuition tells us with whom to bond. Even if a person does not have what some call a "significant other," this does not mean that they will have no soul mate. Perhaps some souls are here on Earth to sprinkle a little love on many people, just as one candle lights many others.

May we be grateful for our primary soul mate, as well as with all whom we form close bonds.

Deep within the eyes is the soul's memory. Our Creator wishes us to look deeper in order to truly see.

Retreat to your inner vision of all you can be.

SPIRITUAL RETREAT

October 9

May we offer ourselves the luxury of a spiritual retreat.

Today, there are many ways to expand our awareness of our inner and outer world. One way is to go on a spiritual retreat. Such a retreat honors the spirit within and uplifts it to honor the spirit within others. Relating to God and others on this level naturally raises our consciousness to a more peaceful and loving level. We can also take time to meditate today, such as a *mini* spiritual retreat with our Creator. We owe it to ourselves to go to a place of beauty to commune with our Higher Nature, traveling to another place physically or in the imagination.

Let us simply give ourselves some time out from a busy day, by taking some slow deep breaths, or by resting our minds on a loving thought or a good or humorous memory. This can help us tremendously. Let us give ourselves the gift of spiritual retreat today.

May we close our eyes at any time and be at one with our Creator.

Some climb mountains to be closer to the Creator.

The outer shell that houses the soul is to be honored.

BODY WORK

October 10

May we respect our body as our vehicle here on Earth and treat it kindly.

There are many ways to respect our bodies—fresh air, healthy foods, water, sunshine, personal hygiene, body massage, and exercise, just to name a few. Therapeutic massages are a wonderful way to begin to love our bodies exactly as they are, coupled with the nurturing warmth, and touch. A professional massage by healing hands can *move* pain and hurtful memories out of the body. The body stores emotions in various places.

Let us treat ourselves to body work today and feel the healthy vibrancy that comes from nurturing the magical child within. As children we were most likely on the move most of the time. Although we do indeed age, this does not mean that we must stop exercising moderately. There is so much information out there these days about taking care of our bodies. Sometimes, all we need is a gentle reminder.

May we do something good for our body today.

Our Creator gave us our body to love and respect. We feel the nurturance of healing hands.

Embrace hatred with the Light of a Higher Power.

HANDLING RESENTMENTS

October 11

May we not harbor resentments against anyone. All humanity is our brother and sister. Therefore, we try to pray for their well-being.

We all have resentments from time to time, for one reason or another, whether we are aware of them or not. Let us transform bitterness into love and compassion by prayer to the Creator to take care of others, just as the Creator takes care of us. This kind of prayer, we find, helps everyone. Our Creator wants us to do this kind of work to better the world and ourselves.

When we pray for those we resent, we raise the vibration of the energy surrounding us all from where we perceive the hurt and harm to be. Where Love is present, the energy is lighter; where there is bitterness, the energy is heavier. Notice how much more freely we move in the lighter atmosphere.

May we be at peace with all others and ourselves today.

Love is healing, as is prayer. Together these powerful spiritual tools can make for a much more pleasant way of living.

We want to care for the subtle energy moving through our
spiritual bodies as much as our physical bodies

CHAKRAS

October 12

May we learn more about our spiritual body today.

The seven chakras, known in yoga, are the energy centers of our bodies, which we may or may not be able to see. Starting at the base of the spine, they extend up to the top of the head. The body/mind/spirit triad is light energy. Each chakra resonates at a certain frequency. Each has a specific color and an element such as fire or water. Healing occurs when the chakras are aligned, balanced, energized, and flowing harmoniously with body and spirit. There are many ways for us to balance all seven chakras, ranging from the food we eat to the type of meditation we choose to practice.

Closing the eyes and visualizing the balance of the chakras is one way to create a healthy mind/body/spirit. All work together as one, relating energetically to the Universal Goodness that connects us all.

May we become aware of the *lightness* of our whole, entire self and create a healing therein.

Our inner spirit is aligned with Light vibrations that reflect a
perfect rainbow for healing and growth.

Sometimes "the grass is greener on the other side,"
yet sometimes, it is not.

SATISFACTION

October 13

May we be satisfied with what we have, what we have learned, and the progress of our life's journey.

At times, we seem to forget the richness of our own lives, our own characters, and our positive qualities. At times we find that we compare ourselves to others, wanting to be more like them or wanting qualities different from those with which we were blessed. With a closer look, we can always find our better qualities, those that perhaps, others appreciate us for, as well. Like Dorothy in the *Wizard of Oz*, we see that everything is already in our own backyards. Our Creator has already made us perfect in the eyes of all Divine Realms. Sometimes there is a delicate balance between our living satisfied—what is too little, what is too much. This can apply to many various aspects of our lives, even down to quenching our physical thirst.

Let us be satisfied with ourselves. The Creator has blessed us with opportunity. Let us work with what we have been given to be the best we can be.

May we look within and see all of our blessings.

We are all of who we are—and that is more than enough. We can shine like a diamond.

When you feel out of sync, beat a drum.

NATURAL RHYTHM

October 14

May we adhere to the natural rhythms of the seasons, honoring our own body rhythms within.

We are in a new season, a season of maturation when more of our energy is guided inward rather than outward. Let us listen to our inner natures and unfold naturally with our body rhythms guiding us. We may be morning people or night owls—according to our particular body rhythms. Let us honor the flow of nature through us.

Let us find our true biological rhythms by noticing when we feel more alive with creativity, energy, and when we better relate to other people. If we are night people and have a daily work schedule, then we can ask the Angels for creative ideas to manifest through our dreaming when we are asleep. If we are morning people and have situations where we work mostly at night, we can simply pray to find the best ways for us to find the beauty of the nighttime. Our Creator has made us each unique individuals, dancing our own dances in accordance to the Highest Good for all concerned.

May we dance to the natural rhythm of our soul and find ultimate peace therein.

Flowing with rhythm, we awaken to our inner light. There is hope, goodness, and peace within us.

Prayers are sacred. Say them with grace.

RELIEF

October 15

May we find relief in our prayers and meditations today.

In this fast paced world filled with hopes and disappointments, love and adversity, and all other paradoxes, let us find an end to confusion and chaos through sincere prayer and meditation with the Creator. When people let us down we have the All Intelligent, All Loving, and All Forgiving Power of a Creator who is just an asking away. Let us be grateful for any amount of faith we have in a Power greater than ourselves. Faith restores us to the Love and Light that we already had, but for an instant, merely forgotten. By resting in peaceful thought, we are better able to access the totality of who we truly are in the eyes of God. As we know, we are free to pray at any time—in gratitude for our blessings and for symptomatic relief from life's pressures, the list goes on infinitely. At times, life may seem as if it is merely an ongoing travail of problem solving. Perhaps this is so, in a sense, because we are given our brains to use. Should our mind feel overworked, let us remember that the mind/body/soul create our entirety.

Let us remember, we are meant to rest the mind, body and soul regularly. Meditation is one way to find this restful state and can be an oasis in the aridity of life's sometimes problematic obstacles.

May we have faith that we are on Earth for a Divine Purpose, and be uplifted.

With years of tears in our eyes, we looked to our Creator. Then we knew what we were on Earth for and what we were moving toward.

Find your gift and joyfully expound upon it.

ENTHUSIASM

October 16

May we enthusiastically work toward our dream today!

The Angels love enthusiasm and spontaneity. Creative actions are reactions from new ideas. Creativity may show itself in many, many ways—by the way we speak and express ourselves, ideas in business, redecorating a room in our house, or a doodle on a piece of scratch paper; the list is endless. Every person is creative in some way. When we feel inspired with enthusiasm, we become proactive in those endeavors or thoughts. Enthusiasm is contagious. When we are enthusiastic, others around us can feel that energy as well. So what is preventing you from achieving your *highest dream*? We all have innate gifts to be discovered and developed. Have we been too serious in our responsibilities and work, overly critical of ourselves, or felt boxed-in? Let's break out of the norm and follow our dreams!

Let us love what we do and do what we love the most. Our Creator wants us to nurture and enjoy the innate gifts that are generously bestowed upon each and every individual.

May we follow our highest dream with spontaneous excitement and feel all of the joy therein.

What we do for Love is with Divine Guidance and the support of Angels. Let us not argue with this innate drive.

Despair will pass. Contribution will last.

PURPOSE

October 17

May we always keep in mind our Highest Purpose and why we are here on this Earth.

In times of despair, we may lose sight of the real purpose of why we exist. Everyone has a right to be on Earth. Some schools of thought say that we chose to be born on Earth in order to fulfill our purpose. In a higher sense, we are on Earth to love and to learn—or to Learn to Love in the Highest, most spiritual way, especially in our relationships with others.

Let us remember the Higher Purpose and not lose faith that we, too, have something to contribute to life. Whether it be a smile, a kind word to someone who feels hopeless, our work, or our family, there are many humanitarian ways to contribute other than monetary contributions. However, if we are able to give monetarily to good, sound causes, then this way is good, too, yet not at all mandatory. It is in our contributions that we begin to live rather than to merely survive.

May we feel validated today in our contribution, however large or small, to this life on Earth.

Just when we felt that all meaning had slipped away, we were reminded of someone else whom we were able to lift up.

Life is more enjoyable when taken step-by-step,
rather than leap-by-leap.

PACING OURSELVES

October 18

May we learn to pace ourselves in our activities and make time for enjoyment.

At times, we may experience *overload* or *burnout.* If we do, let us stop for a moment, take a deep breath, and ask the Creator or the Angels for a well-deserved break. Let us not take on the whole world in one day, but simply do what is in front of us to do. Then we can find time to enjoy healthy entertainment or healthy rest, or whatever is necessary for the moment. Everyone has their own pace in life. It is true that life can be almost too fast for us at times, making us feel that we have difficulty keeping up with everything. Yet, it is important for us not to compare ourselves and what we are able to do in a day's time. If we are always pushing ourselves to *keep up* with those who are able to move at a faster pace, we will usually wear ourselves out trying.

Pausing during a busy day to pray to do something nice for someone else or ourselves is taking care of ourselves.

May we go through this day at our own pace and recognize when to pause for enjoyment and rest.

Just when we experienced burnout, *our Angel gave us a drink of cool water. We paused, became refreshed, then resumed.*

A little willingness can make for big changes.

WILLINGNESS

October 19

May we have the willingness to make changes whenever necessary in our life, which in turn, can make for a better world.

At times, we may have some areas in our lives that we wish to improve upon. For example, we can pray for the willingness to change the old, outdated, less than healthy habits that no longer serve us.

By just being willing to do something a little differently from the normal routine could shed light on a newer, healthier way to live. The Creator sees even the tiniest amount of willingness in our hearts, and will help and guide us to reach our goals; providing the goal is in the spirit of the Highest Good for all concerned.

May we take a little willingness today and let the Angels do the big work.

Our hearts uttered the smallest plea, and the Angels lent us their helping hands naturally and freely.

Each new day is a birthday.

BIRTHDAYS

October 20

May we treat every day like our birthday.

A birthday is a special day for each of us, usually a day of joy and celebration. We feel special on those days, perhaps having fond memories of when we were younger, when we were given birthday parties and all of our friends came to celebrate in fun, food, and games.

Let us try to make every day a birthday with time for fun and entertainment. Remember that we are still those special people every single morning that we open our eyes. Allow that happy child to come out every day, no matter what the circumstances, feeling the creative flow of moments of joy.

May we realize that we are our Creator's children, and we are reborn every single day.

We are reborn into the world each and every day to play with the Angels.

Spontaneity is more loving and creative than impulsiveness.

SPONTANEITY

October 21

May we learn to live more spontaneously within our given limitations.

In our lives, we all have to work within the given limitations that are particular to our own experiences. These may be physical, mental or emotional limitations. Yet, we can find the joy within these boundaries and learn to act a little more spontaneously, rather than always following a rigid routine. If we are the compulsive types, we can channel that energy into creative constructive ways to think, act, and live. Living more spontaneously opens our eyes to new ways of doing old things, which could otherwise prove dull and boring.

Let us act and react with the spirit of our inner child who is magical and so dear to us and others.

May we recognize the creativity in the ways we do things and find the joy of seeing the world with new eyes of perception.

Our Creator made us as individuals in order that we might find joy and peace. Let us see this world as with the eyes of a child.

Giving up can be a spiritual victory.

TURNING IT OVER TO GOD

October 22

May we surrender our worries and burdens to our Creator.

There are times when we all feel burdened by worries. We can surrender these burdens to a Power greater than ourselves by having Faith that our Higher Power will bear our worries. An all Loving and Forgiving God can shoulder anything, no matter what it may be.

If we feel unforgivable, or low in spirits, or oppressed in some way, we can simply say, "We can't, but our Creator can" and "We think we will let our God handle these worries." If we think that surrender means defeat or personal weakness, we can look at spiritual surrender differently. Spiritual surrender is, in the long run, a tremendous victory, a victory over the bondage of self.

May we place all of our cares into the loving care of a Creator who wants us to be free, happy, and joyful.

We felt overwhelmed by the heaviness of our burden, and our Creator said, "Give it to me. Lighten your soul and spirit."

Healing the whole begins with one, and that one
is our own self.

HEALING THE FAMILY

October 23

May we heal in our own time, in our own way, and for the betterment of the whole.

Families can mean different things to different people: an immediate family, a fellowship, a group of people we feel more in tune with, or a spiritual family. If there is any disarray within the family, we can look within ourselves for solutions to the problems through guided Peace and Prayer. When one person heals his or her own wounds, this affects the entire family in a positive way.

Let us take a look inside ourselves, with the given circumstances at hand, and see how we need to heal or change. Looking at ourselves, instead of shaming or blaming other family members, helps us to take responsibility for our own thoughts, words, and deeds. This is where solutions are found.

May we begin our healing in our family by taking responsibility for our own actions and reactions. May we pray for other members to heal and to take responsibility for their own actions and reactions.

We heal, physically, emotionally, and spiritually. The Creator takes us by the hand, guiding and blessing us the entire way.

Paint your day. Create your reality.

MOODS

October 24

May we not identify our whole self by a mood.

There are as many kinds of moods as there are colors. Whatever the mood may be, it can color the day, yet we must keep in mind that our mood is changeable. If we begin a day in a *bad* mood, we must not identify our entirety with this feeling. Moods are like feelings. Like the weather, our moods change— sometimes with outer circumstances. Often, with our prayers to God to help change our attitudes or perspectives, they will change. If we find ourselves uncomfortable in a certain mood, we can use prayer and meditation to change it into a loving feeling. On the other hand, if we find ourselves in wonderful moods, we can say prayers of gratitude to the Creator.

Let us know that we can detach from our moods and feelings, and learn not to label ourselves by them.

May we simply notice our moods today and be grateful that we are alive, growing, and changing for the better.

Our mood was indigo, then sky blue. Our Creator has given us access to every single color and emotion.

A loving soul is the greatest possession.

POSSESSIONS

October 25

May we be content with all that we have, inside and out.

Possessions can be precious to us in this day and time—the *things* that represent who we are, what our tastes are, and the reflection of how we live. Some people constantly want another *thing* in their possession—a piece of furniture, a better car, or even a better life partner.

Let us learn to be more content with what we already have, rather than always wanting something that someone else has. What we have inside of us is what is really important, especially Love. If we possess the Spirit of Love, we have all gifts in entirety and all else is simply a reflection of that Love. We can be grateful for our own inner gifts instead of envying others for what they possess, whether it is material, physical, mental, or spiritual.

May we be content with what we possess on the inside today, instead of what we do not possess on the outside.

He was poor in worldly possessions, yet extremely wealthy in the spirit of Love. He was happy with the blessings his Creator had sent him.

Learn to love. Love to learn.

LEARNING

October 26

May we have the enthusiasm and interest to learn new information, knowledge, wisdom, and ways of constructive living, which involves loving ourselves and others.

If we are aware and conscientious, we naturally learn new information every day. Let us use this information for the betterment of ourselves and how we relate to others. Learning in depth about ourselves helps us to learn in depth about others and more about our purpose here on Earth. Our Creator gave us minds to assimilate information and to communicate.

Let us communicate in the Higher Language of Love, and let us know that learning about ourselves and others is challenging and fun! We grow and change every day. Let us grow toward the Highest Love.

May we learn to love ourselves and others with the Highest Love, generously bestowed upon us by the Creator.

The Angels taught us something new about ourselves, and we applied this information to loving another in the Highest Spiritual sense.

Adversity is a perception.

RISING FROM ADVERSITY

October 27

May we gracefully rise up from adversity and feel the Love of our Creator.

Adversity comes to us in many forms and at different times in our lives. We can either let these fears and situations drag us down or see them as opportunities to use strength and courage, which are gifts from the Creator. The idea is not to deny adversity, but to embrace it and integrate it into our beings, which are good by nature. The Creator made us innocent from the start; it is free will and usually our excessive and various difficult experiences that may create adversity.

When we take responsibility for creating inner adversity, we can then do something to change it, remembering how powerful prayer can be. At other times we must accept outer adversity for what it is, change it if we can, and move on. Sometimes, we need to just avoid adversity and stay out of the line of fire.

May we inhale deeply. We acknowledge, embrace, and integrate adversity in our life today and graciously let it go on an exhale.

We looked down and saw our heavy-laden feet. We looked up, and saw a bird soaring above us, taking our troubles with it as it moved on.

Magic is available to all who believe in miracles.

MAGIC

October 28

May we trust the magic in our soul and see the miracle of healing in ourselves and others.

Twelve-Step programs, in general, can teach us much about life, even if one is addiction free. If we are truly in recovery, we are better able to see the magic happening in our lives as we heal, mature, and reconnect with our Higher Power. We can receive feedback from others who are able to note our progress. We identify with those who have traveled similar roads, and in turn, we are inspired by their progress, growth, and enlightening encounters with their Higher Power.

Living a life free of addiction is indeed a miracle, as the heart of the magic begins and is nurtured. The more magic we experience in our lives, the more magic we can use to help others. Magic is the Higher Power working through others and us.

May we give ourselves the chance to recover and to experience and believe in the magic in our soul, guided by our Higher Power.

We were lost in a world of sorrow that we could not transcend when the magic of prayer transformed us, and we were uplifted and enlightened.

In the midst of fervor, be kind to yourself and to another.
See how it changes things.

KINDNESS

October 29

May we express kindness today to all we encounter.

Kindness is an art form that is cultivated in the heart. The more we practice it, the better we become at developing it and expressing it to others and ourselves. Kindness is God's Grace shining through us and onto others.

Let us remember that we also need to be kind to ourselves. If we are good to ourselves, we can be good to others. Kindness is the type of gift that makes the Angels smile. It takes such little energy to be kind as opposed to being bitter and resentful.

May our soul be happy, our thoughts pure and loving, and our mind clear and focused.

We align our total essence with Higher Will to walk through this life, smiling upon ourselves and all we joyfully encounter.

*Other options are always available. Be open to
see and use them.*

BROADENING THE MIND

October 30

May we broaden our mind today to include other workable
options.

At times, we may feel *stuck* in some way—perhaps in a job
that is not challenging, in a routine that creates boredom, or we
could feel trapped in our own thoughts and feelings. If we do not
like our lives for some reason, it is time for a *mind broadening*
course. Being *stuck* is a signal to do something different.

We could take classes, find new ways to exercise, eat more
conscientiously, dislodge old habits, read about something we
have always wanted to learn, and countless other ways to broaden
our horizons. Sometimes, an inspirational and thought provoking
conversation with a respected person or persons can be enough
for us to see other possibilities. The more options we can create
for ourselves, the less we feel like we are backed up against a
wall—trapped. The mind needs to expand or it becomes dull.

May we use the creativity given to us by our Creator to *create*
a new and different reality for ourselves if the one we are
presently in has ceased working for us.

*Our Creator gave us a good mind. May we direct it toward a
more enriching life.*

Trick or treat? Real or superficial?

COSTUMES

October 31

May we remain ourselves, the way God made us, and give thanks in humility no matter what costume we wear.

Halloween, in our culture, is a time for celebration for many people—the evening before All Saints Day. Many children dress in scary costumes and carry a bag to go door to door in many residential areas and ask for candy. Masks are a large part of the costumes. Many adults, too, have costume parties, with festive foods and drinks to celebrate Halloween. It is a grand affair for those who participate. We wear costumes at other times as well, so to speak. In how we dress, or act, or speak, we sometimes disguise our real feelings. What mask are we putting on this day and what is really going on underneath the costume?

Let us always try to be ourselves in our own truths, the way God made us, regardless of the outer dress. Other people will usually see beneath the costume and mask anyway, so we may as well be *real* inside and out.

May we remain true to our inner nature no matter what costume we wear on any given day.

We remove our mask and reveal who we are behind it. Nothing can block the true nature of the Spirit.

We were quick to judge another by their clothes, until we took time to sit down and talk to them from the heart.

Create fun!

JOYOUS ANTICIPATION

November 1

May we arrange our life so that we always have something to look forward to.

Until recently, I had an aunt who I had nicknamed, "Auntie Mame." There was a real Auntie Mame who was the aunt of writer Patrick Dennis. He wrote a book about growing up in New York in the 1920s with his lively aunt, Mame Dennis. Both humorous and touching, his book was made into a Broadway musical and movie in the 1960s. Auntie Mame was a free spirit and a fun loving character, who also possessed a heart of gold. Fortunately, I had an aunt who was similar to Patrick's.

Once, years ago, when she saw me somewhat low-spirited, she told me that she only had one piece of advice to give me, "Always have a love in your life and always have something to look forward to." I have never forgotten her words of wisdom. Later, when I reflected on her advice, I realized the inter-changeability of the meaning of being *highly spiritual* and *high-spirited*. As we know, being *highly spiritual* does not necessarily mean we mediate for the rest of our lives in a cave in the Himalayas. It simply means that we have a good, sound connection with the given Spiritual Laws and Natural Laws of the Universe

May we keep our heart light, be spontaneous, and create a life of joy.

Light-hearted are the Angels. When we laugh, they celebrate with chimes and bells, whisking away our fears and sorrows.

The quality of Life is a choice.

THWARTING ILLNESS

November 2

May we have the resolve in our mind, body, and spirit not to buy totally into illnesses of any sort.

To a large extent, we are responsible for our health and well-being. Although the medical field is necessary at times, there is a large movement of integrative medicine and holistic approaches to our ailments. We can depend on doctors and specialists for our maladies, yet they only treat the symptoms of illness. There are more holistic ways of treating our ailments by treating the causes. At times, many of our illnesses begin with emotional stress of some sort.

Let us have more faith in the Creator to *uncreate* illness as much as possible, by doing our part to involve ourselves in more holistic approaches. When healing occurs in all aspects of a disease—emotional, physical, and spiritual—then we have a holistic sense of well-being. If we truly look at ourselves honestly, we can usually find the causes of most of our stresses. By simply identifying them, we are already on our way to health.

May we align all of our will and energy with the Creator's will and energy to help in *uncreating* our illness whenever possible.

Our Creator gave us a mind and heart to use and heal ourselves totally.

Kindle your hearth and share the warmth.

HEARTH

November 3

May we nurture ourselves with a hearth and a cozy home.

Now that the weather is getting colder, let us cherish the feeling of warmth in all its versatility. We can be grateful for our homes, our shelters to stay out of the weather when necessary. Staying warm by a fireplace is extremely healing. We can also experience warmth by being at peace with ourselves. When we carry serenity within, we exude warmth, and there is a glow about us. Love and light stream from our eyes, and there is a *softness* about our essences.

Let us make a point in any type of weather, to carry the sense of hearth and home internally and externally. This warmth truly is a gift from the Creator.

May we feel comfortable within our home today and treasure the comforts therein.

We can have the hearth of home at any time, wherever we may travel. May we find Peace in our heart and mind, for this is the gift of the Angels.

We all need to be acknowledged. Do not deny yourself
a friendly hello.

INNER CHILD

November 4

May we be attentive to the child within ourselves, through nurturance and support.

As adults, we act and react to life according to experience and given knowledge of what *works* and what does not *work* for us. Self-knowledge is a blessing from the Creator, giving us the freedom to live within our limits, whatever they may be, and to enjoy life.

Let us also be aware that within us all is a little child who loves spontaneity and laughter, is highly creative, extremely spiritual in nature, and who needs attention. Angels also nurture the inner child and prompt us to open ourselves to the wonder and awe of life. As sophisticated as we may become, let us always remember the little child inside who needs to love and to be loved. We can provide this nurturance in many innocent and creative ways.

May we spend some time today with our inner child, loving him or her with the Love of the Divine Mother.

We heard someone laugh, and we heard someone cry. It was the voice of our inner child, deep inside us. The Angels comfort this child and we, too, can nurture that part of us, which wants to heal and grow.

Deeper understanding of ourselves is found when we are
close to the earth.

NATIVE AMERICAN WISDOM

November 5

May we explore the wisdom of Native American culture.

Native Americans have an unusually basic approach to life, utilizing the four elements—earth, air, water, and fire. They believe in the all-nurturing Mother Earth and the illumination and wisdom of Father Sky, as well as the vision of the Four Directions. Native American wisdom has resurfaced today as many people look for simpler answers in their complicated lives. It is the simplicity of a culture remembered for its strength of heart that brings courage to our own hearts.

Let us be more in tune with the natural elements. Let us incorporate more wisdom in our personal lives and an appreciation for the earth, air, water, and sky. Our Creator wants us to have strong hearts, to love one another, and to forego cynicism and prejudice.

May we take courage and be of strong heart today, as we incorporate the teachings of a people who may share our ancestry.

Mother Earth below and Father Sky above support us and grant us the simple wisdom to love courageously.

Visualization is one of the most powerful tools known to man.

SUNSHINE

November 6

May we use our imagination today to incorporate the sunlight into every cell in our body.

Today, studies are showing the healing power of light. In moderate amounts, some find that the sun is actually good for us. If we find ourselves unable to take the extreme rays of the sun, let us find alternatives such as light bulbs that have the ingredients of the sun in them. When the weather becomes bleak as winter approaches, let us imagine the sun infiltrating our entire bodies with all the healing power it has to administer.

Let us try this *visualization* throughout the holidays and the winter months to create healthy minds, bodies, and spirits and to ward off the low feelings that sometimes accompany the rainy, cold days.

May we let the sunlight of God's spirit permeate our entire being and illuminate our heart and mind.

We stood within the sun's ray to enlighten our soul. Then, we found ourselves dancing in a lush, green forest. Happiness is in our heart. The Angels placed it there for our increasing delight.

Small minds create separation. Big minds unite
with all creation.

SMALL MIND, BIG MIND

November 7

May we learn to differentiate between the *small mind* of worldly concerns and the *big mind*, which is our connection to the Creator.

We all have concerns about certain people and about life itself. When we solely concern ourselves with the problems of mankind and how we relate to others, in either controlling or victimizing ways, we stay within the bondage of the *small mind*. Let us find a healthy balance. When we look to the Creator to solve the problems of the small mind, placing them in competent hands, we are instantly catapulted into the *big mind*. Let our prayers rise up to the Heavens like incense. Have faith that all small mind problems have a resting place with God. Ultimately, we cannot control people, places, or things.

Let us always know that God is in control and that our concerns will be resolved according to the will of our Creator. *Big deals* and *crises* seem to occur when we are in our *small minds*, whereas "all is well," exists in *big minds*.

May we find a healthy balance between the small mind and the big mind, knowing that our Creator will take care of all situations in the way of the Highest Good for all concerned.

When we turned our cares over to a Higher Power, we felt lightened and lifted in faith.

Close your eyes and let God move your feet.

LEAP OF FAITH

November 8

May we take that leap of faith into the unknown and trust that our Creator will take good care of us.

For some of us, trust does not come easily. Perhaps we have been disappointed by certain people and even have felt that our Creator has not clearly understood our prayers. Let us realize that people are fallible and will let us down at times. The Divine does answer our prayers, according to God's will, not ours.

It is when we are able to wholly trust God, with childlike faith, that we know the difference between our self-centered will and the Will of Heaven. This is not the same as leaping before we look. Instead, this is about a more blind faith in spiritual realms. We know that we cannot use our ordinary senses to understand it. Still, our continuous leaps of faith into the unknown can strengthen our intuition, as we get a sense of what will help us and what will not.

May we take that leap of faith to trust our Creator in all situations.

When we close our eyes and acknowledge the Divine, we can take that leap of faith with no doubt in our heart.

To use discernment in knowing when to speak up
is preserving dignity.

SPEAKING UP

November 9

May we learn how to speak up for ourselves with dignity, respecting ourselves and all concerned.

There are times when speaking up for ourselves is paramount. Let us be tactful when we do this, assuring respect for others while not neglecting our own needs. Speaking up for ourselves creates self-esteem, letting others know that we count and refuse to be used as doormats.

If we need assistance in speaking up for ourselves, let us ask our Angels to be present when we do this to insure the Highest Good for all concerned. We may be surprised to learn that, with Divine Assistance, we just may become orators!

May we speak *up* to the Angels when we need to speak up for ourselves.

Our Angels appeared when we asked for guidance, and we spoke with clarity, purity, and self-assurance.

Sometimes, we can cross an entire ocean with one tear.

OCEANS

November 10

May we use the healing quality of the ocean to open the oceans of awareness in our soul and spirit.

Walking on the beach—be it a gulf, a sea, or an ocean—has proven healing qualities. Our skin is able to absorb vitalizing minerals, such as the salt found in ocean water. The healing quality of saltwater can be found in tears as well. Tears are healing for the soul as they cleanse, wash, and restore the body/mind/spirit.

Let us find the awareness within our souls to really *feel* the oceans of different levels of consciousness, praying and meditating accordingly. Then let us ask ourselves if our oceans are turbulent or calm. Do we need to cry? How do we feel after crying? Is the ocean calmer afterward? There is nothing wrong with crying. Crying is a necessary part of life. Laughing to tears is also good for the soul.

May we wash and cleanse our spirit with the salt water offered to us by the ocean and our tears.

When we shed the tears of our soul, we heard the whisper of our Creator, and we were washed, balanced, and totally healed.

All life is a tragicomedy.

TRAGEDY TO COMEDY

November 11

May we look at our life's situations with a new perspective through the eyes of comedy.

There are certain times in life when all looks like doom and gloom. These are the times when it is necessary to step back and ask: Is there something constructive we can do about this situation? If there is, then we do it. If not, then try to accept it *as is*. Try stepping back from a more trying situation of sadness. What would our favorite comic say about using this situation or similar scenario? We can use our imaginations to add to or take away parts of the story to add humor. What could we say to ourselves or others that could help see the humor, if any? As far-fetched as it may seem, there are times when this can be helpful.

Laughter changes things. Laugh until the tears stream forth. It is the most healing thing one can do for oneself. Then just wait a moment, and you will probably feel differently. Think to yourself that this would make a great movie. This kind of thinking may be beneficial as a creative shift in perspective, making hilarious comedies out of horrendous tragedies. This is not to say that life cannot be extremely serious at times, for we are all aware of suffering. This is simply an invitation for us to lighten up a bit. Authors, playwrights, and screenwriters sometimes use this technique in their work. Literature defines this as comic relief! We all need a little comic relief in our lives.

Let us be more objective about ourselves today and see the humor involved.

We laughed and the Angels laughed with us.

Try to be grateful even when the chips are down.

LOW SPIRITS

November 12

May we accept the fact that sometimes we will be low in spirit, and that is all right.

Sometimes we may feel low in spirit, depressed, and just plain down. This does not mean that we are not good people or that our Creator Loves us any less. This is simply a time for introspection. Perhaps we are drained of energy. With less energy to give to others, we can draw upon faith in the Divine to nurture ourselves. After we give ourselves that warranted attention, we pray to move out of this state of mind. We need movement in order for this energy shift to occur. Physical exercise, for example, is a great motivator for low spirits to shift into higher gear.

Let us change our thinking and perspectives to, perhaps, be moving toward a lighter state of mind. As soon as we feel the energy shift, let us give thanks to the Creator for renewed inspiration.

May we not let our depression last too long and may we pray for our energy to return.

No one escapes the dark night of the soul, which is a necessary part of life. Take courage and know that the dawn does indeed exist.

The true source of real power lies with the Creator.

FINDING THE POWER

November 13

May we find strength by praying for our willpower to be aligned with the power of our Creator.

There are those times when we may be too exhausted and drained of strength to go on or to perform even the smallest task. If we have a moment to rest, let us attend to that. If we have obligations, let us pray to our Creator for the power, strength, and courage to keep going. Inside of us lies the will. When we focus on the Will and the Power of the Creator to guide us, we can move mountains. Like a laser beam, we are filled with Light and are once again strong, competent, and confident. There is much hope and faith involved here.

Let us use hope to the utmost. As we visualize each bodily cell rejuvenating and realigning with the Highest Energy, we naturally fill ourselves up with spiritual strength.

May we visualize the laser beam of White Light to connect our willpower in direct proportion to the power of our Creator's Love for us.

We have a purpose on Earth, as told to us by God. Finding this purpose by prayer is like a lightning rod, and the Love of our Creator is food that keeps us strong. We remember to keep our will aligned with God's will.

Vague intentions produce vague results.

CLEAR INTENTIONS

November 14

May our intentions be clear and specific. This way our Creator knows exactly our petitions.

When we pray, we need to have clear intentions in order to be heard. Yet, there are those times when we may feel uncertain as to what specifically to pray for. If our prayers and intentions are sincere, God hears us.

We do not have to be narrators to pray; our Creator sees our hearts and knows what we need even before we ask. However, we can do a little footwork and try to have clarity in our petitions. Perhaps it is as simple as praying for the clarity. As in drawing a map, we want it to be as clear as possible in order for the destination to be reached—so it is with our intentions.

May we pray with all of our energy, knowing that our intention is specific and knowing that the Creator hears our plea and will answer according to our needs, not always to our desires.

We sent our prayers to our Creator, and God knew what we needed.

All opposites exist as one in the same.

ILLNESS

November 15

May we understand that the nature of illness is actually healing.

There are those times when we become ill, no matter how much prevention we may take. Being physically ill can give the body a chance to build up its immune system again. Our bodies are miracle instruments in the way that they can heal themselves. If we find ourselves ill, let us be as compassionate with ourselves as possible, asking for guidance from our Guardian Angels.

Let us take an opportunity to spend some quiet time with ourselves and the Creator. We may want to use this time to be contemplative. This may also mean that the Divine guides us to the appropriate people whom may help us to heal.

May we know that illness may be the Creator's way to slow down our fast-paced lives and to give us the quiet time that we need for restoration and balance.

We were not feeling well, and our Angels told us, "It is time to slow down and treat yourself with compassion."

Good solutions are found by asking the right questions.

QUESTIONS

November 16

May we be Divinely guided to ask the right questions in life.

Much of living life is problem solving. As we age and experience more of life, we may find that living becomes more complicated. Obviously, the problems in adulthood are different than the problems of our adolescence. The elderly experience a different set of problems than do forty-year-olds. Yet, at the base of many of life's problems lies the important questions to ask ourselves in each case. The questions may be kept to ourselves or asked to others. In the asking of our questions, we may want to pray and set a good intention when we need help in finding our solutions, while keeping our motives honest and good.

Let us remember that our prayers are answered in God's time, not necessarily in ours. The important questions to ask in life may, or may not, be readily available to us. This is why prayer is a good spiritual tool to use in order for our questions to be Divinely guided, as well as the solutions found.

May our questions be sound, in order to find sound solutions to our many different problems in life.

Solutions and answers eluded us. We asked for Divine counsel until the most helpful questions to ask were clear and vivid.

One who is driven is inspired.

INSPIRATION

November 17

May we realize that we are guided by our Creator in all things and in all ways, and that we have a spiritual connection that can inspire us at any time.

We do not have to be in the *arts* to be inspired. It is true that artists, writers, and musicians are extremely inspired at times. Yet, we know that the spiritual connection to the Creator can inspire us at any given time and in many different ways. Certain people can inspire us. An uplifting movie, listening to a song, seeing birds in flight, and any number of things can move us into a Higher frame of mind. This could be called God-consciousness.

Let us allow ourselves to be inspired at any time and to express this inspiration in whatever way we choose.

May we use our inspired moments as a chance to connect with our Beloved Creator.

We saw a hawk in flight right in the middle of a large city one day. We knew an Angel had let us see it, and we were inspired by the awe. We had no words to say, only a majestic feeling that ran through our soul, as we were uplifted by the sight.

There is plenty of time to learn our lessons in the school of life.

EASY DOES IT

November 18

May we learn how much we are able to do in a day and to listen to our body's messages, so as to not overload our circuits.

We know that using a battery with too high a voltage for its purpose can burn out the whole connection. The same is true of the body/mind/spirit mechanism. We are composed of energy and light, alive with electrical impulses. It is important that the system rest regularly and eat healthy foods to keep it running smoothly. We also need a certain amount of intellectual stimulation to keep our minds keen. However, we do not need *burnout*, which leaves the mind/body/spirit system smoking with too high a voltage. A bit of physical exercise can be highly beneficial for our systems to work properly. Again, a healthy balance is necessary here as well. We do not want to overload the physical body's circuits with extremes. Out spiritual hunger is another one of the system's *food for life*—a longing and wishing to be uplifted and filled regularly.

Regardless of the way we choose to connect with a Loving Power greater than ourselves, it is sufficient fuel for nurturing our souls. Let us remember to balance and to use our common sense in keeping our bodies and minds healthy.

May we listen to our Creator's creation today—the mind/body/spirit mechanism—and treat it with respect.

It was when our circuits overloaded that we called to our Angels for comfort. They enveloped us in celestial winds of mercy and offered us deep rest and support.

Faith is more than a belief. It is a way of life.

REAFFIRMING FAITH

November 19

May we reaffirm daily faith in our Creator.

Spiritual life, involving a relationship with the Creator, is present every single day in our lives whether we may choose to recognize it or not. We are spiritual beings. Let us not identify too much with the body or worldly affairs. Instead, may we try living our days with more concern for spiritual essence, strong in knowing that our well-being and the well-being of others is in the hands of an all-loving, all-forgiving Creator. We will find that in identifying with our spiritual nature, a healthy body and mind simply fall into place to complete the sacred trinity. Life seems to flow much more smoothly when we loosen our grip on others and ourselves, understanding that all is well in God's world and the Divine Plan.

We are really the instruments through which Divinity flows and manifests itself in our daily lives. It is not necessary for us to have all the answers all of the time for everything. Our Creator has thought of everything already, down to the most minute detail. May we relax in our faith while trying to do, say, and think of our quest.

May we know, beyond a shadow of a doubt, that our entire life is a journey home to be one with our Creator.

Remembering is the soul's way of knowing when it sees the face of an Angel.

Being ignored is worse than negative reinforcement.

ACKNOWLEDGMENT

November 20

May we acknowledge the goodness within ourselves and acknowledge others' goodness as well.

People need to be acknowledged, for we all have goodness within us. When was the last time you told someone you loved them, appreciated them, or made someone's day special by pointing out one or two of their best characteristics? This becomes easier and easier to do when we are acknowledged by the Creator, ourselves, or someone else whom we respect.

Let us make this world a little happier each day by acknowledging each other. Even when another does not acknowledge us, we can still, by God's Grace, find the kindness within our hearts to acknowledge someone else. Sincerely acknowledging other's attributes can quickly put an end to envy, jealousy, and much useless negativity in our lives.

May we give ourselves positive strokes today and, in turn, pass them on to others.

The Angels asked us to help someone today. With their Support and Love, we were able to give a gift to others, without expectation of return.

The greatest strength is to first admit the weakness.

FROM WEAKNESS TO STRENGTH

November 21

May we become honest with ourselves and turn our greatest weakness into our greatest strength.

We all have our strong points as well as our weaknesses. If we are truly and rigorously honest with ourselves, we can identify our greatest weaknesses. After admitting our powerlessness over these weaknesses, we can turn to the Creator for the strength to change them into something Angelic. The real problem is our resistance to change. Yet we must realize that anything is possible with God's help. Once we overcome our difficulties, we can then help others to overcome theirs.

Let us remember that our purpose on Earth is to become as healthy as possible and to serve God and our fellow human beings in whatever capacity that may be.

May we rely on God to help us with our weaknesses and to evolve into the kind of human being, who is useful, aligning our self-will with the Will of our Creator.

We knelt in prayer, beaten down by our self-will gone astray. In our silence, we heard our Creator's voice saying, "We will give you strength to rise above your trouble, and We will transform the darkest night of your soul into Light and Love."

The Creator gives us gifts to give away freely.

CHARITY

November 22

May we do something a little special for someone else today.

Sometimes we become immersed in ourselves, our problems, and our lives. While appropriate time is needed to attend to our needs and daily affairs, let us also be aware of others' needs. Today let us do something a little extra for someone else. We do not need to be philanthropists to show charity. Perhaps a card, a helping hand, a smile, a rose, or a balloon would make someone else's day special.

Anything given with love is appreciated by the recipient. The Love Energy is exchanged and is felt on every level of our humanness. When pure Love is the motive in giving, everyone benefits.

May we step outside ourselves and give of ourselves today, making both our day and someone else's extra special.

We gave money to those less financially fortunate. That was called noble. We gave a hug to the despairing. Heaven called it Divine.

One can have 20/20 vision and still not see.

OPENING OUR EYES

November 23

May we open our eyes from a life clouded over with material darkness.

In our culture, possessions have significance, but only to a point. Sometimes a veil comes over our eyes. It is our responsibility to ask the Creator to gently remove the veil in order that we may see others and ourselves more clearly. Removing the veil is not always easy, and when we open our eyes, we also see deceit as well as beauty. It is our choice to see the good in life, while remaining realistic about the way much of the world is today. As we grow in life's experience and in spiritual awareness, these veils, or outer layers, are slowly shed to reveal our innermost beauty.

If there are obstacles to seeing our perfect souls as they were created, then let us use prayer and meditation to remove them. We will usually find that when we become more aware of God's original creations, the more goodness we can see in and around us.

May we become wise in all aspects of life while asking the Creator to lift our eyes to the illumination of the Heavens.

We have seen the world and choose to be uplifted with clear vision. We seek our own Truth, aligned with that of the Creator.

The heart is the greatest information center.

OPENING OUR HEARTS

November 24

May we go about our day with an open heart.

We may have gone through situations in our lives that have caused us to feel betrayed, disappointed, and unloved. These feelings close our heart. The Angels want us to see that we can trust the Creator and our Guardian Angels wholeheartedly. When we trust in the *unseen*, we are better able to trust ourselves, and eventually, we can trust in others by using our God-given discernment.

Let us open our heart to the possibility that Divine Love surrounds us at all times. When we tap into that Love, we can more clearly see the Love in others and ourselves.

May we open our heart and feel the beauty in our world, giving thanks for our Creator's Unconditional Love and Acceptance of us.

Opening our heart is like opening a new door, and we see the world and humanity in a more Loving Light.

A closed mind is like being trapped in a small room
with no door to open.

OPENING OUR MINDS

November 25

May we keep an open mind today.

We all have opinions and mindsets based on upbringings and personal experiences. However *set* we are in our prejudices, judgments, and opinions, we may want to try to be more open-minded to consider other options that may be involved. Let us create a world of harmony and peace by trying to see other points of view. While it is good to maintain certain beliefs that better others' and our own well-being, there will always be other people's beliefs and opinions in our world.

In our more quiet moments, we may want to reflect upon opening our hearts and minds more, and to think a lot less of who is *right* or *wrong*. Limited thinking can leave us bitter or self-righteous in the way we see the world. If our idea of God is Loving and Forgiving, then it would stand to reason that all people are Loved equally by this Peaceful Higher Power.

May we realize that everyone has different opinions, characteristics, and personalities and that we all have a basic desire to love and to be loved and accepted by God and our fellow human beings.

When we changed our perceptions to include the whole, we found a profound Love and Peace deep within.

One creates every time one speaks, thinks, or takes an action.

ARTISTS

November 26

May we understand that we are all artists in our own right.

We may believe that we cannot see ourselves as artists, unless we are able to draw and paint like Renoir or Picasso. However, we can view this concept a little differently by realizing that we all have our special talents. We each see the world differently from the next person, and it is this unique perception that makes us artists in our own right. Like Renoir or Picasso, we paint our perceptions of the world with our special thoughts, words, and deeds.

Let us paint our own pictures in life, inspired by the Creator and the Angels. Let us not be merely one of the thousands of prints that all look exactly alike.

May we draw our Truth today, and use the color of our personality to create a beautiful work of art.

We picked up the paintbrush of our Truth and Goodness. Our Angel guided our hand and we created a work of art that was beautiful in our sight.

Enchantment is living a full life.

ENCHANTMENT

November 27

May we see and feel the enchantment in life today.

Our imaginations are powerful. We can use this tool to find enchantment and mystery in our daily lives. When we are enchanted, we are able to turn dull situations into enriching, interesting ones. Let us use the eyes of enchantment to see ourselves as our Creator sees us—beautiful and filled with Light. In this way we can make harsh realities into wonderful fantasies of prisms, sunshine, and colorful dreams. The magic of enchantment happens when we allow ourselves to shift our perceptions of any person, place, or thing.

Perhaps we know someone who awes and inspires us. These people are incredibly valuable in our lives as we marvel at their wondrous stories, their positive attitudes, and their colorful slants on life. We, too, have the power to color our world with our God-given imaginations and ways we view life.

May we use our God-given imagination to place a little more color in our life and to see ourselves in a world of wonder and enchantment.

We were cold and shivering in the dungeon of worldly reality. Then an Angel covered us with a purple velvet cape, and our world became an enchanting story.

*Frustration is like quicksand. The more one struggles,
the more problems one creates.*

FRUSTRATION

November 28

May we find constructive ways to let off steam today.

Do you ever feel so frustrated that you feel you could *blow* at any moment? At times, depending upon our personalities and past experiences, we may say we are like "walking time bombs"—feeling restless, irritable, and discontented. There are ways to let the steam out of the pressure cooker. We may have to pound a pillow, or find a way to scream or rant and rave to a trusted friend or therapist, or partake in a vigorous physical workout. In whatever healthy ways we are able to let it out, it is better than keeping it pent up inside and taking the anger and frustration out on others or ourselves.

Watching a movie can also help us live our own drama through the characters involved on the screen. Humor is also a powerful tool to try to use when we feel frustrated. Everyone has a way to let off steam in our sometimes crazy life. Some people yell at God, and that is all right, too. Cosmic demerits are not given for our frustrated moods and actions, as long as we try to conduct them in a constructive manner. Being angry at the Higher Power is usually momentary. We should know we are not judged, but instead, forgiven. We will soon find that beneath the frustration, that we are moved to tears as the fear and hurt surface. It is usually fear and hurt that underlie our feelings of anger and frustration. Let us be assured that the Creator and the Angels never leave us, even when we do not feel as if we have any love to give.

May we receive Unconditional Love and Acceptance from the Creator and try to love ourselves just as we are.

We yelled loudly at the Heavens above. Our voices were heard, and the Heavens rained down Acceptance and Love.

If you want to know human Angels, just ask them into your life.

HUMAN ANGELS

November 29

May we trust our heart to recognize human Angels in our life.

Our Creator places people in our lives for a reason. There are no accidents or coincidences. Some people come into our lives when we need help the most—in whatever capacity. These people are special to us. Let us recognize these people and be glad that they are a part of our lives. At times, we may find ourselves needing new information and inspiration in order to grow and evolve into our own Angelhood. We then can pray to the Creator or a Guardian Angel to place new *Angels* in our lives, and to allow us to be another's human Angel. When we connect with our own Angelhood we can, in turn, be more open to let other Angels into our lives.

Let us make a conscious effort to look within our hearts and into the hearts of others to see pure and simple Human Angelhood.

May we invite the Angels into our life—both Spiritual and Human.

When we are in our Angelhood, miracles are an everyday occurrence.

Feeling uncomfortable can be the greatest motivator.

FEELING UNCOMFORTABLE

November 30

May we realize that there are times in our life when we feel uncomfortable, yet there is peace and serenity on the other side.

Are we willing to feel uncomfortable for a while in order to get to the other side? We need to know what our work is and our attitude toward it. We know, deep down inside, that our Higher Power is in charge and has our life interwoven into the Divine Plan. Let us realize that the effort we put forth in our lives is equally proportionate to the amount of satisfaction, serenity, and gain that we will receive. The Creator urges us to grow and evolve. The Divine will give all of the support needed to help us do what is in the Highest Good for all concerned.

Let us remember not to blame others for our feelings of discomfort. Instead, let us recognize in ourselves whatever the problem concerns. We may wish to pray for the insight to be revealed to us as to the deeper meaning of our discomfort. Then, we can pray for the most constructive solution to it. Ways of healing ourselves, be it physically, emotionally, or spiritually, are always available to us, if we search for them. Solutions sometimes are merely an asking away.

May we understand that when we do something good for ourselves, the Angels act as cheerleaders and will see us through the sweat and tears of our endeavor.

We cried for mercy, and the Angels heard us. They gave comfort to our pleading spirit.

All life is about relationship.

RELATIONSHIPS

December 1

May we cherish our relationships today and be grateful for the people in our life.

Much has been written and spoken about relationships. All of us are involved in relationships to varying degrees, with or without significant others at our sides. Our immediate families, interest groups, pets, coworkers, friends, and the Creator all fall into the category of relationships. Let us nurture our relationships as we would a garden—watering, adding nutrients, weeding, and exposing all parts to the sunlight. All relationships come from the Creator who would have us learn to love all persons who we come in contact with each day.

Let us always remember our relationship to the Creator who has blessed us with people in our lives. It is the most important relationship we can cultivate. Whatever may happen with our human relationships, the Creator is a consistent and steadfast friend who will not betray, disappoint, or leave us.

May we cultivate our relationship with our Creator and give thanks for those people who are a part of our life.

The Angels smiled upon a lonely heart and gave them a friend.

Grandiosity is not following instructions.

FOLLOWING INSTRUCTIONS

December 2

May we recognize the need to follow instructions at those times when certain areas of our life seem out of control.

If we find ourselves overly self-willed and compulsive at times, then we may be the kind of people who have addictive personalities. If we want to rid ourselves of an addiction, we need guidance and support from the Creator and others who have overcome their particular addictions. The first impulse is to try to use willpower and do it alone. Yet, when doing so, we find that it is too difficult. This is when a Twelve-Step program is helpful. Instead, let us gather information about our addictions, lean on others for support for awhile, try to stay out of self-pity, and pray to the Creator for the grace and willingness to go to any lengths to overcome our addictions.

We find if we follow, exactly, the instructions of the healthy people who offer support and love, we will feel as they do in time—free of addiction. This clarifies what it means to surrender our will to the Creator's Will. Peace will come eventually.

May we allow ourselves to follow healthy leaders instead of trying to do everything our way, which, if we are still in the throes of addiction, obviously will not work.

We prayed for willingness to overcome our resistance to instructions, and the Angels were there to comfort and guide us to those with a map to freedom.

We have a choice in being who we want to be.

PROGRAMMING THE MIND

December 3

May we program our mind with positive affirmations regarding the wholeness of sound body/mind/spirit.

Today with certain television shows, radio, music lyrics, computers, and movies, we may be buying into fear-based ways of thinking. The opposite of fear is Love. Let us begin to move away from selective media programming and live more in a world of healing, thinking for ourselves. Frequencies from the media have a profound effect even on the cells in our bodies. We can move toward more positive programming, affirming beauty and Love. The news seems designed to show us a world of prejudice, hate, fear, and worry—all negative programming. Try taking a "news break" for awhile.

Let us explore our own hearts and others' hearts, the healing arts, and nature, thereby exposing our minds to the goodness in the world. Remember, what we put into our minds is what comes out.

May we be aware of the perils of the world, yet not succumb to fear.

We find Love and beauty in the deep meditative state, and this Peace travels with us in the positive world that we create with the Angels by our side.

All we need from emotional pain is understanding.

SUFFERING

December 4

May we learn from our suffering, strive to see the Light, and understand that some pain is necessary on our spiritual path.

Not all people learn by suffering, yet it is likely that some pain will come into ours and others' lives. Some learn simply from past mistakes and move on, having minimal amounts of suffering in their lives. According to the Buddha, suffering is the way to Enlightenment. In our suffering, let us know deeply that the Creator Loves us, as do the Angels.

If we are the type of people who *feel* to a great degree, let us be assured that there are always paths to the Light of Christ, Buddha, Krishna, Mohammed, or whichever Light is our inspirational preference. In the midst of suffering, let us always remember to ask if there is a lesson to be learned. Instead of asking the question, "Why?" We ask, "What for?"

May we realize that though we may have trials of suffering, others also suffer at times, and still others do not know that they suffer at all.

Should we stumble and fall, we pray to be resurrected and know Peace and Oneness within the compassion of the Eternal Womb of Goodness.

*Anything is possible in the Creator's world. All we need to do
is to tap into the line.*

UNCONDITIONAL JOY

December 5

May we learn the Angels' secret of unconditional joy.

Life is not meant to be a laborious struggle all of the time,
according to the Angels. There is joy to be found in our world, if
we choose to see it. At times, we may feel on top of the world for
no apparent reason. If we believe in Angels, we will know that
they are close to us at these times.

The next time we feel unconditional joy, let us thank the
Creator and the Angels. On the same note, when our friends feel
joyful, let us celebrate in their joy—creating what the Buddhists
call Sympathetic Joy. Joy, like laughter, can be contagious.

> *Joy in us—joy in you—*
> *Unhappiness just said, "toot-el-loo."*
> *You laughed first, then we joined in*
> *This is where Unconditional Joy begins.*

May we receive the spontaneity and playfulness of the
Angels today and feel total joy.

The Angels are always near. It is our job to call upon them.

Failure is a misnomer. There is a lesson not yet learned.

LIGHT ON FAILURE

December 6

May we realize that we may have disappointment, but that the most important aspect of *failure* is to keep trying.

What is your definition of failure? Let us not identify ourselves by this limiting term, rather we keep picking ourselves up should we happen to stumble and fall. All life experiences are for the benefit of learning lessons. We can pray to the Creator for the insight and clarity to see our situations more objectively in order to prohibit ourselves from continuing to make the same mistakes.

Let us ask the Angels to comfort us when we are disappointed in ourselves or others, and to see the humor in our situations within the full scope of our lives' journeys. God gives us the strength and courage to keep getting back up should we be struck down.

May we not measure our disappointments in life by society's view of failure, but by our own personal gauge of intuitive happiness.

Should we fall, we will be uplifted once again, and when we look back, we will see the lesson our Creator teaches.

*If the world were not evolving there would be
no such thing as time.*

EVOLVING

December 7

May we evolve more each day into the person our Creator
intended us to be.

Wherever we are in our stages of development, we can
always pray to awaken a little more each day to the dawning of
our inner natures. Our inner natures, our souls, our spiritual
essences are pure and good. These qualities are present in
everyone, and each person's soul awakens to the Light of its
essence in its own time.

Let us accept our personal growth as an awakening process
and realize that we are exactly where we are supposed to be in
our life's journey—all evolving back to the Light from which we
came. In that Perfect Light, we are wise, beautiful, and joyful. We
are loving and filled with goodness. This is how we each come
into this life at birth. This is where we each go back to after our
life's journey is finished.

May we pray for the insight to *wake up* to our Truth and our
soul's Pure Essence.

*We went within and prayed for a revelation. What we found
was a creative well from which to constantly draw inspiration.*

Even a setback is a step toward progress.

PROGRESS

December 8

May we progress upon our spiritual path.

Life is a journey, filled with moments of joy, disappoint-ments, and a rich array of events. It is how we view the events and situations that happen to us that make for a quality life. We can look back on our lives and see how we have progressed. If we believe in a Creator, we can see how this Omnipotent Being has brought us to the point where we are today. It is a relief and a comfort to believe in and depend upon a Creator. As we go through our lives, following a spiritual path, we learn that the journey itself is all that is necessary. We do not have to be perfect in our spiritual quests. As long as we are progressing in our journey, that is what matters most.

Let us keep following spiritual paths realizing that even in the throes of discouragement, we are progressing toward the Love and Light inside us all.

May we continue to look for the Highest Good our Spirit has to offer.

Should we become weary, we can ask an Angel to help us carry our load.

We are on Earth because we choose to be.

REMEMBERING

December 9

May we remember those with whom we have shared special times.

Let us not forget those who have meant something to us during our lives. We are in the holiday season and this time of year is filled with memories, reflections upon others and upon our own lives. There is another form of remembering, too. This is remembering by the soul's definition. Let us remember that we are God's children. We are on a spiritual journey to find the Creator's Essence in our lives. As we grow and evolve on our spiritual paths, let us always remember those special people who have helped us along the way.

We may have glimpses into our true selves, as well, remembering and knowing that we are indeed spiritual beings and are living out our souls' scenarios on Earth, constructed by the Divine, prior to our birth. Our soul chose to come into human form in order to grow and evolve into Our Higher States of Consciousness. According to the Law of Karma, each soul has its work to do here on Earth—perhaps to take care of some unfinished business from a previous lifetime. There comes a time when that soul remembers why it came to live in human form. This moment could be called a spiritual awakening.

May we find the deep meaning of our soul's source by remembering who we truly are—a beautiful and loving child of the Creator.

We looked into the eyes of a child and saw our self and our God.

The Creator is the headmaster of Earth School.

DIVINE TEACHING

December 10

May we teach that which the Divine has so benevolently taught us.

If we should receive insights from communion with the Divine, it may be helpful to share these with others in order to be the most beneficial we can be. Our Creator will teach us many lessons in life. This is what life is all about. The trick is to learn the lessons and then be available to others, be of assistance, and serve through the Divine Power within us. Each of us has much to teach others and much to learn from them as well. One way to look at life is through the eyes of being students and teachers. Sometimes we can be both student and teacher at the same time.

There may be times when we are called on to lead others in some way. In turn, there are times when we need to be followers. Living life has so much to teach us. It may be wise to keep an open heart and mind to receive the deeper understanding therein.

May we use our intuition to give and receive that which the Divine has lovingly bestowed upon us.

We learned something today, and the Angels encouraged us to share it with others.

We can have big goals, as long as we use
little goals to get there.

GOALS

December 11

May we rest assured that when we have a goal that involves the Highest Good for all concerned, our Creator will take care of the details.

We may want to establish those goals that have the best interest for all others and ourselves. We may want to reexamine our goals if we are only concerned with self benefit. We can set more goals that are inspired from the Creator. When we have good-hearted goals, we know that they are in the Highest Good for all concerned. If we are worried about details, let us ask the Angels to arrange the *lights, sound,* and *action* of this picture. It is most wise to allow God to be the Director.

With a little prayer, even a small, short-term goal can be a beautiful work of art. We know when our goals are Divinely Inspired, when our Angels immediately go to work on the details. That which we can envision is that which can be attained.

May we set our goals and attain them, remembering to give the credit to the Divine Master Planner.

Say a prayer and be uplifted. Notice how your whole perspective has shifted toward the Highest Good.

The entire secret to life is contained in one small flower.

FLOWERS

December 12

May our innermost being blossom and grow, in its own time, into a beautiful flower.

We have all witnessed the beauty and aroma of blooming flowers. In budding and blooming, it takes a lot of energy on the part of the plant to put forth a flower. Let us respect this incredible work of nature. When we look at our own essences, we realize that humans, too, can put forth the Spiritual Energy to flower and bloom, radiating beauty from the inside out.

Let us evolve into what the Creator wants us to be—the Spirit of Love and Light, which is what we actually already are, although we may not be aware of it. Like a wildflower growing in the wilds, weathering storms, rain, heat, and wind, we too, have most likely weathered a few storms in our lifetime. Still, in spite of those storms, the wildflower is stronger than we may think they would be—maintaining its beautiful and colorful bloom. Humans, as well, are most likely a lot stronger than they may think they are—especially during tough times. May we be ever grateful for these gifts of beauty and strength.

May we show our true spiritual colors by taking the time to nurture the sunlight within our soul into a flower whose aroma sweetens all of life.

We are a living plant that will someday produce a beautiful flower. The tenderness of the Angels is showered upon our soul.

Wake up! Remember your dreams.

DREAMING

December 13

May we be healed in our dreams.

We, most likely, go through phases in our lives of remembering and not remembering our dreams. Our physical body shuts down when we sleep and our subconscious mind takes over when we are in the dream state. Let us learn from our dreams and know that they are necessary for the deepest healing of the body/mind/spirit. There is much symbolism in our dreams. Some say that we play all the roles found in our dreams. They represent different aspects of ourselves. Even what we consider to be nightmares have a great deal of healing contained in them.

It may be helpful to keep a notebook by our beds at night to record our dreams. This is like keeping a dream diary. We may find those people in our life who are able to give credible interpretations of our dreams. We can go over our dream diary with them to gain deeper understanding. Let us take a deeper look at our lives—conscious and unconscious—to find out what the Creator wants us to know that may be hidden in our Higher selves.

May our dreams be of the Angels and their message.

Dreams come from the Heavens above, and even the most frightening ones contain the Love of the Angels.

Feeling young is not necessarily a state of mind.
It is a state of heart.

YOUNG ENERGY

December 14

May we constantly renew ourselves and keep *young energy* in our hearts and minds.

Do you feel energized right now, or do you feel drawn and worn out? There are many natural and holistic ways to rejuvenate oneself these days. The Angels are expert, natural energizers. We can pray to find ways to relieve the tension held in our bodies and minds. Choices range from yoga, to herbs, to martial arts, to massage, just to name a few. Travel, developing interests, and keeping and open, ever-curious mind helps tremendously. Life is full of wonder and mystery. There are chiropractors who work with the natural flow of *prana* or *chi* (the Indian and Chinese words for the life energy force). We have endless choices today in rejuvenating ourselves.

Let us look forward to staying young in heart and mind. Let us be mindful to breathe young energy into our bodies, coupled with prayer, to reenergize ourselves while treasuring the wisdom we have gained throughout our years. With a little research, we can explore what keeps our bodies and minds young.

May we constantly find natural ways to feel the Life Energy, abundant and flowing through every cell of our body.

The Angels gave us an inspired meditation to use, and we were energized by renewed life flowing through us.

Celebrate all of your Teacher's birthdays.

CHRISTMAS SPIRIT

December 15

May we receive the true gift of Christmas—a loving, Christ-filled spirit of Peace and Compassion in our hearts to share with others.

The most simple and inexpensive gift we can give ourselves and others at Christmastime is to pray and reflect on the qualities of Christ. With the Christ-like Spirit, we can bring joy into this world. Let us take a moment to think about the Christ child and what exactly that child meant to the world. When we meditate on this master's teaching, we can feel Christ's Peace fill our hearts. As our hearts become full of this Peace, Compassion, and Light, we are better able to allow the Spirit to flow from our hearts into the hearts of others.

Let us reflect on the truths that Christ has brought into the world. We need not necessarily be dogmatic Christians to feel this Peace, but simply be open to the Universal Love and Light that exists in all people, creatures, and all things.

May we all carry the Christ Light in our hearts and souls at this wonderful time of year.

Just as an Angel appeared to Mary and Joseph in the Bible, so can an Angel appear to us in a white-spirited glow. We cherish this Christ-Light within our eternal soul and carry a kind and benevolently open heart.

If you fall out of love with another, fall in love with yourself.

BEING IN LOVE WITH LIFE

December 16

May we fall in love with life itself.

Our lives are gifts from the Creator. What we do with them in turn are our gifts to the Infinite and Eternal God. If we seek God first, the Angels align with us, assisting us in being the best we can be at all times. When one seeks the Divine, it becomes one's life focus instead of merely a task to do. Loving God comes naturally to us when we get a glimpse of the Unconditional Love and Acceptance, which the Creator never ceases to have for every soul. This is when we fall in love with our lives, assured that the Creator is guiding us in all that we do, say, think, and feel.

Let us always remember that we are held in the loving arms of the Universe and that we are Divinely guided and protected each and every day. When we find our true purpose, the Divine Universe itself employs us. We are working for the Heavenly Father and the Divine Mother—our Spiritual Parents and Employers.

May we receive the greatest gift of loving God and of falling deeply in love with our life.

We see the Beauty and Love in our God and in our life. When we awaken to the Divine, suffering diminishes.

Any gift should be received as a gift from the Creator.

THE THOUGHT THAT COUNTS

December 17

May we be grateful for all gifts given to us, however great or small, and have the clarity to acknowledge the thought and love that goes with them.

There is an art to receiving a gift from someone, even more than our giving to another. It is customary, for most of us in America, to give presents to others at Christmastime. A lot of people become a bit overwhelmed during this gift-giving season. One reason for stress may be due to the costs of buying those gifts. Out gifts to others do not necessarily need to cost a lot to bring joy to another's eyes. The loving thought behind gift-giving is what really matters. Let us be grateful for what we receive from others. It could be a loving smile, a soft look in the eyes, a short note during the holidays, or any number of other pleasant gestures.

Let us be open and sensitive enough to see the Spirit that goes with any gift given to us. Let us be grateful for the gifts from the Divine that we receive each day.

May we awaken to the God behind all gifts we receive.

We see the Love in the smallest gesture and accept it as a great gift.

Be rich in Spirit. Your cup is overflowing with what
you already have been given.

ABUNDANCE

December 18

May we be wealthy in Spirit, Character, and Goodness.

A dictionary definition of abundance is "an overflowing fullness." What does an overflowing fullness mean to you? Money? Prestige? Decadence? Chocolate? Worldly Possessions? Let us examine the deeper meaning of this word. Let us look within our souls. Our Creator wants us to live lives of overflowing fullness, rich in Spirit, Love, and Harmony. We are truly fortunate if we possess loving hearts, overflowing to others. The Angels want us to be filled up with Love, as well.

For all that we have, let us give thanks to God and the Angels, and know that they have our best interests at heart. Should monetary wealth be included in our abundance, let us spend it or give it away wisely and be forever grateful to the Creator for this energy force.

May we live abundantly in the spirit of Love and Light.

We all have Love and Light available to us in enormous quantities. The Heavens supply us with all that we need to be healthy, spiritual, and free from suffering.

Champagne comes in other forms besides alcohol.

NATURAL HIGH

December 19

May we be inspired and live in a world of natural highs.

The Angels are experts on natural highs! They love to inspire us to raise our consciousness to spiritual bliss. The Angels also love it when we laugh and think humorous thoughts. Perhaps a breath of cold, fresh air can awaken us or inspire us. You can find your own natural highs in life. Endorphins, the body's natural opiates, are released when we feel love flowing into or out of us.

When we lift our minds from the world to the Heavens, when we laugh, and in countless other ways, the body releases these natural *feel goods*. Nothing is more real and lasting than a natural high. When was the last time you sat out in the open night air and looked up at the billions of stars and the moon, feeling the breeze blow across your face? Whatever it may be that uplifts your spirits in the natural world, that is your joy and blessing from above.

May we find natural ways of being Divinely inspired and uplifted.

We found a friend who encouraged us, and we were uplifted to a more natural and spiritual reality.

Be a beacon of light in the dark so that someone else may see.

STRONG HEART

December 20

May we be of strong heart, radiating a beam of light from our heart-centers out into the world.

To be strong in heart means to possess the humility to be open and vulnerable, without fear, loving all humanity unconditionally. Visualize, in your moments of quietness, a beam of white light traveling from your heart-center to the outside world. Send your love and peace to all beings. This is how world peace is activated. Can you imagine that if every human practiced this, what kind of world we would have? Remember: world peace starts with each of us individually, and then spreads the peace to all others. Others will feel this love, consciously or subconsciously, and will be the better for it.

When sending out the Beacon of Love, let us feel the Angels smile. When we have been awakened to the Light of the Universe inside of us, it is our responsibility to shed the light upon others.

May we radiate our strong heart to all beings; sending Love and Peace unconditionally out into the world.

We connect our open heart to the entire Universe. The magnitude of our profound strength from God opens the door for another soul to lightly tread in this world.

The mere thought of lighting a candle is a prayer in itself.

LIGHTING CANDLES

December 21

May the Love of our Creator be a flame to enlighten ourselves and to light the candles in the hearts of others.

Let us notice what happens when we light a candle: total darkness ends, a soft glow appears around the candle, and a mood is set. It is our Creator who lights the candle flame in our hearts. This flame is Love and can be acknowledged as a symbol for the Unconditional Love that our Creator has for us. Let this flame grow in our hearts and enlighten our minds, and let the glow flow out to others.

We may want to light white candles often as a symbol of the Divine Healing Light of the Universe. Some use different colored candles for different reasons, assigning different meanings to each color. Some light a black candle to represent the Loving Light of the Creator in the midst of darkness. Catholic ceremonies utilize the lighting of candles as prayers to heal themselves or others. Scented candles are popular these days to enhance the air that surrounds us. This may be a part of aromatherapy that many use for healing and creating different moods.

May we feel the glow of Love in our heart and mind, lighting candles for ourselves and other people.

We lit a candle and prayed, and we saw Love and Light everywhere.

Love all seasons equally and know balance.

WINTER

December 22

May we celebrate each day of winter, as the days grow longer and more light is available to us, little by little every day.

The day of darkness is past. The day before the first day of winter is the shortest day of the year. Now today, the first day of winter, we turn our faces toward the Light. Today, the winter solstice is truly one of celebration. Let us be joyful that more Light is coming our way. Let the Angels lighten our hearts and uplift us—turning our faces toward the sun—uplifting our minds and souls to the Creator.

May the light of longer days shed light onto all issues that we may have processed during the fall. We may want to allow our deeper and busier thoughts to lie semidormant in the cold, like seeds that will come alive in the nearing springtime. We let ourselves relax more now, coupled with the anticipation of busier days ahead in the warmer seasons.

May we see the Light within our soul as well as the sunshine that illuminates our entire being.

Light, light, light! A celebration! We turn our faces to the sun at our Creator's invitation.

Fellowship is love personified.

UNITY

December 23

May we feel the closeness of friends, family, and other significant people in our life in the unity of the Holy Spirit this season.

We all have made progress in our lives, whether subtle or profound. Whether we see it or not, we can rest assured that we indeed are in the process of growing toward the Light. Let us remember all those who have helped us along and always keep the Creator close in our hearts. As we gather this Christmas season, let us really feel the unity of the Holy Spirit and acknowledge the Light within our souls. Let us feel connected to others who may also share like-minded ideas or those who have new ideas to share.

At Christmastime, unity may mean gathering with family members. Whatever our ideas of fellowship are, we carry the Spirit of Love within our beings each and every day. Remember that humans are not meant to be isolated. If we know of those persons who may not have a family of any kind, we may wish to include them in our own gatherings, making them feel warm and welcomed by our hearth.

May we always remember that we are one with our Creator and all souls. This connection is Love, Light, and Goodness.

The age of separateness is past. We can all work together for the Love of God, which is the True Lasting Love.

Should you find yourself alone, let the Creator be your
"significant other."

RELATIONSHIP WITH GOD

December 24

May we nurture and cultivate our relationship with the God of our understanding.

Do you have a concept of God? People around the world, whatever their beliefs, usually know about a Higher Power in their culture. When we think of God, we think of a Good Force, a Light, a Refuge, and a Higher Love.

Let us nurture and grow in our personal relationship to God, with a deep and sound knowing that we are guided by our Creator in all things and in all ways. Let us place God first in our lives, realizing that this is the First Relationship. When we fall in Love with God, we fall in love with ourselves and eventually with others, wishing only Goodwill to all in the Highest Spiritual Sense. This is truly the Highest Love. We are all Divinely guided and protected each day, whether we maintain any belief at all. Notice how fear diminishes when compared to the profundity of God's Love.

May we learn to love God with our entire body/mind/spirit.

"Give Thanks to God," say our Angels. "Let the Almighty be the wind for your sails. The direction is Holy, Good, and Pure. The Divine ship is sound, strong, and sure."

Christ is a perfect example of a spiritual being having a human experience.

THE CHRIST-LIGHT

December 25

May we carry in our heart the compassion and grace of the Christ-Light.

Christ is known as the Savior in many parts of the world. Our Creator gave us His Light and Love on Earth through this man. He performed miracles and healed many people in the name of God. Jesus claimed to be the Son of God, and many followed his teaching during his lifetime. We are all aware of how Christ's impact on Earth resonated out to touch the lives of billions of people to date.

Christianity is the largest religion in the world today. Many, many people put their trust and lives into the hands of Jesus Christ and find peace and refuge there. Whether we follow Jesus' teachings totally or not, whether we celebrate the birth of Christ today or not, we can still align our consciousness with the gentle, loving spirit of Christ's Light. Whatever our conception of a Creator may be, we always have available to us, throughout the world, a Loving image of Christ. May we rest in the assurance that we are never alone in this world. Christ loves all beings and creatures on Earth equally.

May we contemplate the immense Love and Compassion of Christ today and know that we are Loved and Accepted Unconditionally.

With gentleness of Spirit and Grace we see Christ's glowing face in the Light.

Receiving in grace is a virtue not to be taken lightly.

RECEIVING

December 26

May we learn to receive others and their gifts with grace and enthusiasm.

We all know how to give of ourselves, our time, and our service to others. Yet do we know how to receive these same gifts from others? Do we appreciate the quality of their time, their kind words, and their offerings and tell them so? Let us learn to receive in grace and joy as well as to give. Let us remember that others love to give just as much as we do. Most people like to feel useful and needed to a substantial degree. When we shun their compliments or discount what they are sincerely trying to say to us, we are saying to that person that their thoughts and feelings do not count.

Whether we truly believe a compliment that is given to us or not, let us thank the other person for it and acknowledge their thoughts. Appreciation of what others give to us helps them to feel useful, as well as happy to be the giver. Let us allow others to feel appreciated by their giving to us. Let us rejoice in the true spirit of reciprocity.

May we give others the benefit of showing their affection and love to us, and to see their gifts in the Divine Light.

We allowed another the pleasure of their heartfelt giving and saw within their eyes the joy that softens and uplifts.

*One who can thank God at the end of a hellacious day
will know delight.*

DELIGHT

December 27

May we delight in the beauty of the physical and spiritual realms.

The word delight simply implies a *joy*, and this word even sounds joyful. We all know this word according to the senses—when we giggle, or eat something new that tastes marvelous, when we observe nature in new ways, and also when we are inspired by the Divine. Delight means different things to different people. Let us be aware of what delights us and take it a step further, spreading the joy to others. As in the physical realm, let us also delight in the spiritual realm, our relationship with the Creator.

Let us take delight in meaningful meditation, a spiritual walk in the woods, or any other way we make conscious contact with God. Let us remember to share our joy and live in delight.

May we delight in the world of the senses in healthy ways, as well as in the Angelic world of the Divine.

*When our Angels took our hand and smiled, we delighted in
their gentle Peace that helped our Spirits to soar.*

Only the Creator can see the sincerity placed into effort.

EFFORT

December 28

May we take credit for our efforts and turn the outcome over to the Divine Creator.

The Creator sees our innermost hearts. For example, when we pray for a change of heart or to live in a more God-like way, the Divine hears these prayers. God will give us the strength to place our prayers into action. Even if we fall short of our Highest Goals, our Creator sees and smiles upon our efforts. If we are persistent in our efforts, the Highest Goal will eventually be attained. Let us not be discouraged by our unsuccessful efforts, yet have faith and take comfort in our beliefs. The enthusiasm that we put forth in our efforts makes the Angels want to help us even more.

Let us remember that when we make a God-centered decision, the entire Universe aligns with us in all that we think, say, and do. Everything works for us in the manifestation of our goals. Then we notice how our efforts become effortless when guided by the Divine.

May we make our petitions wholesome.

We prayed and then let go of the outcome. We knew our Creator and our Angels had our best interest in their hearts.

Is there only one road leading to a large city?

MANY PATHS TO GOD

December 29

May we walk a spiritual path that speaks to us—body/mind/spirit—and realize that all paths lead to the Supreme One.

Let not a harsh, strict, or fearful doctrine of religion discourage you from your idea of a Loving Creator. Dogma is of man; spiritual Truths are of God. Do not limit yourself with guilt from a vengeful, fear-producing God. Times are changing. We are fortunate in America to choose, believe, and follow any spiritual path we choose.

Let us choose paths where Love and Light prevail. Let us shake off the old conditioning and think for ourselves, knowing that our sincerest requests are acknowledged by a Loving and Forgiving Creator. God speaks to many different people in many different ways.

May we use our own discernment in choosing a path to the Creator, not simply and blindly following the flock.

> *We met a Hindu—he loved God,*
> *We met a Buddhist—she loved God,*
> *We met Christians—they loved God,*
> *We met ourselves face to face*
> *in the quiet realm of our meditation,*
> *And tears flowed from our eyes,*
> *We comprehended God's Love for us*
> *And our own love for the Divine.*

We can, indeed, have Heaven on Earth.

EGO VERSUS SPIRIT

December 30

May we rest assured that one day our ego will no longer wrestle with our spirit.

As we live and evolve, each day growing closer to the Creator, we may feel the anguish, at times, of our egos fighting with our spirits. Let us not be discouraged by these feelings or thoughts. Rather, let us be encouraged that we are on a road to progress, not perfection As we meditate, the struggle between spirit and ego lessens and is replaced with the calm peace of knowing that we are embraced by the arms of the Creator and the Divine Mother. The key is to persevere in our growth toward God. The spirit world can be ours on Earth.

Each day, as we remember to center ourselves in God consciousness and as we surrender our wills to the will of Heaven, we notice that we have less of the fear, which is basically egocentric in nature. When the focus is on the Unconditional Love that God has for us, our egos seem minuscule in comparison.

May we set our eyes upon the spirit world and cease the struggle between ego and spirit.

We knew the spirit world before our birth, and we realize that it is possible to have Heaven on Earth.

Take a day off from self-criticism.

CONGRATULATING YOURSELF

December 31

May we review the past year and congratulate ourselves for the work we have done on ourselves and for others.

As we review the past year, let us take stock of the good we have done. Of course, we have also had tribulation. Yet, let us concentrate on the positives of the year as we reflect. We are more mature and wise. We have learned more lessons from our experiences and are more connected to the Creator.

Let us be proud of ourselves, hug ourselves, and congratulate ourselves for any and all work well done. When was the last time you gave yourself a hug? Hug yourself tightly and stand tall in the acknowledgment of all of your accomplishments thus far in life. The Angels are indeed, smiling down upon us. Heaven thanks us for those we have helped. Allow yourself to hug another for any or no reason. Living life can be tough at times; people need a pat on the back. Let us give ourselves a few as well.

May we look forward to the New Year in anticipation of more of the Good; may we be excited about new opportunities that await us on our spiritual journey.

We may not be perfect, but we are willing and excited to learn. Our Creator reveals more of our true self to us as we travel on our spiritual journey.

About the Author

In the highest sense of the word, Ann Blakely Rice is a true survivor. In her life thus far, she has survived childhood abuse, divorce, depression/anxiety, alcoholism, and cancer, the recent death of both of her parents, among being a witness to numerous other tragedies. She, indeed, knows what suffering is all about firsthand. In this book, she hopes to pass on to her readers various healthy coping methods that she has gathered over the years.

Ann graduated from college with a Fine Arts degree, yet considers life itself to be the "real school" for living. She continued on to graduate from the Yoga Institute in Houston in 1979 and has maintained a home practice of the science ever since. She has taught yoga and meditation on several occasions near her home in the Texas Hill Country. She holds a degree from the University of Metaphysics in Yoga and in Spiritual Healing. She has studied with many teachers, including Ram Dass, Timothy Leary, Deepak Chopra, Stephen Levine, Carolyn Myss and Joan Borysenko. She has attended numerous seminars with all the above and more. She has spent much of her time traveling and studying with various Hawaiian Healers, Shamans, and Native Americans. While having had several mystical experiences, her "down to earth" approach to life and relationships have assisted her in walking a mystical path with practical feet.

In spite of her difficult life challenges, she loves life, people, nature, music, animals and having fun. She considers laughter extremely important in holistic healing. She believes that it is everyone's birthright to heal from any traumatic event and/or illness in their life. She writes only from personal experiences and invites the reader to celebrate life with her, while stressing the importance of maintaining a relationship with their Higher Power that some will call by a different name. She is not affiliated with any particular religion, yet has researched most of the world's religions over the years. Her broadminded approach to spirituality has helped her communicate her message to people all over the world. She strongly considers it an honor to communicate anything that may be of help to her readers, day by day.